Mr. CLEAN

Cash, Drugs and the CIA

The True Story of a Master Money Launderer

Bruce Aitken

Foreword by
Howard Marks (aka Mr. Nice)

One Hour Asia Media Limited
onehour.asia

Editing and Publishing
Johan Nylander & Kenny Hodgart
johannylander.asia | kennyhodgart.co.uk

Cover design
Megan Tanner | thetravellingdesignstudio.com

Cover photo
Anna Gru | unsplash.com

Back cover and PR photos
Ali Ghorbani from Ali G Studios | aligstudios.com

Layout and formatting
Pankaj Runthala | manuscript2ebook.com

Disclaimer: This is a work of non-fiction. The events and experiences detailed herein are all true and have been faithfully rendered as the author remembers them to the best of his abilities. Some names and identities have been changed to protect the privacy of those individuals. All dialogue is as close an approximation as possible to actual conversations that took place, to the best of the author's recollection.

ISBN (e-book): 978-988-75155-2-4
ISBN (paperback): 978-988-75155-3-1
ISBN (hardcover): 978-988-75155-4-8

One Hour Asia Media Limited
onehour.asia
Published in Hong Kong

To the Reader

THIS BOOK HAS been difficult to write on several levels.

Firstly, it brings back memories of a very wonderful and exciting time in my life, but also of some incredibly trying and challenging moments. In fact, although it is all in the past now, just thinking about those years causes me to well up with conflicting feelings of hopelessness, despair... and pure, adrenaline-pumping bliss. It feels as if it all happened yesterday.

What's more, writing these words has been a soul-searching experience. So much of my professional life was lived in a shadowland where the boundaries of what's legal and not legal, moral and not moral, are blurred, and this choice of life affected people around me. I leave it up to you to judge the rights and wrongs for yourself.

What started innocently enough led me to a world of money-laundering, and of moving millions of dollars for some of the world's most notorious and shady characters — including the CIA, government officials, financiers and well-known drug lords. It was a life of first-class flights and five-star hotels — a lavish, globe-trotting lifestyle, yes, but one always fraught with the risk of failing on a money run or being caught by the authorities. And in the end, it all caught up with me. I was illegally kidnapped by American agents, and suddenly found myself staring down the possibility of spending the rest of my life behind bars in a US prison.

Before I started writing, I decided I would tell the truth and nothing but the truth, according to my best recollection. Names have not been changed unless explicitly stated. The sequence of events is unchanged, and nothing has been added to the story for dramatic effect — allowing you to focus on events, put yourself in my shoes and try to feel what I felt at crucial moments.

I have tried to make sure that only the facts as I remember them are recorded. I have also pieced together additional information from many of the thousands of documents connected to my ordeal and trials that I still have stashed away in dozens of boxes. The deceptions, the double crosses, the lies, the broken promises, the illegal activities of each person involved: all are exposed in the pages that follow. And without wishing to give the whole game away, more often than not the US government's alphabet agencies — especially the CIA and DEA — and its investigators and prosecutors, are among the key protagonists and perpetrators.

Invariably, I found that it was those of us accused of wrongdoing who evinced the kind of integrity one would expect from law enforcement. It was the accused who looked out for one another and showed some serious *cojones*. These are the people I respect more than ever as I look back. This is as much their story as it is mine, although both theirs and mine are certainly interwoven. Their lives, and many others, were and continue to be impacted by government policy relating to the war on drugs, particularly as regards questions of legality, the growth of the prison industry and the large number of fellow citizens now experiencing incarceration, as well as by other changes that have taken place in society over several decades.

As for the writing style you will encounter, I sought and was offered varied opinions from several literary agents. In the end, I decided to keep my own style, which might include flaws and a lack of literary know-how; however, two veteran international journalist friends came to my rescue to help create a fluid manuscript for the benefit of the overall "read." I hope you will enjoy the book and find a few gems of meaning along the way.

As I was writing, it also became apparent to me that, although I had not always been especially religious in the past, a powerful spiritual element of faith permeates the events of my life. This accounts in large part for the very detailed autobiographical slant of *Mr. Clean*.

My education into the wider world began in Saigon in 1969, as far as the "moving money" aspect of it was concerned. However, the feeling I had in my spirit, that Asia was to have a profound impact on my life, was born in a different school, and in a different place, when I was just a young boy in fact.

In this life when you cast your fate to the wind, there are surely turning points — or certain people that you meet — that are destined to have a major impact on your future. This was such a turning point. Staring at a map in school one day, I felt something stir in my soul. I was fascinated by Asia, with all its exotic names and places: Hong Kong, Saigon, Bangkok, Jakarta, to name just a few. Back then Southeast Asia was called Indo-China.

That early feeling must have been a premonition — something deeply spiritual — because I knew in my soul and spirit that one day I would see all of these amazing places.

At the heart of my story, all the same, is a kid who was born in Hackensack, New Jersey, and grew up in Hasbrouck Heights, a kid who — through chance and circumstance — grew up to become one of the world's most successful money launderers.

In taking that path, there were to be some unintended, and at times devastating, consequences.

Bruce Aitken
AKA Mr. Clean
Hong Kong

Foreword

MANY OF US have traveled through customs or airport security carrying something we should not. Possibilities include a scintilla of the finest squidgy Afghan hash, an extra bottle of duty-free booze, or a few thousand dollars that did not seem worth mentioning to the authorities. We know it can be a nerve-wrenching experience that precipitates sweaty palms, a pounding heart, and the persistent fear that the little old lady in the corner is actually an undercover drug squad officer, and we are aware it does not usually facilitate a relaxed journey. Imagine doing that day-in, day-out for two decades. That is precisely what master money launderer Bruce Aitken did in the 1970s and 1980s. I can well understand why he turned to God in later life.

I never fully understood the terms "smuggling" or "money-laundering" or why they became crimes. When I was "smuggling" or Bruce was "money-laundering" all it meant was that we were moving beneficial herbs, in my case, or official banknotes in Bruce's, around the world. We happened to cross some artificial man-made boundaries called borders, but how could transporting something from A to B possibly be illegal? It never made sense to me and still does not.

The beauty of the book you hold in your hands is that it offers a unique and perfect insight into the money-laundering world of 30-odd years ago. That was a time when, at one point, Bruce and his colleagues would be moving around huge amounts of currency by using golf bags with secret compartments within them. Indeed, Bruce estimates that his favorite golf bag, "Old Faithful," would alone have transported many millions of dollars worth of notes between locations such as Guam, Japan, Vietnam, Hong Kong, Switzerland, the Philippines and Australia. As with everything, it is often the simplest solutions that work best.

I first met Bruce in the early 1980s in Hong Kong, and we immediately formed a solid rapport. He was a master of his chosen trade and helped me clean up some cash that I had earned through smuggling. Reading about his two decades of laundering vividly brought back to me all the excitement, glamor and sheer fun that an international jet-setting life of crime invariably imparts.

In the first two years of his career, Bruce visited 30 countries and then escalated to going through two 48-page passports a year. I traveled almost as extensively, but I tended to do so under several different identities backed by false passports. I could not build up a collection of air miles. Bruce, as far as I am aware, always traveled under his real name, and I cannot even hazard a guess at how many miles he managed to accumulate.

While Bruce fell into his vocation by accident, he took to it like a duck to water and was soon the go-to man for those who did not feel the need to tell the tax authorities about every penny they had earned, or were slightly cagey about exactly how they had earned the money. Bruce never asked many questions but, as with all these stories, governments began to ask too many questions, and snitches, that most vile sub-species of criminal, were eventually very happy to provide them with answers. I found Bruce's heartfelt tirades against grasses to be one of the funniest and most incisive parts of this fascinating account.

Bruce also captures brilliantly the paranoia and nerve-racking horror of his chosen lifestyle. There were so many near misses that it was only sheer luck and quick thinking that kept him out of trouble for so long. For example, who would have thought that one of the main ways to avoid a pull by airport customs was to join the queue directly behind someone of Indian descent? It turns out that our so-called color-blind airport officials will generally pick on our Indian brothers, who they assume are "always smuggling something," thus allowing the man with $600,000 wrapped around his number-five iron to pass through unimpeded.

Mr. Clean introduces us to a host of incredible characters straight off the pages of a Len Deighton novel. These include Nicolas Deak — a Hungarian-born United States citizen, an ex-secret service soldier and former hero of the war in Asia. Deak established and was chairman of Deak-Perera, a worldwide network of currency agents and smugglers, to service a multitude of clients, mainly the Central Intelligence Agency. Deak's murder, theoretically by a lone, demented female, is one of several mysteries that Bruce believes ends up at the feet of the biggest money-laundering, drug-dealing operation of them all: the CIA, Deak-Perera's main client.

We also meet Father Jose, a Spanish Jesuit priest who lugged bags of money all over Tokyo making payments for Bruce's firm, Deak and Company, and sending all of his hard-earned commission of half a percent back to a church he founded for prostitutes in Mexico City. The eventual arrest of this kind-hearted money launderer played a major role in the

1975 Lockheed disgrace that forced the then Japanese Prime Minister, Kakuei Tanaka, to resign.

Bruce's activities were also interwoven with two of the most famous scandals ever to humiliate Australia's authorities: the drug-dealing Cessna-Milner affair and the Nugan Hand affair, which involved the Vietnamese heroin trade (the Golden Triangle), corrupt bankers, and, of course, the CIA.

When the net finally catches Bruce, we get first-hand insight into the nefarious activities of that most hypocritical of organizations, the United States government. The legal wrangling that could have resulted in at least two decades in prison for Bruce went on for many years, and Bruce's ability to survive the seemingly endless horrors that faced him is a true testament to the quality of his character and the strength that his powerful faith has imbued in him.

We are both proud of ourselves for explicitly refusing to cooperate with the institutionalized forces of injustice that wanted us to testify against any of our co-defendants. Although I got sentenced to 25 years, and you will read of Bruce's several hardships in the pages ahead, it was worth it.

Bruce now hosts a weekly Christian radio show in Hong Kong that has a phenomenal number of listeners.

Read this book and learn how good men can sometimes end up doing things that many regard as not so good. Learn as well how to ensure you do not get pulled by that nasty-looking customs official who seems to be staring directly at you.

Howard Marks, AKA Mr. Nice

Howard Marks authored this foreword shortly before he passed away from cancer in 2016, aged 70. Born in Wales, he was known for being an international cannabis smuggler and the best-selling author of several books, including: Mr. Nice; Señor Nice: Straight Life From Wales to South America; and Mr. Smiley: My Last Pill and Testament.

Table of Contents

Prologue

The pickup

STANDING IN the lobby on the 12th floor of the MLC Centre in downtown Sydney, Australia, I suddenly felt very conspicuous. The year was 1978, and the time was about 11:30am, a half hour before the crowds in the offices would start heading out for lunch. I did not want to meet or see anybody. *What the hell is keeping that lift?*

Impatiently pushing the button, I felt a lingering tiredness and irritability from my overnight flight and the nylon Compass Travel bag over my shoulder felt uncomfortably heavy. Fifteen minutes earlier it had been empty. Now it contained A$500,000, equivalent to about US$600,000 at the going rate. Just the thought of that kind of money was enough to change my mood to one of exhilaration and anticipation.

Suddenly the bell on the lift rang. It seemed louder than normal and startled me. My senses were now extremely alert. The door opened and I instinctively cast an eye in to see if it was occupied. *Good, it's empty!*

I punched the button for the sixth floor. On six, I got out, hurried down the corridor, and stopped at room 606. I took one last casual glance around and rang the buzzer.

"Mr. Bruce Walker, come in," exclaimed the shy, granny-like receptionist facing me, referring to me using the alias she'd come to know me by. "Harry has been waiting for you."

EARLIER that morning I had flown in on the red-eye from Hong Kong. I'd gone straight to my hotel and checked in. No chance for sleep. It was just before 11:00am when I headed out of the Hilton, walked a couple of blocks down Pitt Street, and then circled back around

1

through a few crowded arcades. Finally, I entered the lobby of the nearby MLC building. That was my routine. First stop was Jeff on the 12th floor to pick up the money.

Jeff was expecting me. It was normal to pay him a visit several times a year. He was one of Sydney's many prosperous diamond dealers, and wanted to get his money offshore to avoid Australia's punishing income taxes.

Jeff motioned me into his library-like office. Of medium height and build, he wore a lightly starched white shirt with light brown trousers, fashionable for someone in his mid-forties. He was always nervous, and I could see beads of perspiration dotting his pale wrinkled forehead and the bridge of his nose, shining as they reflected on his expensive horn-rimmed glasses. Yet there was a bond between us — a trust. His piercing brown eyes were clear and confident. It was not easy to hand over half a million dollars to someone on a handshake. He never hesitated, though. I quickly bundle-counted the money: each bundle of 100 bills, in Aussie $50 notes, totaled $5,000. The A$500,000 fitted nicely into my empty Compass Travel bag. Ten minutes later and we were done.

"Please tell Brink to credit my account in Bank Leumi, Zurich, as soon as possible!" His departing words rang in my ears.

The "Brink," whom you will be introduced to in full later, was Mr. Dirk M. Brink, Managing Director at the company I worked for, Deak & Company (Far East) Ltd., Hong Kong. He was both my mentor and direct boss. Not only was he one of the world's most eccentric characters, he also possessed a certain creative genius for sneakily moving money.

"Harry," in Room 606, was also expecting me. Always matter-of-fact and probably in his early fifties, Harry stood about 6 feet tall, with a marine-like posture that gave him an impression of fitness. He was brown-eyed and well-tanned, and dressed like a banker in a dark-blue business suit and conservative gray tie.

He quickly bundle-counted the cash I had received from Jeff, and — in his trademark aristocratic voice — bade me farewell. Job done.

You see, Harry always had clients, most of them Aussie businessmen and many of them also clients of the "Big Ten" international accounting firms, who had a habit of stashing their gains offshore, usually without paying taxes. They periodically wanted to enjoy some of it back home without the government getting wind of it. And we were happy to accommodate: *"Need cash? Call Deak & Company. No questions asked."* That was our motto.

Unbeknownst to either Jeff or Harry, the "swap" took place right under their respective noses. It was a total cakewalk, took little more than half an hour and earned Deak & Company a tidy five percent commission. This for me was a typical day's work. And I relished it. In fact, truth be told, I loved every Goddamn minute of it.

Somehow I'd not only fallen into a career as a money launderer, but I excelled at it. This profession changed my life in a multitude of ways — some that you might expect, others that I for one did not.

The *expected* ways included the perks of working for an internationally prestigious and trusted company. We provided a service that was in high demand among wealthy people, government agencies, world leaders and industry tycoons, not to mention plenty of ordinary people and plenty of plain old misfits, all over the globe.

The profession commanded a certain amount of awe among clients, many of them mesmerized by the secrecy and mystery of how huge sums of cash could somehow magically be made to disappear right before their very eyes and reappear in their offshore accounts. It involved a lot of glamor. I also made life-long friendships and was treated very well and with respect by clients and associates.

And the *unexpected*…. Well, read on and you'll see for yourself. All I can say is fasten your seatbelt and enjoy the ride.

God knows it all started out innocently enough.

CHAPTER 1

Chasing Dreams

MONEY FOR ME always held some fascination, because as a youth it was a scarce commodity in our household. I grew up in a small town — Hasbrouck Heights, New Jersey, just eight miles from New York City. On a clear day, you could see the George Washington Bridge on the River Hudson.

In the 1940s and 1950s, life there was simple. We never locked our doors at night, and during the hot and humid summers both the front and back doors were left open so you could catch the breeze. Life was beautiful, although we were poor. I look back with particular nostalgia on lazy Sundays; so-called "blue laws" required many enterprises to be closed, but Mom and Dad usually had enough for an especially delicious noonday meal.

The population of the town was about 12,000. We had a corner candy store, a Jewish butcher, a Polish ice-man who delivered ice for the icebox, and an Italian man who sold strawberries. I played baseball from early morning until late at night with other young baseball fanatics, and developed good skills playing in Little League.

Once, after pitching a great game, the father of the pitcher on the opposing team got into an argument with my dad and told him: "Bruce is so damn lucky; if you dropped him into a sewer, he would come up with a gold watch." I never forgot that. The luck of the Irish: I almost felt blessed.

My dad, "Irish" Jay Aitken — his mom was Irish and his dad Scottish — was born in 1893. My mom was born Alice Schonemann, Swedish on her mom's side and German on her dad's. My stern German grandfather had at one time been head waiter at the Waldorf Astoria Hotel in New York, while my Scottish grandfather was Catholic and had been a sailor on a ship that frequently came to New York before he settled in New Jersey.

Before Dad met Mom, he had been married to another woman and they'd had a daughter together. Unfortunately, I never met either of them. When Dad took off with young

Alice — a real beauty, ten years his junior — they must have created quite a scandal at a time when going off and starting a new family just wasn't the done thing.

Dad and the other woman never got divorced but the new union proved to be a lasting one — and produced five "illegitimate" children. I grew up with a sister, Honey, 17 years my senior; a brother Jim, ten years older; and twin sisters, Janice and Joanne, two years older. The twins and I were inseparable, partly because we had been born and grew up in a slightly different era than the others.

I made my introduction to the world as a menopause baby in 1945. Story goes that when the neighborhood doctor, Dr. Basralian, found out my mom was pregnant at the age of 42, he was frantic and recommended she not go through with it. Mom replied without hesitation: "Dr. Basralian, you can go to hell!" Dad said it was the first and only time he'd ever heard my mother curse.

As I grew up, our family felt quite ostracized. Dad took to drinking a lot — like a true Irishman in both custom and appearance. His real estate business failed, and he didn't feel welcome in the Catholic Church — he told people the church had declined to give him some painting job he'd wanted, and so out of spite we never went to church. We lived downstairs in a family house, with various aunts and uncles living upstairs. Our small flat had two bedrooms and extra sleeping space in the living room. I was 14 years old and in high school when Dad begrudgingly installed the first shower in our bathroom.

Dad had his talents. For example, he could play the piano by ear — as soon as he heard a song, he could play it. But since we lived next door to Leo's Tavern, his partiality for drinking and playing music created something of a recipe for disaster. Many nights I had to pick him up off the bench outside the house and drag him home.

But I loved him dearly; after all, he was my dad. And besides, he was the one who taught me how to play baseball. Once, he'd even met Babe Ruth, probably the most legendary baseball player of all time.

Both my mom, who looked angelic with her beautiful head of natural white hair, and my dad, were ahead of their times. Not only did they live together unmarried well before that way of life came into vogue, but my mom also had to work to support the family: she was the bread-winner, and worked as a switchboard operator at the Physicians & Surgeons Exchange in Hackensack. She worked like a slave, putting in long hours for a pittance of 40 cents an hour, although in later years she reached the lofty heights of a dollar an hour. She got paid every Friday.

As a consequence, my adorable — though not identical — twin sisters and I came to love Friday nights. By most Wednesdays, we had already run out of food and the cupboard was bare. So, on Fridays, we would meet my mom as soon as she got off work and head for the Safeway Supermarket. We'd then board the 102 bus to go home and feast.

For my part, I became an entrepreneur early on, and took odd jobs whenever I could: I was a shoeshine boy, sold lemonade with my sisters, cut grass, shoveled snow and worked as a newspaper boy for the *Bergen Evening Record.* Later on, I set pins at the Pioneer Club bowling alley.

Our hero! Dad was a real 'ham'

THERE were times when my father demonstrated extraordinary *chutzpah*, extreme self-confidence. I remember one hot summer Sunday, when Mom had been sick for a week. She couldn't go to work, and we were broke and famished.

Leo's Bar was an excellent restaurant, normally jam-packed with hungry diners on a Sunday afternoon, and it was within stumbling distance. Suddenly, I heard the screen door open, shaking me out of a hot and hungry, sleepy summer trance. Dad came running in, breathing hard, with a huge ham in his arms. The aroma was tantalizing.

"Quick!" said Dad. "Close the doors. Be quiet! No one is home!" My sisters and I ran for cover, but not before each of us grabbed a large chunk of ham which my dad sliced off for us. *Hallelujah, this was heaven!* I quietly rejoiced at the thought that we were going to feast on ham sandwiches for the next two weeks.

Suddenly, Leo — six foot tall, muscular, wearing a snarling face creased with a mean and ruddy complexion — came running out of the restaurant screaming and yelling, "Where is my ham?! Goddammit! Who took my ham?! Who stole my goddamn ham?!"

We froze.

Leo was followed closely by a herd of hungry diners who had been patiently waiting for Sunday lunch. Apparently, the big ham had just come out of the oven and had been placed on the window sill to cool off. We heard banging on our door. My dad finally answered, and found a mean crowd of diners standing there. Despite whiffs of delicious ham wafting throughout our house, Dad mustered up a look of total astonishment and bellowed: "What ham!?"

I was damn proud of my Dad. He was a real character.

Problem was, he just could not hold down a job. He worked mainly as a house painter and eked out a living sporadically. He taught my brother Jim and myself how to paint houses, and Jim eventually went on to make a good business out of it. In fact, Dad actually ended up working for Jim — when he kept off the booze. When he got his own painting jobs from time to time, I would sometimes have to go finish them so he could get paid.

One day he came home and announced he had been hired to be a janitor at the nearby synagogue. We were so happy. He had the keys and all he had to do was keep the place straight. I laughed when he got the job because for reasons I never understood, his whole life had been spent blaming Jews (as well as Blacks, Italians and Puerto Ricans) for all the problems in the world. I can still hear my mom telling him, "Oh Jay, they are not all like that!" My mom loved everyone. Fortunately, I took after her. My best friends have been Christians, Muslims, Buddhists, and Jews — all sorts of people.

(More importantly, the neighborhood's Jewish butcher actually saved my life when I was four years old. From his shop window, he saw me riding my tricycle into the path of an oncoming car; he dashed out, and snatched me off the cycle just in the nick of time.)

Anyway, my dad started the janitorial job on a Friday, and immediately discovered the ceremonial wine cabinet. After all, he had the key.

The next morning being Saturday, the Sabbath, the Rabbi and some of his flock arrived early, only to find Dad and a couple of his red-faced Irish friends passed out on the synagogue floor, empty bottles of wine strewn all around the wine cabinet. He was fired on the spot.

Back at home, Dad continued to connive at every opportunity. We kids dreaded the unexpected, and jumped out of our skins whenever the doorbell rang. We were instructed *never* to answer the door — *never* to open it — because it might be a bailiff serving a subpoena to appear in court for an unpaid debt. We normally had the TV on, blasting away, and when the doorbell rang we'd turn everything off and run out the back door, so technically nobody would be home.

The TV and radio were part of a deal we had with Amana, a household appliance firm, that included a freezer and food plan. A salesman appeared one day and we signed up. The deal was that you placed a quarter into the TV and it came on for two hours. We could watch baseball — usually the New York Giants or the Brooklyn Dodgers, whose games were preceded by *Happy Felton's Knot-Hole Gang* pre-game show. We hated the Yankees. When we ran out of money, we listened to the radio. Radio was great. You only had to use your imagination — that gift from God that can take a lifetime to appreciate.

When the big Amana freezer arrived, it was stocked full of food. What a deal. We ate all the food and, when it was gone, my father called the suppliers and told them to come and take the freezer back because we couldn't pay. We were all sad to see it go.

Being poor was often challenging. When the electricity bill could not be paid and the power was cut off, we studied by candle light. When we couldn't pay the heating bill, we froze.

During my freshman year in high school, my aged and senile Aunt Mary, who lived upstairs, suddenly got a wild hair up her butt and decided she'd had enough of us. Since the family house was in her name, she went to court and had us kicked out on the street for not paying her rent.

Rolling with the punches

I WAS a typically confused teenager, confronting all the challenges that teenagers face, although being poor had made me tough. If anyone said anything against my family or anyone in it, there would be a big fight, for sure. As we grew up, we learned not to take any crap from anyone.

I don't know why, but some of the kids in my neighborhood were always fighting. I never wanted to fight anyone, but I fought from time to time. It was all about earning something called "respect."

I was an honor student, but I was losing interest in school. I lost interest in everything, in fact, except maybe girls — and they were a mystery. Sure, I knew I should go to college, but on what — thin air? Where was the money going to come from?

Ultimately, I decided — along with my best friends Vic Dragon, Richie Jaeger, Bob Soel, Phil Stroh, Eddie Geleski and Jeff Draesel — that I should go to the prestigious Rutgers University and become a doctor.

When the mail came one day, Bobby found out he was going off to Lycoming on a football scholarship, while Vic, Richie and Jeff all got letters saying they had been accepted to Rutgers. So I rushed off home and found my own letter waiting for me, also from Rutgers. I was so happy! When I tore it open, though, it looked different than the others. In a few short words, I was told the university was returning my application, and that the check for the admission fee in the amount of five dollars was being returned because of "insufficient funds."

I was so mad. I had given my dad the five dollars I had earned setting up pins at the local bowling alley every Friday and Saturday night.

When I told him, I could see that Dad felt hurt, so I gave him another five dollars and resubmitted the application. Two weeks later, another letter from Rutgers arrived. Yet again, the check had been returned for insufficient funds. "Do not re-apply," was the stern advice. All my friends were going away to college. I felt left behind, alone and lost.

It was a time of deep despair and disappointment.

I knew I needed to get away, and in fact even although I was not of a religious disposition as a young man, I always felt that God had a special plan for me. During the many times when I felt I had no guidance and had to learn from my own mistakes, I always felt everything would turn out OK. And I prayed a lot. No doubt this was a result of my mother's influence. She always said: "If you don't have anything good to say about anyone, then don't say anything at all." I found out much later than many of her words of wisdom came from the New Testament. She was an angel, for sure.

My greatest dream, however, was not to become a doctor. It was to become a professional baseball player. That was my greatest passion in life, and I followed the games almost religiously on TV or the radio. I had played baseball throughout high school, and you might say that I was a star pitcher, managing a couple of no-hitters and a perfect game.

One day, after one of my last games in high school, I got a call. It was from a fellow named Bob Potts, manager of the Paterson Phillies, a New Jersey baseball team. Bespectacled, rotund and non-athletic in appearance, Bob was a baseball lover at heart and a quiet, nice fellow. He said he had been following my career via the newspaper, the *Bergen County Record*.

"How would you like to pitch for the Phillies this Sunday?" he asked.

This was a massive break. It was one of those phone calls all ambitious athletes dream about, but fear never will come. I was in heaven. First big step into the pros!

"Come to the field in Hackensack at noon Sunday, and we'll have a uniform ready for you."

Sunday came, and it turned out I pitched a good game. We won — and I was on my way. Semi-pro baseball was a great delight. I started looking forward to every Sunday.

(I got to rub shoulders with some real characters in my baseball days. On one occasion I was about to leave for the game in Paterson when the phone rang. It was Mr. Dragon, the father of my best friend Vic. Mr. Dragon was a pretty tough guy who umpired semi-pro games on Sundays. "Bruce," he said, "are you pitching in Paterson today?" I was and he breathed a sigh of relief. "That's great. My car won't start. Can I hitch a ride with you?" As we approached the field in Paterson, Mr. Dragon thought for a moment and suddenly yelled out: "Stop the car a couple of blocks from the field and let me out. I'll walk from there. It'll be a scandal if the pitcher arrives bringing along the umpire!")

The following week, we played in New York City, then in Garfield, New Jersey, the Sunday after. One of the best players on the Garfield team was an outstanding baseball player named Ken Huebner. In both appearance and raw natural ability, Ken — who was one year ahead of me — reminded me of a modern-day Babe Ruth. We knew each other from reading about one another's exploits in the newspapers and we became instant friends. In fact, we would remain friends right up until his passing in 2018.

Ken asked me about my college plans, and he seemed surprised when I told him about my failed attempts.

"Listen," he said. "Let me see what I can do."

Ken had a full baseball scholarship at Florida Southern College in Lakeland, Florida, an excellent college with a great baseball program.

It was mid-July, 1963. A couple of days later, I had just arrived home after painting a house all day when Mom informed me I had received a call from a man named Hal Smeltzly. He turned out to be the baseball coach at Florida Southern College.

I took a deep breath and dialed his number. "Hello, Mr. Smeltzly?"

For over an hour, we talked about my good academic and baseball records. He said I had been highly recommended to him by his star player, Ken Huebner. He said if Ken thought I was a great pitcher, that was good enough for him. An application for admission to Florida Southern would be coming in the mail.

"Fill it out as soon as you receive it, and ask your high school to send me your transcripts. Don't worry about anything, but don't delay! You will be on a full scholarship for four years, half baseball and half academic."

I was speechless.

In late August, 1963, I met Ken at the airport in Newark, New Jersey. I was 18 years old, and it was the first time I had flown on a plane. Always gracious, Ken let me sit by the window. First destination was Tampa, then Lakeland, Florida.

Playing baseball for Florida Southern was a dream come true. Over the four years I spent there, we won the Florida Conference Championships, and I made the All-American College Baseball Team in 1965, with the lowest ERA (Earned Run Average) in the nation. My record still stands at Florida Southern. The highlight of the year was playing against the Detroit Tigers during spring training. I was even called a "college baseball star" by the *New York Times*, in a story about how scouts were looking for new players for the major leagues.

New York Times, Friday, June 4, 1965 / St. Petersburg Independent

College Baseball:
*Draft Choices... Guerrant of Michigan, Fred Mazeruk of Pittsburg, Bill Monday of Arizona State, **Bruce Aitken of Florida Southern**....Terry Craven of San Francisco State, John Fause of Arizona....These are just some of the college baseball stars being watched eagerly by the scouts of the twenty major league clubs which will meet in New York next week to conduct their first free agent draft of college, high school, and sandlot players. Aitken, a right-hander,*

led all pitchers in earned run percentage with a 0.63 mark. He had an 8-2 won-lost record for Florida Southern, permitting only 42 hits in 71 innings. He walked 16 and struck out 61.

In addition, I had been invited to two back-to-back tryouts at the great Yankee Stadium, "the house that Ruth built." I recall pitching on the mound, mesmerized by the aura of the place; and, although it was frowned upon, I scooped up a handful of dirt as a keepsake.

My enthusiasm had me thinking: pro baseball, that's the next step for me, no doubt about it!

Florida Southern College was a great school both academically and athletically. I studied Economics, worked hard, and — to my surprise, at a Methodist school — I even enjoyed the mandatory Wednesday religious hour in the school chapel.

What I did not enjoy was the mandatory Reserve Officer Training Corps drills. By this time, the war in Vietnam was in full rage and ROTC graduates from schools like ours could go to Vietnam as Second Lieutenants. I still recall one of the lectures by a sergeant: "Gentlemen, this is the M-1 rifle. It weighs 9.5 pounds; with the bayonet attached it weighs 10.5 pounds. Therefore, the bayonet weighs 1 pound." There was a lot of laughter over that comment. As for me, I just wanted to get back to baseball.

Hopes shattered

BEFORE I knew it, I had graduated from Florida Southern. I was 22 and still poor as a church mouse.

I returned to New Jersey for the summer to play baseball, expecting to get drafted by a pro team. Ken went on to play for the Kansas City Royals and I was talking to scouts from several major league clubs. I was among the top picks in the upcoming pro baseball draft, and was expected to be offered contracts worth over $50,000, which was a fortune at that time.

Then, one hot New York City Sunday in June, while scouts were in the stands watching, it happened.

I had been pitching a great game, when all of a sudden I felt a sharp pain in my right knee from an old injury suffered in college. Then it locked. I could not straighten out my leg. The pain was excruciating, and so was my panic about potential serious damage. Soon, I was on the way to the hospital. The doctor at the Emergency Room applied enough force on my knee to straighten out my leg and put a cast on it. A month later, the cast was off, but so were the baseball offers. I had thrown my last pitch in organized baseball.

My dreams were shattered.

In fact, it felt like everything was shattered. I had no money and my future prospects looked dim. It was hard to find the motivation after my injury and having been so close to fulfilling my baseball dreams, but I knew life had to go on.

On a lark, I had applied for a job in Ft. Meade, Maryland, along with a good college buddy, George Kerekes. I passed the test and suddenly found myself being offered a job at the National Security Agency, a national-level intelligence agency of the United States Department of Defense, as a cryptographer.

Looking back at it now, and considering my later career of choice, it feels a bit ironic that my first job offer after graduating was from a US government intelligence organization. The training was due to start in September.

As mentioned, this was the height of the Vietnam War, however, and the bloody NSA job was not draft-exempt. In September 1967, just as I was preparing to go to Maryland and start my new life as a cog in the government intelligence machine, I received a notice from the draft board to report to Newark, New Jersey, for the Army induction physical.

I was very much against the Vietnam War and personally regarded it as total madness. I thought to myself: "I'll be damned if I am ever going to shoot anyone. America can go to hell first!" At the time, I was protesting in Greenwich Village and listening to Bob Dylan.

But there we were, my high school buddies and I, all together on the way to Newark to get physicals; and before long we'd surely be on our way to the killing fields of Vietnam.

A couple of hours later, we were on the bus back to Hasbrouck Heights, comparing notes. When it came to my turn, I was able to report that I would not be going to war.

The doctor had moved my knee around and announced: "Torn lateral meniscus, you fail."

This was the first time in my life I'd felt a sense of joy at being a failure. The injury had turned into a blessing. But I still wasn't clear what the hell I was going to do with my life. Because of the draft process, my start at the NSA had been postponed until the following April, seven months away — and I needed to get a job before then.

Salad days

I HAD a 1954 Chevrolet I had bought for $200 and it took me three days to drive it from New Jersey back to Florida, where I still had many friends.

I was taking the Lakeland exit off I-4 when the car shuddered violently and stopped. I got out and looked underneath it only to see that the drive shaft had embedded itself in the blacktop. I only had a couple of miles to go. My friends, Ellis Shaw, a college basketball player from Coral Gables, and Norm Wolfinger, from Easton, Pennsylvania, were expecting me soon.

After pushing the car onto the grass and removing the license plates, I said good-bye to my Chevy and started to walk down the ramp to hitch-hike the rest of the way. Suddenly, a big semi-tractor trailer blew its horn and stopped to help me. The driver looked the car over, and pronounced: "I can fix it, if you let me buy it."

Happily, I signed the Bill of Sale over to him and took him up on his kind offer of $25 for the car and a ride into Lakeland.

My friend Norm, who was later decorated after being wounded in Vietnam, was destined to become a top lawyer, a well-respected prosecutor for the State of Florida. But in the first summer out of college, in 1967, he drove a potato chip delivery truck. We'd shared some wild times during our college days, and they were about to continue.

Norm turned me on to Colt 45 malt liquor beer and, taking after my Irish dad, I found myself getting drunk with my friends every weekend and chasing girls around in the boondock phosphate pits we called "High Tension" on account of the electricity pylons at the entrance gate. Our Friday night ritual was to wander down to Lakeland to "colored town," as African-American neighborhoods in every city in the South were known. There, we found ourselves treated like honored guests by the "sisters" and friendly bar owners. One time, Norm got so drunk he was arrested for peeing on the nearby Golden Arches at McDonalds.

Years later, as a Florida prosecuting attorney who'd put his wild days to bed, he would go out of his way, as only a true best friend could, to write a letter on my behalf to a prosecuting attorney in support of my bid for freedom from incarceration.

Ellis, meanwhile, went on to Vietnam as a soldier and caught some mysterious illness while on tour. Learning of his death was one of the saddest moments in my life.

My luck turns

THAT same spell in '67, I got a job working in Bartow, Florida — in the phosphate mines. The job title was "dam tender" and it was hard and tedious work.

Long pipes gushed water and built up gravel underneath, and when the gravel came to the top of the pipe, you had to call for another pipe to be connected, otherwise it would back up into the system. That was the job — watching the end of a pipe all day.

It was 40 miles away from where I was living and I had no car. Work started at 7am sharp and ended at 3pm. I really had no choice, though; I had to eat. Every day I woke up at 5am. It was pitch dark.

I started to hitchhike to work. You could still hitchhike in America in those days and with luck I would usually arrive in time. I'd do it over again on the way home.

I soon realized I needed a real job, however. So, after a few weeks, I went to Orlando to see Terri, a girl I had dated in college.

(While spending time with Terry and her family, something odd happened. Her parents were interested in psychic or supernatural forces, and they made an appointment for me to visit a mystic they thought very highly of, to get "checked out." With nothing to lose, I agreed to try it out. The mystic, named Robert Bos, looked me in the eyes; in return I looked into his, which were bright gray. Suddenly, he said: "I'm getting something." What happened next was weird: he told me a few details about my early life that no one knew about, then concluded by saying that — to his amazement — I had 13 guardian angels, which meant I would have a life graced with amazing luck. Almost nothing could go wrong, he stressed. However, he saw something else, too — something not so great. He frowned and I read fear and sadness in his mysterious eyes. I pleaded with him to tell me but he flatly refused. This would bother me for years to come, and I always wondered if one fine day I would find out what he'd seen.)

I started doing random daily jobs in Orlando through Manpower, the staffing firm, and stayed in a cheap hotel near the local "colored town." I was feeling increasingly adrift and knew I needed to get serious about my future, so I paid a visit to the office of a local headhunter and made a detailed résumé. After all, I had a college degree in Economics.

When I returned to the fleabag hotel one day, I found a message waiting. I had an interview the next day for a job as a claims adjustor. If I got it, I'd have a company car — just imagine! This was to be another major turning point in my life.

The next day I put on my only white shirt and a tie, and hitchhiked across Orlando to a small office building: Employers Insurance of Wausau.

"Hi, I'm Ron Langa," said the athletic-looking young fellow interviewing me. Ron wore a brilliant, broad welcoming smile, and a white short-sleeved shirt and tie, formal but at the same time carefree and casual.

In essence, adjusters inspect personal injury claims or property damage to determine how much an insurance company should pay for a loss. And Ron was the only adjuster in Orlando at that time, a one-man operation. A sharp, witty and fun-loving young bachelor, he hired me, and we became instant lifelong friends.

Later, we even attended law school together, and while I lasted only a year, Ron went on to become a top lawyer in Orlando.

By the time I got back from a six-week claims adjuster training course in Wausau, Wisconsin, I had pretty much forgotten any vague ambitions of getting a knee operation and playing baseball — or indeed of going to work for the NSA. I had a decent salary, a company car, and a big South Florida territory to work in. Sometimes I would take off on company business and return a couple of days later, spending Friday in the office doing the paperwork. I soon moved into a nice house with Ron, and on weekends we partied.

At last, I had enough money to eat what I wanted, whenever I wanted — three big meals a day on the road! In less than two months, my weight quickly ballooned from the same 165 pounds I'd weighed when I graduated from high school, to a staggering 203. When I stepped on the scale, I was shocked, and started running. I also switched to cottage cheese and stopped eating like a pig, rapidly returning to 165.

My family was still in New Jersey, and poor as hell, so about three months after returning to Orlando, in the Fall of '67, and after getting my first pay-checks, I sent for Mom and Dad. I rented a trailer home for them to stay in temporarily, and asked Joanne, one of the twins, to drive them down from New Jersey.

Family reunion

A WEEK later, expecting my parents to arrive at any moment, I was staying close to the phone. When it rang, it was Janice. "We are almost there. We just passed Daytona Beach."

"We," to my amazement, turned out to be not only my mom and dad, but my twin sisters and their families, plus Honey and her current wild boyfriend, Lonny. Soon, the whole caravan arrived at our house. All my plans were upset. Ron was equally surprised. All I could think was: *it will take all my salary to support this family*.

Soon, the situation degenerated into an Irish fighting match. The small trailer home was packed. And then, all of sudden, it was emptied of Mom and Dad.

Honey had forced them to move into a room at a boarding house with her and Lonny, and together they were sucking up the little cash I had given to Mom. I was livid. Arriving at their room, I threw a fit: I took Mom and Dad, and, much to their relief, returned them to the trailer.

Back home that night, there was a knock at the door. A police car with flashing red lights was parked outside. Ron answered. I waited, then came out.

"Are you Bruce Aitken?" the officer asked. "Come with me; you are under arrest."

This was the first time I had ever been arrested — although years later I would have a few more of these unpleasant experiences.

"Your sister has charged you with assault," the officer advised me.

Ron was enraged and told the police the truth about what had happened, but the officer insisted: "Sorry, come with me and let the judge decide."

I went to the police station and was formally charged, and ended up posting bail of $100.

"Ok, you can go now," said the same officer.

"Not so fast," I said.

"What is it?"

"I want to file a complaint. Can I do that?"

"Certainly!"

So, I filed a complaint against Honey — for assault. Within an hour, she was picked up and charged and brought to the same police station. I had gone home long before I got the call from Mom bearing the news.

She asked: "Is Honey going to spend the night in the police station? She can't post the $100 bail." The next morning, I dropped the charges.

Honey had a penchant for having people arrested whenever they disagreed with her. It must have been the Irish blood. Years earlier, in New Jersey, she got into a big fight with my brother Jim about who was to pay for the burial of my father when he passed away. My dad, still very much alive, had to go to the police station and bail them *both* out.

Get me out of here

AFTER a year or so, I lost interest in claims adjusting. I was driving down the interstate one day, listening to Glen Campbell's version of *Take Me Home, Country Roads* on the radio, and I pulled into a rest area and looked at the stack of files on the car seat. I just felt I'd come to a point where I couldn't continue doing this job any more.

At heart, I missed the excitement of playing baseball — the sport was still a big part of me. Confused and unhappy, I turned around, drove back to the office and gave my notice.

Once again, I found myself at a loss, albeit a self-inflicted one. Thankfully, Honey had got a job and moved out — all was forgiven on that front. But I had gone and rented a nice little house for Mom and Dad, even though I was constantly broke.

As I joined the ranks of the unemployed, I had about a month's savings in the bank. I needed another miracle. Luckily, one Sunday morning soon after I'd quit my job, fate struck again.

I had one hell of a hangover from the night before, so I got up late. Ron was out of town for the weekend and I was alone in the house. Slowly relishing a second cup of coffee and feeling quite depressed, I turned to the jobs section of the *Orlando Sentinel.* There, I saw my future in large black letters right there in front of me: American Express International Banking Corporation.

They were interviewing in Orlando for overseas assignments in something called military banking. Of all places, AmEx was looking to send staff to Vietnam. College graduates with a bachelor degree in Business or Economics were "most welcome." My hangover suddenly disappeared and my spirits soared. I could see excitement returning to my life, and for a second I forgot about the horrors and dangers of the war. My imagination rushed. *Where would this lead me to?* Vietnam to start with, but after that? London? Paris? Amsterdam?

Suddenly, the world felt full of opportunities.

Excitement beckons

I APPLIED for the job, got it, and went to New York for training. It was early Fall of 1969 and I was 24 years old. It felt great to be back in the Big Apple and to be employed by a big company.

The interview with Amex in Orlando had gone smoothly. In fact, it seemed like the main requirement for Vietnam was that you had a warm body.

The training class was into its second week when one of the executives walked into our class and dropped the bomb.

"Will the three staff assigned to Vietnam identify yourselves?" he said. "Urgent openings are available right now, for a bonus."

Suddenly, three hands went up — the hands of the poor and hungry; me and two colleagues, Vince and Bill.

"Come with me right now," said the executive. "You'll go to AmEx Travel and make the flight arrangements. You can finish your training on the way at Kadena Air Force Base in Okinawa."

Calling my family and friends in Florida with the news, they thought I was totally nuts. "Are you crazy? There is a war going on in Vietnam. You protested it! Don't go!" But the decision was a no-brainer. I felt driven by a sense of fate and excitement. I had to get away.

Forty-eight hours later, I was staring out the window as the plane descended over the mountains on our final approach into Fairbanks, Alaska. Next stop, Japan. Things seemed to be rushing forward at ultra-rapid speed and I was just hanging on as best as I could.

After finally arriving in Tokyo I took a taxi downtown, watching the lights and the crowds. I didn't have much time. I found a bar, chatted with the bar girl, was overcharged, and felt I'd had my first taste of the exotic Far East. It felt surreal to suddenly be in Asia, on the other side of the planet.

Next destination was the Kadena Air Force Base. The Japanese island of Okinawa had been a critical strategic location for the United States Armed Forces since the end of World War II and the base was a sprawling structure. We stayed off-base and commuted back and forth with other AmEx staff for a couple of weeks. Even in that short space of time, we met a steady flow of staff coming back through from Saigon, Vietnam on military flights. They were full of war stories and constantly telling us to change our minds while we still had the chance.

We were booked into a tiny hotel, the Koza Kanko, and found ourselves suffering from all kinds of culture shock. And yet it was exhilarating just to be out of the USA and in a foreign country. Quite frankly, I didn't give a damn which country it was: I just wanted excitement in my life again. I had also discovered rice. Rice with sauces. We had never eaten the stuff. We ate potatoes, because we had been told rice was for weaklings — "the little people."

There was a street in Koza City — now part of Okinawa City — called BC Street, a seedy, run-down place with lots of bars and girls catering to the US military. It was there that I came upon a row of small shacks linked up together, each about the size of an outhouse. There must have been a peephole for each occupant, because each time I approached one of the shacks, the door would swing open and a woman in her fifties — a *mama-san* — would jump out and, with an alluring smile, offer a menu of "services."

I was surprised and quite horrified. This was my first exposure to the ubiquitous "skin trade" in Asia, and to the availability of women from the world's oldest profession, about which I had been totally naive. This was a new world.

Next stop, Vietnam. There, an ongoing war and new levels of debauchery awaited.

CHAPTER 2

Saigon

I WAS FEELING happy to be leaving Okinawa and the Kadena Air Force Base. I'd had a good time there, and I was excited to be abroad, but Okinawa's daily rain and cold were getting to me. There was hardly any sunshine at that time of year.

I had a growing sense of anticipation about seeing Vietnam. There would be time to think about that later, though, because first we had a stopover on the way to Saigon: Hong Kong.

Before my arrival, I didn't know much about Hong Kong or what to expect. Did they speak English or Chinese there? How would I get around, or order a meal?

It was a sunny day in late November 1969 as we landed at the legendary Kai Tak airport, located close to a densely populated residential neighborhood of the same name. Most anyone who ever landed there has a story involving a hair-raising descent in which their plane almost grazed some buildings on approach to the runway.

Soon I was gazing out over an amazing sight, one of the most beautiful I have ever seen. I was on the Star Ferry crossing Victoria Harbor, from the Kowloon peninsula to Hong Kong Island.

The sunlight shimmered on the water like a million bright lights, while the sound of ships' horns wailed in the distance. There was a huge amount of traffic on the harbor, all of it vying for space and the right of way. Large ships, small ships. Dozens of Chinese junks with their big red sails, weaving their way between tiny boats.

The Chinese boats were called "wala-walas" and almost all of them seemed to be steered by smiling little old Chinese ladies dressed in black and wearing conical bamboo hats, their gold teeth sparkling in the sunlight.

Strange exotic smells assailed my nostrils and the salty water slammed rhythmically against the side of the ferry. Straight ahead of me was Hong Kong: Victoria Peak rose up from the central business district like a proud Phoenix, and beneath it skyscrapers — many half-built — sprouted everywhere like in a concrete forest.

I had read about the city in James Clavell's novel *Tai-Pan*, a colorful portrait of European and American traders who moved into Hong Kong in 1842 following the end of the First Opium War and Britain's seizure of the island, but to actually be there held me and my AmEx companions, Bill and Vince, in awe. Hong Kong was also still very much a British Crown Colony, a fact I found reassuring. I loved it at first sight.

Across the border in Mainland China, however, Mao Zedong's Cultural Revolution was raging and the political upheavals had spilled over to Hong Kong. Demonstrations led by local communists in the city had escalated to large-scale riots two years before my arrival, and Maoist slogans could still be seen across town.

"Down with American Imperialists and their running dogs!" read a big banner draped across the wall in a little shop called the China Products Store, across from the Peninsula Hotel on Nathan Road, Kowloon. Quotations from Chairman Mao were posted everywhere, and copies of Mao's Little Red Book were piled high on the counter. A pretty and very tiny Chinese sales girl noticed me frowning at the sign, and asked me where I came from. I told her I was American.

"Are you a tourist?" she asked.

"No, I am on my way to work in Vietnam," I replied.

"Vietnam? Oh, yes," she said, glancing and smiling at the sign. I could read her mind: *An American imperialist running dog!*

Because I had been totally against the Vietnam War from day one, I saw the irony, and realized I was about to discover the truth for myself.

My new colleagues and I became so fascinated with Hong Kong we decided to stay an extra day, a decision that would turn out to be a huge mistake as far as our employer was concerned.

We went to the beach at Repulse Bay, up to Victoria Peak, to the Night Market, and to Causeway Bay Typhoon Shelter, where those very same little boats played music and sold seafood and San Miguel beer. The place was a beehive of activity. The trams, the ferries, the people — it was magic. Here I was in the Far East, with a good dose of England thrown in. There was even a cricket pitch in front of the Hilton.

The next day, we tried to rebook our flights through AmEx and learned that all flights to Saigon were booked for the next three days. Great news, we thought: three more days in Hong Kong. We dived right back into the city and its excitements and temptations.

Expect the unexpected

THREE days later, we flew out.

Staring out of the window as the plane descended towards Saigon through light clouds, the voice of a pretty young Chinese stewardess brought me back to my senses. It was the age of the mini-skirt and I could hardly keep my eyes off her lovely legs: I was 24 years old, and the attractions of the local girls had me mesmerized. They were just very... *feminine*.

"Fasten your seat belts," she commanded in a perfect British accent.

Cathay Pacific Flight CX 106 from Hong Kong was on its final approach into Ton Son Nhut Airport. It was noon on a Sunday in early December and the flight had taken longer than we'd been expecting due to a stopover in Cambodia. I'd managed to get off the plane and have a short walk around outside the terminal at Phnom Penh. The place looked just like Florida to me — flat with palm trees.

At Phnom Penh I'd also recognized one of my fellow passengers lining up to board: none other than the former Prime Minister of Thailand, Kukrit Pramoj. The only reason I recognized him was because he had once played himself in a famous movie, *The Ugly American*.

On our onward flight to Saigon, my thoughts had also been suddenly disturbed by Bill asking aloud the question that was probably on all of our minds.

"What the hell are we doing here?"

Almost simultaneously, Vince and I replied: "The bread, man, the bread."

Why else would anyone in his right mind be going to war-torn Vietnam unless he had to?

In fact, we were about to find out that we were already up shit creek without a paddle. Really, we were nothing but naive country bumpkins; we didn't think we were, but oh yes, we were. Like most Americans, we didn't know a hell of a lot about anywhere but the United States, which we were told constituted the greatest country on the planet. Hong Kong had been an eye-opener. We didn't know anything at all about Vietnam.

On our approach into Ton Son Nhut, I could see military aircraft on the tarmac, and dozens of helicopters parked under half-moon-shaped bomb shelters. It felt both nerve-racking and exciting to finally be there.

Getting out of the plane, we had to wait for 20 minutes for a green military shuttle to take us to the terminal. The heat and humidity were heavy and close, like someone had thrown a wet blanket over me. Gasping, I could hardly breathe. The heat shimmering off the tarmac burned my face and eyes. This place made Florida look cold.

After clearing customs and immigration, we piled into a taxi and headed to the American Express office. The streets were filled with people riding bicycles and motorcycles, or driving old French Citroen cars, while the city's myriad smells were simultaneously strange, exotic and intoxicating. Whatever the French colonial regime had gotten wrong here, they had also left some great things behind. The smell of freshly baked baguettes, coupled with rich Vietnamese coffee, tantalized the senses. Back then, like today in fact, Saigon — or Ho Chi Minh City as it's called now — was one of Asia's most dizzying and high-octane cities.

Arriving at the AmEx office, we were met by a wall of yelling.

"Where the hell have you three morons been? What the hell are they doing in New York, sending me a bunch of morons?" A stream of expletives followed.

This was Reed Vauter, In-Country Manager for American Express International Banking Corporation, Vietnam, or AMEXVN.

We had arrived three days late due to our "mistake" in Hong Kong, and now we were paying for it.

Reed was six feet, three inches tall and looked a bit anorexic. He wore faded blue jeans and a short-sleeved white shirt that looked like it needed a good washing. His thin face, the bags under his eyes, and three days' worth of stubble reflected a torturous and extreme lack of sleep.

"Don't you morons know how to send a cable or make an international telephone call?"

In fact, we had no idea how to send a cable or make an international phone call. Not to mention that the thought had never crossed our minds.

"Check into the Astor Hotel on Tu Do Street, and get your stupid fat asses back here by 6am tomorrow morning," he said.

Then he turned to me: "Bruce Aitken, you moron, you're going up-country to Chu Lai."

Bill was to be dispatched to Pleiku in the Central Highlands, and Vince, if I remember correctly, to Phan Rang.

Picking up my bags, reality hit me. *Saigon. I'm in Saigon!*

The walk to the Astor Hotel, just a couple of blocks from the office, seemed to take forever. I was sweating like a pig. I noticed that the Vietnamese were not sweating at all.

Every two steps someone approached, asking me if I wanted to change money.

"Hey, you got green dolla! No sweat! Me no cheap Charlie, I give you good rate, G.I.!"

Startling, also, were the hordes of beggars, many of them missing limbs. Some were soldiers from the Army of the Republic of Vietnam, or ARVN, the South Vietnamese military force affiliated with the United States. Casualties of battle, they pressed themselves close to us, begging for money while simultaneously trying to steal our watches.

Checking into the six-story Astor was a different matter. The front door was guarded by two Indian hotel doormen who chased away the street people. There was a curious mixture of furniture in the lobby: lots of rosewood with in-laid mother-of-pearl, and a big tropical fish tank in the corner. I glanced at the ladies working at the reception; they were all attired in national dress, the *au dai* — sleek and sexy. Score one on the plus side, I thought to myself. These Vietnamese ladies are something to look at, all right.

After checking into the room and taking a cold shower, I had the urge to get out onto the streets and look around. It was early evening, and the sun was starting to go down. Along with the night came a refreshing breeze and a remarkable drop in heat.

As I walked through the crowded streets, I thought about the black money market. On the way over, we had been indoctrinated as to its perils — that it was illegal and to be avoided. But when I went to a small makeshift food stall to buy a Coke, I was introduced to how finance really worked on the streets of Saigon.

The little old Vietnamese man who ran the shack smiled broadly through his sharp-eyed, wrinkled face, and betel-nut-red stained teeth. Handing me my Coke, he demanded: *"Hi Tram Dong, please."*

I quickly calculated that the 200 hundred piasters he was asking for amounted to about $2. At the time, a can of Coke would not have cost more than five cents in the US.

Pointing this out, I said: "That's outrageous! Are you nuts?"

"Dollar?!" asked the old man, his eyes lighting up, then darting around to see if anyone was listening. "You have dollar? You give me one dollar, no sweat. I give you Coke and give you back 400 piasters. You have MPC, I give you Coke plus 200 P."

He was mistaken about me having any MPC, short for Military Payment Certificate — a form of currency used to pay US military personnel. P was short for piasters, and you heard it everywhere on the streets. But I knew I had just been introduced to the black market, or as the local businessmen called it, the free market.

It was bullshit, of course. I had just changed $20 at the hotel at the official rate of P118 and this little drink stall was offering me a rate of almost P600? I knew something was not kosher, and that I needed to figure it out before I went broke. However, the knowledge that there were three kinds of money in circulation — US dollars, MPCs and piasters — and that they were coveted in that order, would be very useful indeed.

Good morning, Vietnam

THE following day, I woke early. I hadn't slept well in the Astor: the constant drone of helicopters dropping flares along the Saigon River had kept me awake, and I was still annoyed about having been ripped off by the hotel's money changers.

We were told the helicopters were looking for Viet Cong infiltrators.

"Happens every night. Get used to it," the AmEx staff told us.

I had been issued with a Military Assistance Command Vietnam ID card. MACV was a joint-service command of the United States Department of Defense, and although we were officially civilians, the affiliation gave us a certain standing. (Believe it or not, my so-called GS13 rating gave me privileges equivalent to those of a colonel in the military.)

Soon after sunrise I boarded a C-130, a four-engine turboprop transport aircraft that was to take me to my posting in Chu Lai. It was a very different experience to the commercial air travel I'd enjoyed up until that moment.

On a plane like the C-130, you have to sit along the sides in canvas seats, and there are no windows, so you don't know where the hell you are. I just listened to the engines for four hours and finally the thing touched down in Chu Lai, which was to be my home for the next nine months.

Chu Lai was a Marine Corps military base and also the headquarters for the US 23rd (Americal) Infantry Division. In all, there were over 13,000 souls stationed there at any one time.

It was hot and the place was a real dust bowl. Imagine an American Express bank in a place like that. Still, the US military and personnel needed all kinds of support. Neither life nor money stop because you are on the other side of the world fighting a war. Quite the opposite: we bring America to you.

It was an odd experience being a civilian in the middle of a war. As civilians, we could go off the base at our own risk. There was a little village called Tam Ky a few klicks (kilometers) down the road, and we visited it as often as possible for a few cold beers and a massage. The beer tasted better in the "vil." And most importantly, there were women there.

Nights spent on the base were either in the Officers' Club, perched on a hill, where you could silently watch the Medivac helicopters land the wounded at the field hospital, or at the NCO Club, where we'd drink and listen to rock 'n' roll belted out by some outstanding Filipino bands.

Then there were the Red Cross "Donut Dollies," an interesting mix of American girls who'd braved all to come to Vietnam to support the troops. And real troopers they were.

In Vietnam, outnumbered a thousand to one by American men, they were treated like goddesses. Of course, some may have been lonely young ladies who had been unable to find love or companionship back home. But to the last, they were a bunch of good-hearted chicks, and as American as apple pie.

What really amazed me were the unexpected things you could find right there in a war zone. The US government spent a fortune bringing all kinds of civilian services to Vietnam. Not only had the Navy contracted a construction consortium, RMK-BRJ, to build various forms of infrastructure, but the troops also had easy access to banking, base exchange and life insurance. There were even car salesmen. That's right. A soldier could buy a Corvette and have it waiting in his driveway on the day he got home — a short-timer's dream.

But the horrors of the war were constantly present, too. One day in early 1970, Chu Lai made the headlines in the USA by weathering the largest Viet Cong rocket attack of the war up until that time. I remember the morning well — running from the mess hall, my breakfast in hand, to the underground bunker beside it. Over 200 rockets were launched from the nearby mountain and the field hospital was busy that day. It could have been much worse, but fortunately most of the rockets overshot the base and landed in the South China Sea.

The US response to the assault was typical of the war: Wait for several hours for permission to respond to the incoming fire, then eventually send up the Phantom jets and bomb the hell out of a mountainside, killing plants and trees — once the Viet Cong had all moved on.

Cold comfort

I MOVED into a port-camp, one of the little housing units provided by the company for staff. These were actually a leg above anything else on the base except maybe the general's quarters. You could call them small trailers, but they were good enough: air-conditioned, with hot and cold running water. There was also a loaded .45 caliber pistol under the bed.

On the first night, I took the bullets out of the gun, walked up to a cliff overlooking the beach and tossed the damn things into the ocean. How the hell could I sleep with a loaded gun under my bed? I might end up shooting myself. Not all Americans are cowboys from Texas.

American Express International Banking Corporation, Military Banking Division, Chu Lai, Vietnam, APO 96302, was no slouch of an operation. I was surprised to find the place staffed with several expats: three Americans, two Germans, and a Japanese guy named Dick Hase. The job was nothing special, though, and the Vietnamese staff did most of the work.

Dick and I became best friends within the work group. He was a quiet fellow, and wise in many ways. He taught me many things about how the military circus worked. It was the sergeants who ran the military, he explained. They were the "wheelers and dealers," making all kinds of business deals on the back of military operations.

This I found to be particularly true of a man named Sergeant Cruz. If you wanted anything, no problem: call Cruz. The guy was running a 24-hour on-call operation: Need a crate of steaks? "How many?" "How many cases of beer you need, man?" It was party time!

One night, peering through cigarette smoke at the Officers' Club, I suddenly heard someone yell out my name. "Bruce! Unbelievable. What the hell are you doing here?" Amazing! One of my frat buddies from the Florida Southern college, Bob Kimbrough, was here on the same piece of sand. Bob was half way through a tour as a second lieutenant pilot, flying Huey helicopters. Damn, I thought, this was the result of staying in the college Reserve Officer Training Corps. I was happy to learn later that he made it out of the place unscathed. (And while he was there, I was very pleased to procure an occasional case of steaks for him and his troops, courtesy of Sergeant Cruz).

Back to the subject of party time, though…

One Saturday morning, I heard Dick calling out to me.

I never did like working on Saturday mornings, but he had an urgent message — more like a warning, in fact.

"Sergeant Cruz came by and said to remind you to come to the party up on the hill behind the NCO Club in the afternoon." Dick advised: "Don't go. These G.I.s all no good, all smoke that stuff, that 'mariana."

"Oh, marijuana, really? Any ladies there?" I replied.

"Oh no, don't know, he didn't say; don't go."

"Dick, do you have anything better to do in this dust bowl?"

I was an athlete and did not smoke. I had smoked one joint with a friend as a teenager in New Jersey and I remembered it because, after smoking it, we went for a beer at a topless bar in Garfield and made fools out of ourselves ogling the girls.

Against the advice of my friend, however, I went to the hill to check out what was going down. Curiosity got the better of me. It was late afternoon and the sweet smell of marijuana was already heavy.

"Where the hell is the truck?" shouted Sergeant Cruz, taking a long slow hit on a freshly-rolled, foot-long reefer before passing it around. "Shit. It is five o'clock, and they were supposed to be here an hour ago."

"What truck you talking about, man?" mumbled one of the soldiers as he exhaled smoke rings.

The soldier was a young black fellow from Georgia named Al, about 19 years old and a "grunt," as infantry foot soldiers were called. These were the young guys that went out in the bush looking for the enemy for days at a time — the ones who did the actual fighting. They were all great young men serving their country in a senseless war that was not popular. I looked up to them and prayed they would all make it back home safely. But for every one of these fellows, there were at least another ten military staff providing support and various other services. It all felt like a big scam. My mind went wild at times. It seemed the war was much more about business, about money, than any "domino theory" about stopping Communism. It was a huge mistake, and a shameful disgrace on the part of America. I digress…

"The ice cream truck, you idiot!" Cruz shouted back.

Just then, we heard the sound of a vehicle approaching. Everyone jumped up.

"That's the big fucking surprise, Cruz? Ice cream?"

From the hilltop, we could see a big white truck with the Foremost Ice Cream logo written in red on its front and sides. It was about a mile down the road but it was approaching at a very high rate of speed and kicking up one hell of a dust trail. Five minutes later, there it was, screeching to a halt right in front of us.

"What the hell took you so long?" screamed Cruz at the young driver, who was sweating profusely. (Murphy's Law! He'd got stuck behind a convoy and couldn't pass it!)

The truck had been off-base early in the morning, delivering a load of ice-cream to the next base, a small Marine outpost about 20 klicks down the road. On the way back, it had picked up some very precious cargo.

"Quick. Open the goddamn truck door! The girls!" screamed Cruz.

Suddenly a half dozen of us were at the back of the truck refrigerator door as it sprang open.

Our jaws dropped! There they were, six local ladies. Three were throwing up, and the other three were passed out. I thought they might be dead. Just in time, they got out of the truck — crying, and screaming in Vietnamese. The situation was chaos. Holy shit, it was pandemonium. All survived, thank God, but they were really shook up.

Sergeant Cruz was worried, but worried only about one thing.

"The mama-san in Tam Ky is going to be so pissed off. No more party girls now or ever. It's a disaster."

Again, everything was for sale in this goddamn war and it was rarely pretty.

Later that night, I went home feeling drunk and uneasy. Cruz came in the following Monday, his usual smiling self.

"What happened to the girls?" I asked, genuinely concerned, amazed at the stupidity of what had happened, and terrified at the thought of what *might* have happened.

"Oh, no problem," Cruz casually replied. "Took them back off the base the next morning the same way they came in, in the ice cream truck. They refused at first and put up one hell of a commotion. I had to put a gun to their heads, haha."

Nine long months later, I finally got my transfer notice. Due to the rapid rotation of AmEx employees, many of whom decided to quit and go home early, a chance had opened for me to move closer to Saigon. I was to be sent to an air force base in Tuy Hoa, halfway back to Saigon in time and distance.

Ambush

THE difference between an army base and an air force base is like night and day. Chu Lai was a shit-hole compared to Tuy Hoa, at least on the surface. The roads in Tuy Hoa were paved, and the place was maintained. There was grass and trees. At Chu Lai, the only green I saw was that of army fatigues.

The American Express office in Tuy Hoa was run by a happy-go-lucky character named Kerry Murphy, a really great guy with whom I became instant friends. He was Irish, a hard worker and a real fun-loving fellow. We hit it off instantly.

Soon we got into a good working routine, covering for each other. Because Vietnam is hotter than hell, we got thirsty. By noon we would have our first beer, but in disguise. We would pop open a can of Coke, pour out the soda and fill it with cold beer. By the time the staff had balanced out and gone home for the day, we were already drunk and heading for the Officers' Club to continue our revelry.

Kerry had a cute Vietnamese girlfriend who worked for the bank, and he was constantly worried that she would get pregnant. More and more, we started leaving the security and boredom of the base and heading downtown to Tuy Hoa, where we each rented a room in his girlfriend's house. Transportation was in the form of Honda 90 motorcycles we had bought, and the distance from the base to the village was about 20 kilometers. The journey entailed riding down the highway, then turning onto a narrow two-lane road which passed straight through ten klicks of rice paddies, separated by two bridges over two rivers.

The bridges were the dangerous part. They held the railroad tracks for the trains, and the railings were separated by wooden planks, many of which were missing. You had to be damn careful and sharp-eyed, switching from plank to plank, when you saw one that was missing. Hit a pothole and you and the bike could be flipped over the side of the bridge and into the water, which seemed to be at least 100 feet below.

One night we had to make a quick decision. One of our staff, Miss Phung, was getting married, and we were invited to the party. But this also turned out to be the night when we had a shitload of problems at the bank. Saigon was calling about a shipment of American Express Travelers Checks that had not arrived. The courier was hours late and we couldn't get in contact with him. We could not leave until they determined where the hell the checks were, and it was already dusk. The phone rang again and again, with either Saigon or the wedding party in Tuy Hoa calling. Finally, around 8pm, we got word by telex. The courier had taken the $100,000 T/C shipment and boarded the C-130 from Saigon to Pleiku by mistake.

It was already 9pm and we were facing a dilemma. We were guests of honor at the wedding. But we'd never left the base this late, and there was a curfew. It was dangerous driving in the dark.

By then we were pretty drunk, however. We looked at each other and made a decision: What the hell, let's do it.

All the traffic was by then traveling back to base; and there we were, trying to leave. The guard at the gate motioned us over to stop.

"Where the hell are you two arseholes going? You fucking crazy?" he said.

"Yeah, we're crazy," we replied. "Just lift the gate so we can get our fat asses off this shit-hole base. We're heading to a party."

"You're totally nuts! Don't you know there are Viet Cong operating in the area?"

It was a clear night, with a full moon. As Kerry led the way, there wasn't another vehicle in sight. Once we passed through the mountainous area, the road sloped down a bit until it leveled out. Then it became an absolutely straight road for about five klicks through rice paddies. It was a beautiful sight; beautiful, that is, until clouds passed in front of the brilliant full moon and everything went pitch black. For the first time, I began to think the guard had been right. Kerry was about 50 meters ahead of me. In the silence of the night, the sound of our motorcycles could be heard for miles, and we were only about halfway there.

All of a sudden, there was a flash of light, and the red brake lights on Kerry's Honda lit up. I heard his bike skidding on the asphalt, along with a strange hissing sound. Adrenaline coursed through my body and I was instantly sober. As I drove towards him, my heart racing, I tried to gaze into the dark fields to see if we were being attacked by the VC. Memories of my family flashed up in my mind. I thought about my friends, who'd told me I was nuts going to Vietnam.

"Kerry!" I shouted out as I drove towards him.

I realized the hissing sound was on account of the razor-sharp concertina wire that had been stretched across the road, causing both tires of Kerry's bike to burst. A second coil rolled out behind him and in front of me, but I was able to skid off to the side and slam the bike into the gravel so the wire hit the side of my bike and missed me. I saw blood on my scraped hands, but strangely felt nothing. I was totally numb. This is it, I thought. It's a VC ambush. I was just waiting to hear the sound of shots fired from the darkness.

Suddenly, Kerry was surrounded. Ten, maybe 20, soldiers jumped from the rice paddies from both sides of the road. I was a few meters behind. Brandishing M-16 rifles, they started screaming at us in Vietnamese. We started screaming back in English.

Then one said: "Where you go, G.I.?"

They were all wearing green. We had been ambushed all right, but not by the Viet Cong. We'd been ambushed by "friendlies" — by the ARVN, our allies. The soldiers had been sitting waiting for VC.

Instead of shooting us, an old Vietnamese man appeared with a set of wire cutters and cut the wires out of Kerry's bike. It took about 15 minutes to get the job done, and another two hours for us to get back to the air base. We took turns walking the bike with two flat tires and riding mine next to it. We got back to the base just before the Officers' Club closed at midnight. Just in time for another cold beer.

A close call — and a call from home

AS THE months passed, Amex staff seemed to be bailing out and heading home in increasing numbers. Inevitably, I found myself on the move once again, this time to Saigon.

Hailing a small white taxi outside Tan Son Nhut Airport, it felt pretty good to be back in the capital. Saying good-bye first to Chu Lai, and then to Tuy Hoa, had not been a problem for me. It felt something like going from the desert to a village and then finally arriving in the big city. For the next couple of months, I was to be assigned to American Express at the Military Assistance Command Vietnam (MACV) headquarters in Saigon.

The compound was a sprawling set of buildings and facilities located between Tan Son Nhut and ARVN General Command. The big guns, including General William Westmoreland — who was Chief of Staff of the US Army for four years — worked here. MACV came to be known as "Pentagon East."

I stayed in a villa rented on the base by AmEx: 127 Ly Tran Quan was a nice place on a quiet, shady street two blocks from the Saigon downtown cemetery. I remember the cemetery because it was the same one where the Viet Cong had hidden most of the ammo they'd used during the Tet Lunar New Year Offensive of 1968.

The villa had six bedrooms and a pool on the roof. It was ideal for rounding up a few girls from one of the local bars and throwing a party. The company also employed a little old lady named Cupa, who was a great cook. She could only speak two English words: "Eat now." Each time she said it, she giggled heartily.

Being young and single — and a civilian — in Saigon meant there were some crazy times. Vietnam was full of women who spoiled a young, healthy bachelor rotten. I routinely had my drinks, which were plentiful, in the presence of beautiful young ladies in the wall-to-wall bars on Tu Do Street or Nguyen Hue Boulevard. Just before the 11pm curfew all the military fled, leaving all the women behind and at the mercy of us civilians.

Instinctively, however, I knew these experiences would change me. The vibe of the place naturally included the backdrop of an ongoing, brutal war — in fact, even as a civilian, you never knew when you might be in the wrong place at the wrong time and get your ass blown off. It was "live for today," because tomorrow you may not exist. That also created a somewhat heedless attitude of "I don't give a damn about anything," which risked leading to a complete breakdown of what would normally be considered moral and ethical behavior. For some people, the breakdown was real. Every day was lived on the edge. And sometimes — usually before the military curfew — shit happened.

One hot evening, I was slurping a cold beer in My-My, a bar on Tu Do Street. It was nearing curfew and I had a young lady sitting on my lap when we suddenly heard a massive explosion out on the street — bam! The whole bar shook like an earthquake.

Someone screamed: "What the fuck was that??" We ran outside with our ears ringing, and looked across the street. The Bristol Bar had just been hit. We later learned that a Viet Cong sympathizer had driven by on a motorbike and flipped in a couple of grenades. Of the half-dozen unlucky civilians and G.I.s who had been sitting at the bar, not much remained. The Bristol had actually been one of my favorite hangouts, and it was purely by chance that I'd gone to My-My instead on this particular day. The chaos that followed and the smell of explosives and flesh was nauseating. "Fucking gooks!" everybody screamed, some shooting into the air.

FROM the MACV office, I was sent on different assignments and I got to know my way around the region. I often worked in Di An and Phu Loi, about 40 kilometers past the sprawling Ben Hoa Air Force Base, and at Cu Chi, on the outskirts of Saigon. (Years later, it emerged that Cu Chi base had been underlaid by an amazing series of tunnels *right under the base,* allowing the VC freedom of movement. It became a major tourist attraction after the war.)

On New Year's Eve, the last day of 1970, a couple of the office girls, myself and another fellow all decided to go to the beach town of Vung Tau, about a two-hour drive south, for a party.

We checked into our little hotel and I took a shower before heading to the lobby bar, where we were to meet for a few beers before dinner. I was almost dressed when someone started banging on my door. I mean *banging.* I opened it to find a colleague almost yelling at me: "Bruce, they are looking for you. I heard your name on the Armed Forces radio."

"What… *my name?* What the hell are you talking about?"

"Your name, damn it. No joke, man. The message is to tell you to contact the Saigon Red Cross immediately."

The air in my lungs turned hot and heavy. Whatever this was about, it could not be good. I called the Red Cross, and as I waited for the operator to come on the line, I became aware that it was almost New Year's Eve in America. All I could think was: This has to be about my dad. My dad. I felt sick.

The Red Cross told me Dad had suffered a heart attack and passed away. I was to return immediately to Saigon, where the company would get me on the first flight to America. I just stood there, stunned, as a feeling of ineffable sadness and disbelief overcame me. My eyes reddened as the tears welled, and each heartbeat reverberated in my head.

After the initial shock hit me, I fumbled through getting my things together and my friend drove me to Saigon that night, even though it was after curfew. We braved it and drove as fast as possible. Before we got to the highway, we passed through a small village at breakneck speed. Suddenly a dog ran out in front of us, and *bam*! It glanced off the side of the jeep and made the most harrowing — and the loudest — wailing sounds you could possibly imagine. Shit! That poor dog! The neighborhood was waking up. Lights were coming on. What could we do? My friend put his foot down and we lammed it. Albeit accidentally, we'd probably killed that hapless dog, but there was really nothing we could do about it now.

MEMORIES of my dad flooded my consciousness over the days I spent traveling to Orlando: a 40-hour trip in those days. I felt especially sad that he had died before my home leave, which was scheduled for the following month. It was a profoundly sad time.

Looking down from heaven, he would have seen the humor in my arrival in Orlando, though. My sister Honey, being a proud former US Marine, had calculated when my flight would be arriving at the Orlando Air Force Base and called our sister, Janice. "Come, drive me there right now. Our brother is arriving from Vietnam."

Honey and Janice arrived at the gate of the Air Force Base, and Honey flashed her 20-year-old Marine ID right in the guard's face, while shouting, "Pull up the gates right now!"

This agitated him somewhat. He said: "Let me have a look at that!" The guard looked at her long-expired ID and refused to hand it back.

"You should not have this. This is the property of the US government."

"Give it back!" Honey demanded.

"Hell, no."

Honey threw such a fit she had to be restrained by the Military Police. Meanwhile, Janice was doubled over in a fit of uncontrollable laughter. And at about the same time as this whole fiasco was happening, I was landing at Orlando International Airport on a Delta Airlines flight from San Francisco — nowhere near the Air Force base.

WE GOT through Dad's memorial service as best we could, but by the time I had been in America for two weeks, I was itching to get out. My family and friends asked me to stay. Disney World was opening in Orlando, and the city was expected to grow; there would be good opportunities. But I missed the Far East, and to my surprise, I missed Vietnam in particular. I had the itch, and I had to scratch it. Orlando seemed dull by comparison.

As I prepared to return to Asia, I was sad to be saying good-bye to my mom again, but I also couldn't wait to get back to the excitement of travel and Vietnam. I had a lot to look forward to. Kurt Leutsch, who was the country manager of AmEx, and German, had promised me a new position near Saigon that involved covering the two area offices mentioned previously — at Phu Loi and Di An — and I'd decided it made sense for me to set up digs downtown.

(Kurt was about five feet six and rotund, with a Santa Claus-like red face. He was also one hell of a nice guy. In fact, all the Germans working for AmEx came across as hard-working and humble. It seemed their only pleasure in life, after work, was to get stuck into a couple of six-packs of Budweiser. I always gave my ration card to Kurt so he could buy another case every month.)

On my way back to Vietnam, however, I first had a stopover in Hong Kong.

Twenty-four hours after leaving Orlando, I was drifting in and out of sleep when I heard the Pan Am stewardess on the intercom: "Fasten your seat belts; we are on our final approach to Kai Tak Airport in Hong Kong." It was 8am.

I was so happy to be back in Hong Kong, and had made a reservation at the Hilton for the night. I would be leaving for Saigon the following afternoon. The same day I landed, I was looking forward to having dinner with a lovely Chinese girl named Jenny, whom I'd met last time I was in town, at what would soon become our usual spot, Jimmy's Kitchen. I loved the escargot there. Jimmy's Kitchen to this day remains one of the city's most legendary restaurants.

The next morning, I breakfasted on the balcony of the Hilton, which overlooked the Hong Kong cricket pitch. And as I tucked into my chicken-liver omelet, drained several cups of coffee and thumbed the pages of *Time* and *Newsweek* whilst listening to the BBC World Service broadcast murmuring in the background, I thought to myself: I could get used to this kind of pure decadence.

Looking back, I sometimes think it was fate that dictated my decision to go back to Asia. Already in my youth in New Jersey I could feel a premonition about that part of the world. I remember staring at a map as a young schoolboy and feeling something in my soul. I was fascinated by Asia with all its exotic names and places: Hong Kong, Saigon, Bangkok and Jakarta, just to name a few. Now, I just felt happy to be back, and I knew my adventures were only just beginning.

A taste of things to come

WHILE in Hong Kong, I also prepared a little money scam. In Vietnam, as an AmEx banker, I was able to change money at ridiculous rates, and had access to US dollars, military coupons and Vietnamese piasters — all tradeable on the black money market.

First stop, the Hong Kong office of American Express. Next, the chemist. You could never be sure about customs when arriving in Saigon, so I cashed a check for $2,000, asking for 20 crisp US hundred-dollar bills. That was a hell of a lot of money in those days.

Returning to my hotel, I wrapped the money in plastic and stuffed it into the back of a large tube of Colgate toothpaste I had sliced open with a razor blade.

The flight to Saigon the next afternoon arrived on time. After dropping my things off at the company villa, I jumped into a taxi and headed downtown to the Astor Hotel. The smell of Saigon was exhilarating.

At the hotel, I closed the screeching gate of the old French-built lobby lift and pressed the button for the sixth floor, where I had to get out and walk up a flight of stairs to the rooftop bar, which is where I knew I would find Mr. Tai, my good Chinese friend, and to my knowledge the best black-market money changer in Saigon. (Next best were the Indians who hung around on the street across from the Mosque.)

"Mr. Tai, good to see you."

"Mr. Bruce! You been up-country? Long time no see."

"Yes, up-country. What's the rate, Mr. Tai?"

"How much you got?"

"Two thousand US *green*."

"Dollars! Great, man, great! I'll give you MPC 4,000 or 1,600,000 Vietnamese piasters."

"Give me the MPC."

Being manager of a bank, I had access to all three currencies. I would put MPC 2,000 away for now, and then over time exchange the remaining MPC 2,000 at 1:1 for another $2,000 at my bank. Poof! I was doubling my money like magic. I felt just like the Fed and the US government — creating money out of thin air.

Had I been really greedy, or perhaps smarter, I could have made a small fortune, but I was happy enough stashing away a couple of thousand every few months. At the time I thought that was big money. Little did I know how the black market would direct my future, but looking back it was here that I discovered my mission in life. I just didn't know that yet.

Dealing in the black market was not always easy, though, and you had to learn who to trust and who not to trust. You never knew whether a person smiling at you was a friend or foe.

I learned my lesson the hard way when a guy on the street offered me a rate to exchange $100 green for 300 MPC. He even brought me a couple beers while I waited down an alley for the money to arrive. My guard was down. I took the bundle but when I got back to my hotel to count it, it turned out to be a load of piaster wrapped up in a 20 MPC note. I took a loss of $75 on the transaction and learned a couple of big lessons, one of which was not to be greedy. (Some GIs took being ripped off by money changers on the street a little harder — and would start shooting their guns in the air.)

———•❧•❦•———

LIFE IN Saigon had a rhythm to it: working all day in the office, scamming to find ways to earn extra bread, partying every night until midnight.

Living at the company villa was nice, but it did restrict my ability to go out at night, whether to change money at the top of the Astor or to party. It was not long before I moved out, therefore — and into the Cach San Vo Thanh, a place managed by Mr. Tai.

The Cach San Vo Thanh also happened to be just across from a new pub, Club 147 Vo Thanh, that had been opened by a G.I. from South Carolina. He had married a local girl and decided to stay.

The 147 Vo Thanh would become my virtual oasis.

Decorated with red-velvet wallpaper, it was where you could go for southern-fried chicken and sizzling steaks served on metal-and-wood platters. But the real attraction had to be the bevy of beautiful girls who poured the beer, served the food, lit cigarettes and made conversation. The place was cozy, with less than a dozen tables and a small winding stairway leading up to a tiny bar in the loft. After dinner, you could invite one of the girls for a Saigon Tea ("You buy me Saigon Tea? No tea, no talk.") I soon got to know all six of them — and they soon learned that I lived in the building across the street in an apartment on the top floor, and had a roof garden. Thanks to the curfews in place, often I'd hear a knock at my door and find one of the girls looking for a place to stay for the night. Neither the Vietnamese police, known as "little white mice" because of their white uniforms, nor the military, took kindly to girls roaming around after midnight.

For me, the attraction of Saigon at that time was that it was just a truly tantalizing place. The city bewitched and intoxicated like the exotic beauty she was, her myriad and sensuous charms just waiting to be discovered. I never knew what to expect, but expected something new every day. What's more, because I was changing green for piasters at anything up to P800/1, whereas the official rate was P118/1, I was able to live like a king in the local economy.

More and more each day, however, the horrors of the war started to creep in under my skin. The war really dehumanized people. One Cobra pilot, for example, went around with a tape he'd made. On it you could hear him singing "Here Comes Santa Claus" over and over, followed by artillery fire as he blew away a dozen Viet Cong. The people he gunned down were human beings just like us: people who had mothers and fathers, sisters and brothers, grandmothers and grandfathers.

Another thing that always bothered me — besides the killing and destruction — was seeing how some people were really living it up even as the country went to ruin. Spending most of 1971 working for American Express at MACV Headquarters next to the airport provided a glimpse of where and how the top brass military lived — the colonels and generals who were running the war. And what I remember most were the amenities: Olympic-sized swimming pools, golf courses, good restaurants, sports clubs like the famous colonial-era Cercle Sportif, and a so-called BX discount store on the base that was stocked with just about everything you could imagine.

MPC was used to buy anything and everything on base — stereos, cameras, watches, you name it — and most items were almost immediately sold on at a tidy profit. You would soon find them on sale at street markets all over Saigon and in particular at Cholon, the large Chinatown at the far end of the city.

Surrounded by extravagance and profiteering in the midst of bloodshed, it helped to make light of things however you could.

I don't know the term used by the other military banks there — Chase and Bank of America — but for AmEx, overdrawn accounts, which were a huge percentage of all our accounts, were called TIDs, or Transactions in Difficulty. G.I.s who were rotated home left behind a heck of a lot of checks that would bounce. We wrote them letters, but the only reply I ever saw came with a picture. Our debtor had traced around his hand with a pencil — middle finger extended. What he probably didn't know was that under our contract with the US Department of Defense, the losses were all written off by the US Treasury, which meant that in effect AmEx really didn't give a shit. On another occasion, we were about to ship a load of canceled checks back to New York when one of the girls spilled a whole bottle of *nuc mum* on top of them. *Nuc mum* is a liquid shrimp sauce the Vietnamese eat with everything, and it has a powerful, foul stench that can knock your socks off.

What to do? Nothing. We packed it up and sent it through the Army Post Office to the New York office. About ten days later, we got a call from New York asking what the hell was in that box. I was told that when they opened it, half the staff in the New York office freaked out and started looking for a dead cat.

Many of the Transactions in Difficulty we handled, though, were for poor souls, barely out of high school, who had been killed in action. The TID slips were collected and shipped home with their personal belongings. Often, blood-stained checkbooks would be handed to us for account reconciliation.

Perhaps all this degradation accounted somehow for a certain permissive approach to wrongdoing. I remember there was one AmEx staff member who got caught after he had made some $100,000 on the black market. We thought he would be tarred and feathered. Instead, he was sent out of the country within 24 hours, later to be hired by Chase in Germany, and given a good reference by AmEx to boot. The bank obviously did not want to be embarrassed by the incident.

As time went on, I found I just couldn't tolerate the job — or the war — anymore. I went to the USO to call home and tell my family I was coming back.

I knew I would miss several things about Vietnam — the French restaurants and the good food at the Mosque, visiting my friends the Indian money changers, seeing Cobra gunships close up and Huey helicopter pilots showing off as they skimmed the streets showing off, to name but a few. But where I had once seen excitement and adventure, I now saw dread and degeneracy. The lyric to Edwin Starr's song ran constantly through my head: "War! What is it good for? Absolutely nothing."

Last orders

HAVING decided not to be part of the machine any longer — small a cog though I was —

I resigned my position as I neared the end of my second tour.

As I did so, many impressions flooded my mind. I remember sitting in a bar with a lady on my lap, one of several too many cold beers in my hand, and realizing that nothing seemed to matter anymore. It was June 1971 and the US was starting to bring the troops home in large numbers, turning everything over to the Vietnamese. AmEx was closing offices rapidly.

During my final stretch in Vietnam, I slept on the couch at the home of my good buddy and colleague John Langer and his beautiful Vietnamese wife (both of whom I remain friends with to this day.)

Having secured assurances from Miss Tuy, the company secretary, that she would delay notifying immigration about my departure until I gave her the OK, I decided to do a little more dollar salting before I left. I had to be careful, though. Other AmEx staff pulling similar stunts on the black money market had been caught by the Army's criminal investigators, the CID. But I needed the money to support myself and to pay for some more education when I returned home.

So I went on one last spree.

I had about one month to fill my coffers, and I sensed the Army investigators were watching me. Finally, on my last day at AmEx, I was approached in the bank by a military intelligence operative in civilian clothes. He introduced himself as Albert and asked me to meet him later for a drink.

I knew I would be carrying a bundle of US dollars and some traveler's checks that evening, so I had a queasy feeling that it was a set-up. Either that or he wanted in on the action. I said I would meet him at the Roxy Bar on Tu Do Street at 10pm. I knew the *mama-san* and many of the girls working there.

When I finally arrived, however, it was after 11pm, and all the military personnel had gone home. I had been to see Mr. Tai, who — unusually — had kept me waiting at the Astor Hotel bar for almost two hours. "Bruce," said the *mama-san*, "someone was here waiting for you and just left. He had a few beers and asked a lot of questions. He very pissed off you no come on time! When he left, I watch him cross street and meet up with two army MPs and take off in their jeep."

A chill ran down the back of my neck.

I knew the walls were closing in and it was time for me to get out. So, I made a little money and at the same time embarked on a month-long going away party that only stopped because PanAm was threatening not to allow any further changes to my travel dates.

My plan was to get back to the States and study law — and who could say, maybe even one day run for some kind of office and do some good. *It was a good plan.* My ticket to New York was written as follows: Saigon/ Bangkok/ Rangoon/ Calcutta/ Delhi/ Karachi/ Tehran/ Tel Aviv/ Athens/ Rome/ London/ New York.

The last thing I could have known then was that many years later, just as the United States government seemed hellbent on locking me up and throwing away the key, connections in Vietnam would be my saving grace.

What I did know was that I had caught the travel and adventure bug — and when you have an itch, you have to scratch it. Scratching it would lead me to become friends with one of the world's most charismatic intelligence operatives of the 20th Century, a man described as "The James Bond of money." Fate was about to deal me an exciting new hand.

CHAPTER 3

Deak & Company

SOME PEOPLE ARE very calculating and plan their futures step by step. In my life, I've tended to prefer casting my fate to the wind, confident that the only direction to go is up. Part of the magic and beauty of life is that things do not always turn out the way you expect them to.

I returned to America and began studying law at Memphis State University, in Tennessee, alongside my old buddy Ron Langa, with whom I'd lived when we worked as claims adjusters in Orlando.

After a year at law school, however, it was clear to me that I would be a lousy lawyer. When I analyzed legal cases, I often came up with the wrong conclusions — I believe because I was basing my answers on common sense. I also yearned for the sense of adventure I had had in the Far East. There, I had felt alive every minute — whereas spending endless hours at the university library, plowing through pages of legal literature, felt increasingly pointless. I decided to drop out.

During this time, I'd continued to have regular contact with Jenny, the shy Chinese girl whom I'd dated in Hong Kong. While I was still at law school, she traveled to Toronto in Canada to study at a secretarial college. She would fly down and visit me in Memphis regularly, and we'd have a fantastic time together. From the start, I had seen something wonderful in her and I knew it would last a lifetime.

On one of those trips after Jenny's course had finished we decided, on a whim, to get married. My good friend Ron, who carried on at law school, was my best man, and in fact he and his future wife, Lynda, were the only witnesses at our civil ceremony.

That night, Jenny and I shared a quiet dinner at a simple restaurant before heading back to our tiny rented nest on top of a garage, just behind a big Southern mansion. Pooling our funds, we had a grand total of $1,800 — one hell of a start.

Jenny had a strong faith, though. Every Sunday she went to the Catholic Church near-by for Mass, while I stayed home drinking coffee and reading the Sunday newspaper.

I was — once again — in the market for a job, and Jenny suggested I reach out to a company in Hong Kong that she knew about: an international foreign exchange firm called Deak & Company, which happened to be the same firm that I had used to buy the US dollar notes I had smuggled back to Saigon in toothpaste tubes. At the time, Deak had been known in Saigon as the biggest operator in the black market.

I had actually also met the Managing Director of Deak & Company's Hong Kong office on one of my visits there. Dirk Brink had come running out of his office to the exchange counter that day, yelling: "Goddammit. Doesn't anybody have a visa to go to Jakarta?" Calming down somewhat, he'd then flashed me a smile that indicated this sort of thing happened all the time.

We'd had a chat. I told him I would like to work in Hong Kong some day.

"Ah," he said. "You have an American passport. Good, very easy for you to get visas. Give me a call. Stay in touch."

Now, after opting out of law school and desperately trying to find a job, I searched around for that business card from Dirk Brink. Jenny found it — and I made the most important call of my life.

"Deak and Company Far East Hong Kong," the voice of the receptionist trilled confi-dently.

"Hi, my name is Bruce Aitken," I said, "and I am calling from the United States. May I speak to Mr. Dirk Brink?"

"Hold on," she replied. I did.

I took a deep breath and prayed hard. I had no Plan B. After several seconds, which seemed to last an hour, Brink's deep voice answered on the other end, with a tone of wari-ness as to who could possibly be calling him from America and for what.

SURPRISINGLY, Mr. Brink remembered me almost instantly. He said that, as a matter of fact, he had an opening in Hong Kong right there and then, and he was looking for a new assistant.

"I'll arrange for you to go to Deak & Company in New York as soon as possible to apply for the job and undergo training," he told me in what I would come to know as his charac-teristic deep voice. "If you pass, you'll come to Hong Kong in a couple of months. Get one of those big fat passports with 48 pages. The job involves a lot of traveling."

My heart was racing. I hugged Jenny, and thanked God and her. A miracle had just happened. From here on, our lives were going to speed up considerably.

On a cold day in January, I was scheduled to take a 4pm flight from Memphis to New York for my interview. However, Jenny and I were nearly broke, and I'd decided to earn a few dollars before I went. I was doing hours as a laborer, working high up on the new bridge that was being built over the Mississippi River. It was dangerous work, but the pay was good.

I got to the bridge and started to climb to the top level. It was snowing, but they had a good warm fire burning up there. "Good morning all," I said. Then, as I bent down to pick up a wrench…CRACK. I felt the cold steel of another one slam into one of my upper front teeth, breaking half of it.

The pain was excruciating, but I was more worried about the interview in New York.

"You *moron!*" I screamed at my co-worker. "Look what you've done. I have a job interview tomorrow morning."

Poor fellow. He thought he'd been doing me a favor by handing me a wrench just at the moment I'd been bending down to pick one up myself. I regained my composure and ran down from the bridge as fast as I could, then made straight for home. I was panicking. Just like many times in my life when I was in deep shit, I prayed.

"Jenny," I yelled as I burst into the little apartment we rented over the garage. "Look what happened!" Much to my surprise, she looked at me and laughed! She said I looked funny with a broken tooth.

"Oh, Lord, what am I going to do now? *Think,* Jenny!"

The solution? Call Dan Dooley. Yes! Memphis State University had a fine dental school, and our friend Dan was a graduate student. A couple of hours later, I was out of the dental chair, with a new state-of-the-art, high-tech half-tooth called an "enamel etch" in my mouth. I asked Dan how long it would last. "Well," he said. "When you are in New York, chew all your food on the other side."

I caught a late evening flight to New York and arrived at my hotel after midnight. I had a bad headache and one hell of a toothache. In fact, I was afraid the whole tooth was going to come out.

The next morning, I woke up very early. I showered and dressed in my best suit — or more accurately, my only suit. I thanked God the tooth was still there!

I took the subway to Wall Street. The winter sun was rising, but it was very cold. It was 8am and the diner I stopped in for a cup of real New York coffee was already crowded.

Across the street, I could see a neon light in the foreign exchange shop at street level: "Deak-Perera Foreign Exchange." I felt a big knot in my stomach.

By nine in the morning, I was being introduced to the traders at Deak: Chief Trader Raoul Del Cristo from Cuba, Lallo from Columbia, Michel from Egypt, and Manuel Van Gelderan, who was visiting from Buenos Aires. All of them were laughing like hell over a joke in Spanish they said they would not dare translate. No doubt about it, I liked this place.

After several meetings, and as the day was winding down, the secretary on the eighth floor finally motioned to me. "Mr. Roethenmund is ready to see you now."

This was it. Otto Roethenmund, the number two guy — Senior VP. "Hello, Bruce," he said. "Welcome to Deak New York. What do you think of this place?"

Otto could not have been nicer or made me feel more comfortable. He was a Swiss banker and had the savoir faire of a gentleman. In the '70s, Swiss and other international bankers were held in awe by Americans — and envied because they could buy and own gold. At the time, the Gold Reserve Act made it a criminal offense for US citizens to own or trade gold anywhere in the world. I would later learn that Deak & Company had ways around that.

After an extended and pleasant conversation, he got straight to the point.

"Well, Bruce, you are doing fine, and you are the kind of guy we feel is a good fit for the position in Hong Kong. Dirk Brink needs help. You have been in the Far East, you have a Chinese wife, and you speak a bit of the language."

By now, it was already about 6pm and my headache was returning. No-one had mentioned anything about my broken tooth, but the pain was unrelenting.

Then Otto Roethenmund dropped the bomb: "One more thing before you meet Mr. Deak tomorrow morning."

Meet Mr Deak? Holy Jesus. I'd never expected to meet Mr. Deak, the legendary founder of the company, in person!

But first things first: they wanted me to go and take a lie detector test.

"Have you ever taken a polygraph test?" Otto asked. "If you hurry, you can still make it up town tonight in time for one. Here is the address."

As a matter of fact, I had. When I had interviewed for the National Security Agency job at Fort Meade, Maryland, during my last year of college, I'd had to take one then. (I suddenly had a flashback to the blinking signs that graced the walls of the agency's corridors: "Monitor Your Conversation.")

Being fastened to the machine whilst indicators such as your blood pressure and skin conductivity are measured and recorded is quite an irksome experience, especially when you have a thumping headache. The operator in charge of my test in New York, a surprisingly congenial chap named Mr. Wilson, told me to come back in the morning for my results.

Mr. Deak

MEETING with Hungarian-born Nicholas Deak was like meeting with a celebrity, a real international heavyweight. As founder and chairman of Deak-Perera, the worldwide currency exchange and precious-metals dealer, he was at the time one of the financial world's best-known figures. An article in *Time* magazine from 1964 called him "the James Bond of the world of money." He held a doctorate in economics and talked money in five languages. What's more, he was a decorated war hero and a former US intelligence agent.

"Good morning, Mr. Aitken. Mr. Deak will see you now."

This was it. I had awoken early again, once more relieved that my tooth was still there. I really needed this job. All I could think was: What will happen to Jenny and me if I don't get hired? *Please God, please God…*

Mr. Deak stood up from his desk, motioning for me to come shake hands and sit down. The eight or ten steps to the desk seemed to take forever. I felt his awesome presence, no-nonsense and stern. And yet he had warmth in his eyes. The first thing he said was: "What did you think of the polygraph test?"

The only thing I could think of saying, with a nervous smile, was that I thought I had passed. I'd told the truth, although I had felt my heart beating very fast a few times.

"Yes, you did," replied Mr. Deak. "But, actually, in real life it means nothing. In real life we often *have to* lie. We work with a lot of money in this company and with a lot of private clients who trust us to keep their identity and affairs confidential — no matter what happens."

Our talk was friendly and ranged across numerous topics. When the intercom rang to remind Mr. Deak of another appointment, I glanced at my watch and was surprised to find that most of an hour had passed.

"Well, Bruce," he said. My heart sank — and then rose when he finally uttered the words: "Welcome to Deak & Company."

I was overwhelmed with joy and gratitude. He told me training would start the following week, and that I would start downstairs with Deak-Perera, the holding company of Mr Deak's financial services empire. He knew that my wife was a trained secretary, and offered a job for her too with Deak-Perera while I trained in New York.

My starting salary was to be $1,000 a month, and Jenny's $600. Our combined earnings didn't amount to a whole lot of money in New York, even by the standards of 1974, but still — I couldn't wait to get to a phone and call Jenny with the good news. Although she would not say so, I knew she must have been worried. I felt so proud to have been offered this job, like I'd regained my dignity as a person who could provide for his wife. Again, I had rolled the dice in life and come out okay. The thought of returning to Hong Kong — this time employed — was exhilarating.

Sometimes, people just click. Thank God that was what had happened with Mr. Deak and me. Over the years to come, we would become quite close, as he would often come to Hong Kong and invite Jenny and me to join him for dinner. Sometimes he would ask me to check something out for him on the lowdown and report back to him. And, like almost everyone who ever met her, Mr. Deak really took a liking to Jenny and no doubt felt I must be a wise man to have found such a special girl.

Coming to know Mr. Deak made a lifelong impression on me. Small wonder, as he was an altogether impressive man — charismatic and brilliant.

Although in his late 60s when I first met him, he was extremely fit: every morning he would jog around the track he'd had built at his mansion in Scarsdale, New York. He was also a strict vegetarian and seemed disciplined in every aspect of his life; nothing was left to chance.

I remember once during my training period rushing out for a quick lunch break and grabbing a hot dog from my favorite vendor at the corner of Battery Park, across the street from our Broadway office. As I was stuffing a second one into my mouth, I looked up and saw Mr. Deak standing in front of me. "Do you know what's in that hot dog you are eating?" he asked. Sheepishly, I said I had no idea, but that it sure tasted good. Seemed like he was probably just teasing me. On our walk back to the office, he said he would be coming to Hong Kong before the end of the year, and that he would contact me via Brink in case of any special assignments.

As I would later find out, during World War II — then in his late 30s — Deak had parachuted into the Burmese jungle and the Balkans on numerous covert missions as an agent of the Office of Strategic Services — a wartime intelligence agency of the United States, and the predecessor of the CIA. As a major in the US Army, he was also the officer who took the Japanese flag of surrender in Burma.

Immediately after the war, he was stationed in Hanoi, where he headed US intelligence operations in what was then still French Indochina.

Before long, he was back on US soil for good, however. Having opened Deak & Company, a foreign exchange business, in 1939, after the war he picked up where he'd left off before it in the business world. He soon acquired Perera US Inc, and in the decades prior to my joining the company he'd built a worldwide network of currency agents and smugglers to service a multitude of private clients — and intelligence operatives.

(These intelligence connections were in fact instrumental to Mr. Deak's rise. His colleagues in the OSS included future CIA directors William Colby and William Casey, and it's now well-established that the CIA gave Deak-Perera financial backing in its early years. As we shall see, there was an enormous *quid pro quo* at play.)

Meanwhile, Mr. Deak's stellar connections in the financial realm also extended to his personal life: his wife was the daughter of a Mr. Potter, an Austrian banker I would meet a couple of years later when I made a courtesy call to Bankhaus Deak — one of Mr Deak's overseas banks — in Vienna.

"In the world of foreign exchange and precious metals, no name glitters like Deak-Perera," the *New York Times* would write of Mr. Deak's creation in 1984, and it was hard to disagree with that assessment.

However, while some of the Deak-Perera methods were quite sophisticated, others involved a lot of smoke and mirrors. And in fact, some were ridiculously plain and simple — such as crossing borders over mountainous terrain in South America with bags of money loaded on the backs of donkeys. The expression "Where there is a will, there is a way" rang true at Deak. It didn't have to glitter, it only had to work.

JENNY and I enjoyed the time we spent working in New York City. We were squeezed into a tiny studio flat on 33rd Street and we worked long and hard during the week, but on Friday nights we went uptown to a pub called The Great British Disaster, where we would meet friends, including some buddies of mine from my Vietnam days. Saturdays were spent hanging around the city, and Sundays we read the *Times* and walked around in Central Park. The *Sunday Times* took all week to read; it weighed about ten pounds back then. For the first time in a long time, I was really happy.

Winter turned gradually into spring in New York, and just when Jenny and I were preparing for our move to Hong Kong, Otto Roethenmund called me into his office one day.

"Bruce, would you mind going to Guam for a few months before going to Hong Kong? It is on your way."

He explained that they needed someone to run the office while the established manager there, Tony Evans, was away. (When I later met Tony, I found him to be extremely hard-working, intelligent and likable. Unfortunately he was also extremely overweight — and a couple of years later we learned from Mr. Deak that he had suffered a massive heart attack and passed away at the age of 35.)

I had heard about Guam — a US island territory — but I didn't know much about it. "Sure, of course," I said.

Two weeks later, Jenny and I were on the famous Pan Am 001 round-the-world flight from New York through Los Angeles and Honolulu to Guam. I got off in Guam, and Jenny continued on to her family in Hong Kong.

Deak & Company (Guam)

WHAT A contrast between the island of Guam and the island of Hong Kong. I wondered why on earth Deak would bother to have an office in such a backwater territory. With its small indigenous population, almost all of whom worked for the government, Guam seemed the ideal tropical island location for anyone looking to just chill out, and it was suitably dotted with Korean and Taiwanese bars and clubs to help you do just that.

What the island also had going for it was a mix of very nice local people and interesting outsiders. There were a lot of American libertarian thinkers hanging around Deak and buying gold, and I made friends easily. In fact, some of those friendships have lasted until this day — including those I forged with Mickey Howard, Chuck Nordquist, Ted Pope and Dennis Mankini, four entrepreneurs selling insurance to the military. (Indeed, much later Mickey, along with two others — Roger Slater and Steve Deutsch — would testify on my behalf in court.)

Another notable friend was Bill Thomasson, the manager of a local finance company. Bill would later join me as a partner when I started my own company in Hong Kong — First Financial Services Ltd. And then there was Thomas O'Donnell, a fine young fellow who worked for Bank of America. Tom later went on to become the representative for Philadelphia National Bank in Manila, and then also joined me in Hong Kong as a partner in First Financial.

Last but not least was Charles Provini. "Chuck" was a US Marine captain, a decorated Vietnam vet who'd really seen some action thanks to his involvement with special teams dropped into North Vietnam to clean up after B-52 runs. Chuck ultimately became my ticket off the island: he replaced me at Deak Guam so I could return to Hong Kong.

But I digress. What was Deak's main business in Guam? Knowing Mr. Deak to be no fool, I soon came to realize the island's lucrative potential.

For one thing, there was a brisk business in Japanese yen, involving mainly young tourists, often on their honeymoons, who flocked there by the thousands. We also did some business with the US military. The island's sprawling Anderson Air Force Base played host to B-52 bombers flying from Guam to North Vietnam and back again. It seems I could not escape the damn Vietnam War.

The office's main trade, however, was in peso remittances to the Philippines, which were collected from Deak offices worldwide. Remittance is when migrant workers send home earnings to support their families; indeed, this often forms the financial backbone for both individual households and entire economies. At the same time, many wealthy people in the Philippines wanted to get their money *out* of the country and exchange it into US dollars. Mr. Deak had created an ingenious foreign exchange system to please everyone.

Payment lists of remittances would come in day and night by telex from Deak offices around the world. But instead of going through the Central Bank of the Philippines at the official rate, Deak offered a better rate.

How?

Black money markets exist because governments often restrict flows of capital in order to hoard foreign exchange, while their citizens prefer the freedom to do what they want with their money. Black markets also exist because of greed and ill-gotten wealth.

We used to say: "Clean money exists — but only after Deak launders it."

Many people in Manila, the Philippine capital, were happy to give us pesos in cash, paying up to seven percent over the Central Bank's rate just to get US dollars into their accounts offshore, with no record of any transactions happening. And the biggest sources of cash pesos were some of the banks themselves — or, more accurately, executives of those banks, as well as some prominent stockbrokers. Simultaneously, tons of overseas Filipino workers all over the world were ready to give us US dollars in exchange for pesos in cash delivered to their families at three percentage points better than the bank rate.

We did the swaps and pocketed the difference, making a cool three to four percent on every dollar.

Deak's partner company in the Philippines making our deliveries could not have been more ideal — it was a franchise of DHL, the package delivery giant. DHL already had heaps of workers on motorcycles delivering documents all day, so why not deliver cash pesos, too? Oddly enough, each day the Central Bank of the Philippines quoted two rates: their "official rate" and then next to it — can you believe it? — the "black market rate" offered by Deak & Company (Far East) Ltd.

Little did I realize when I arrived that my experience in Guam would last the better part of a year. I'd dropped out of law school — but this was an education of its own.

The Guam connection would in fact go on to play an important role in my future career as a money mover. As a US territory, it provided easy customs entry to most destinations in the region, especially Japan, the Philippines, Taiwan and Korea. And from the Guam office I made some very important contacts, many of whom would later become good clients of Deak & Company in Hong Kong.

Since Deak's business interests ranged across several different but connected sectors, I also discovered I was able to wear more than one hat at the same time, depending on where I was and who I was meeting. Working in Guam, I became accustomed to using four business cards: one each for Deak & Company Guam, Horizon Travel Guam, Deak & Company Far East, and Compass Travel. Carrying these four cards allowed me to be a chameleon, blending in anywhere, relevant to any discussion.

Kim Thanh Gold

THEN it happened — the Fall of Saigon. April 30, 1975.

For several days before the fall — also known as the Liberation of Saigon, depending on where you stood — I stayed on the telex in Guam frantically contacting American Express friends still in Saigon. I had just been to Saigon a few months before, on a holiday, and I couldn't believe this was happening, or that everything was unraveling so fast. The People's Army of Vietnam and the Viet Cong had captured the capital, marking the end of the war.

Three weeks before the city actually fell, planeload after planeload of Vietnamese started arriving at Anderson Air Force Base in Guam. A refugee camp sprang up near the Naval Air Station at Oroti Point. American Express staff I had worked with in Vietnam started arriving as well.

Fearing reprisals, anyone who had worked for the Americans was scared as hell of being taken prisoner by the Viet Cong or North Vietnamese troops who were approaching Saigon.

But something unexpected was also arriving. Among those getting out of the country were rich Vietnamese who feared what the Communists would have in store for them. Old ladies dressed in their black pajamas would arrive in Guam and set off the metal detectors. They were carrying taels of Vietnamese gold wafers called "Kim Thanh": Vietnamese-style gold, thin and pure; so thin, in fact, that you could easily smuggle or hide it by bending it around anything, including your body.

I received an urgent call from the State Department asking if Deak & Company could help to manage the huge amount of gold flooding in. My answer was a big yes.

Because I had been in Vietnam, I knew exactly what taels were, and I knew what they were worth. I offered the State Department a deal, and they accepted.

The deal was that Deak would buy the taels at the US dollar price per ounce, one tael for the price of one ounce. Simple. Since a tael was 1.2033 ounces, we had a good 20 percent spread.

The gold would have to be bought for cash and then transported to Hong Kong to be immediately melted into Chinese-style donut-shaped taels. The price was not hedged, so we took the risk of fluctuations, but gold was in a bull-market trend.

After I'd struck the deal with the State Department, and notified Mr. Deak in New York via telex, I called a meeting with trusted staff, all of them Filipino residents of Guam. I told them: "Cancel everything and plan to put in some insane overtime."

Next, I called Dirk Brink in Hong Kong, and he immediately set up a daily courier service, which involved Hong Kong employees flying to Guam with cash then returning to Hong Kong with as much gold as they could fit into their hand-carry backpacks, which was about 20 kilos each. We called it "the Gold Train."

Planes were landing from Saigon daily, and pouring out passengers who had thousands of taels hidden in their clothing. Most were being housed in a temporary tent city set up at Oroti Point. The military fenced it in, guarded it, and constructed a small shack on-site, outside which we placed our sign: "Deak & Company Kim Thanh GOLD."

I had secured about $1m in cash. The State Department gave us strictly enforced operating hours of 9am until 5pm. By 9am the next day we were open for business.

FOR the best part of the next two months, we worked all day. At 5pm, we'd rush back to the office to sort and weigh the gold, pack it into the backpacks of at least three or four couriers sent from Deak daily, and get them to the airport by midnight. More Hong Kong couriers carrying more cash for the next day arrived at 2am. The Gold Train was in full gear.

Soon we were attracting one hell of a lot of attention in the Hong Kong physical gold market. The *South China Morning Post*, Hong Kong's leading English-language newspaper, picked up on it, and suddenly my office was besieged by journalists. When the *Post* ran its story, the State Department started receiving applications from several other Hong Kong gold dealers, all asking for space to set up their own trade and offering to buy at a much better price. Obviously, this was a problem for us.

To make matters worse, the State Department started to come down on me hard. They accused me of screwing the Vietnamese with our gross margins. Even worse, they claimed that I was operating after hours and staying open until midnight, hence breaking our agreement.

I was furious at the accusation, and stated I did not think 20 percent was too large a gross margin, given the expenses, the price exchange risk, and that fact we were the only company who had been immediately able to provide the service. But I was confused about the allegations that our shop was open in the evenings.

I decided to lay a trap and find out if anyone was really using the shack to buy gold after hours. Much to my amazement, I pounced on several expat friends of Dirk Brink's who were sneaking into the camp at night and doing business at my shack.

"Calm down, don't worry, Bruce," they said. "There will be a big fat envelope waiting for you in Hong Kong when you get back."

"Bullshit," I said. "Tell Brink to keep his fat fucking envelope. Pack up, and get the hell out of here."

They refused, so I called my good friends — the Guam police.

Soon after, Brink's buddies were escorted to the airport and placed on the next plane to Hong Kong, mightily pissed off at me. It was years before we ever spoke again.

Meanwhile, Deak-Perera would in fact successfully fend off its rival dealers to become the exclusive "money changer" for all five of the Vietnamese refugee camps around the region after the war. A later newspaper account got the facts spot-on: "Deak-Perera was one of the few financial institutions in the US with a combined expertise in precious metals, foreign currencies and international banking. As a result of this knowledge, they were invited by the US State Department in April 1975 to assist the South Vietnamese refugees that were pouring into Guam and the US as Saigon fell."

Our gold-buying operation catapulted Deak into the national limelight in the US, however; and for a company that preferred to operate in the shadows, this would have serious unforeseen consequences. Little did I realize it at the time but we had attracted unwanted notice and criticism from higher-ups in the government intelligence community.

Within months, though, the operation was all over. When the plane loads stopped arriving, the Gold Train had reached its final station. I returned to the Hong Kong office — and as promised found a nice bonus from Mr. Deak waiting for me.

CHAPTER 4

Deak House Rules

SHELL HOUSE, 26 Queens Road Central, was a famous address in the heart of Hong Kong's commercial and financial district. Looking straight down Pedder Street from Des Voeux Road Central, the grand building commanded your attention. Across its length, and four floors up, a bright-red neon sign read "Deak & Company (Far East) Ltd."

This was the nerve center of Deak's Asian business. Outside of New York, it was the group's most important and most profitable operation in the world. In Asia, it represented three of Deak's banks: Foreign Commerce Bank (FOCO) of Zurich and Geneva, Bankhaus Deak of Vienna, and Deak National Bank of Fleischmanns, New York.

Dirk Brink ran the place like a well-oiled machine. A brilliant thinker and risk-taker, he was also cunning; definitely one of a kind.

He would usually arrive at the office before 8am and was always the last to leave, normally just before midnight. He poured out more work in a day than most people do in a week.

Dirk could also pour on the charm, and almost everyone who met him liked him. All day long there would be a queue of people outside his office waiting to see him, plus dozens of phone messages from all over the world, a pile of telexes needing replies, and journalists waiting to interview him. Everyone wanted Deak's point of view and predictions.

Dirk told me what he expected. "Bruce, you are now my assistant. What I cannot do, I will send to you to do. You handle it. If you don't know the answer, please do not bother me, just use your head; it's all common sense, so say anything you like. Most people are idiots; they don't have a clue what the gold price will be tomorrow. Always tell them it is going to go sky high, you better buy now. It's always going up."

Dirk spoke to the boys behind the counter in their respective native languages — predominantly Chinese or Bahasa Indonesian — and struck a casual air of knowledgeable, respectable authority.

Of average height and in his mid-40s, he appeared fit and healthy, and wore an almond-colored safari suit that matched his tan complexion. He had a full head of rust-brown hair, and his face was well-shaped, his piercing green eyes sharp and bright.

Dirk Brink in fact turned out to be one of the most interesting people I would ever know. He had an amazingly clever mind for moving money, and a ruthless character.

Born to Dutch parents in Indonesia, where his father was a high school principal, he had led a colorful life. He was fluent in many languages — Indonesian, Cantonese, English, German, Dutch, French, Esperanto and Afrikaans — and had an instant opinion on just about every subject in the world.

The *South China Morning Post* called Dirk almost every day, and he never hesitated to offer sometimes quite outlandish predictions about tomorrow's prices — for currencies, precious metals or the stock market. No problem.

Brink's office was a large space cluttered with heaps of newspapers, books and magazines. A huge desk sat in the center of the room and was covered with telephones of all different colors, each denoting a distinct language. Sometimes as many as three calls were on hold at a time as he switched back and forth effortlessly between them, quoting FX rates or whatever the moment required.

COMPANY dress for Brink and all foreign management staff was not the customary coat and tie; no sir, that was for bankers, lawyers and nerds. At Deak & Company, only safari suits were allowed. The company motto might as well have been: *Have safari suit, will travel.* And since the company also owned and shared the floor with a major travel agency, Compass Travel Limited, travel we did.

In addition to myself, the non-Asian staff included Ron Pulgar-Frame — a barrel-chested, chain-smoking Englishman — and three English ladies who worked as secretaries: Jill Lovatt, Julia Hayes, and Bernie Layfield.

We were surrounded by about 50 Chinese who did one hell of a lot of work. They were led by Anthony S.C. "Tony" Pong, the expert head FX Trader, and Mr. K. M. Leung, Treasurer and Chief Accountant, who also happened to be Tony's father-in-law. Leung was known to all of us as "Dr. No." Brink would come rushing out of the office looking for huge sums to cover deals in progress. He would first ask Tony at the FX counter, who always said "yes," then go and get the deal nixed by asking Dr. No. When Brink threatened to chop off Dr. No's head, he invariably changed his answer "yes!"

Tony ran a team of super-efficient "counter boys" who could handle multiple FX transactions in a flash. But he was more than simply an office man. At night, he turned into the "Emperor of Entertainment" for financially well-oiled Deak clients who wanted a night on the town. He kept a little black book of ladies' telephone numbers — including those of bored and lonely (but attractive) housewives of local bankers; women whose husbands traveled a lot and who were looking for a little romance on the side. I also often suspected there was significant under-the-table private business going on between Pong and Brink.

Deak Far East was making millions, and sending millions back to New York. Often the timing of such deals was given away by the tell-tale action of Brink sending anyone overly inquisitive and their prying eyes off on a trip to nowhere.

Over the years, the company had built a network of off-shore banking resources — and it was expected that our clients kept their savings inside Deak's ecosystem.

In short, if Deak laundered it, you better open an account with one of Deak's banks and let it stay right there. Deak's banks issued ICDs (International Certificates of Deposit) at high interest rates, and paid a one percent commission to the selling agent or staff member who completed the deal.

For example, I might do a "pickup" from a client, and if I then convinced the client to place the money I'd collected in a Deak account, I would get the commission. If the client rolled the deposit over the following year, I received another one percent. Right from the get-go, I truly loved Deak & Company.

THE CORPORATE philosophy and culture of our business was very much steeped in a feeling of normalcy around things that weren't strictly by the book. It felt perfectly moral and just, for example, to avoid or evade taxes and insure your future well-being — after all, didn't we all have a God-given right to privacy? And didn't this also justify the need for nominees and Swiss bank accounts? I mean, even the Central bank of the Philippines — as I mentioned earlier — quoted the black-market rate offered by Deak & Company. This bolstered my belief that laundering money was not to be taken too seriously as an act of wrongdoing.

The nature of our business also meant I soon became accustomed to dealing with all types of unusual and sometimes very eccentric characters — from tax evaders and drug dealers to government agents and sometimes just plain old lunatics. There was rarely a dull moment and I got to know about all manner of skeletons in all manner of closets.

But the sense of normalcy around all of this was probably reinforced by our professionalism. For example, even if our business was in large part based on trust and personal contacts, there was a methodology to how we worked to build this trust.

Most businesses operate with rules and regulations, by-laws and Articles of Incorporation. Why should the black-market money-laundering business be any different? If you are going to do it right, you need rules for all to work by. It just so happened that in our profession the rules were incredibly simple — and written in code.

At Deak & Company in Hong Kong, we followed the rules of the Little Blue Book — a play on Chairman Mao's Little Red Book. For us, this was the bible of free market foreign exchange. It was a clever little piece of work created by Dirk Brink and laid out a simple method of encoding that could easily be used to create almost any message by means of a series of two-letter combinations.

The key component of this little manual, however, was what we referred to as the "Two-Dollar-Bill Rule" — our own admittedly basic version of the KYC ("Know Your Customer") rules that are now part of banking's multi-billion dollar compliance industry.

For Deak's part, the company was totally up-front about its business: all you had to do was walk in and ask. On the other side of the table, meanwhile, clients' legitimacy and trustworthiness were established based on referrals from existing, trustworthy clients. But to ensure that potential customers were indeed *bona fide*, we needed some kind of paper trail.

The Two-Dollar-Bill Rule was the answer, and it was simplicity itself. It usually worked something like this: As we traveled around the Far East, or indeed wherever we had an "agent," we would from time to time leave the agent with a supply of US two-dollar banknotes. What made these notes unique, however, was that we had cut them in half. The agent would give half a note to anyone he decided to refer to our Hong Kong office for the purposes of discussing confidential business.

For example, our Taiwan agent, "Sam," might send a telex to Compass Travel advising that his friend, Mr. Chan, would be coming to Hong Kong on such and such a date, and request that we assist him by arranging his "tour." When Mr. Chan arrived at our office, he would be accorded a warm welcome, and at some point in the conversation he would present half of the two-dollar bill he had been given by Sam. His half would then be matched with the other half of the same two-dollar bill kept on file in our office, and the discussion would immediately move on to the nitty-gritty of moving cash.

We would tell the client: "Mr. Chan, you wish to sell us New Taiwan dollars (NT$), equivalent to $100,000, and we are happy to buy them from you. You realize, of course, that Taiwan has very strict exchange controls and this is a very dangerous business. Our requirements are as follows: We need 24 hours' notice and a good-faith non-refundable deposit of $3,000 to cover the expense of sending someone from our office to Taipei for one day. The NT$ we buy from you must be in cash, in circulated currency, and never brand-new bills in consecutive numbers. We will quote you the exchange rate of the day and charge you a total fee of four percent. Agreed? Good."

In Sam's case he would take the cash… and buy fish with it (more of this in the next chapter but Sam's deal was that we gave him a better FX rate than the official one: he'd use the client's NT$ to buy fish, then pay us back offshore in US dollars earned from exporting it to Japan). Back in Hong Kong, Deak would credit the client's account with the agreed sum in US dollars.

The four percent we charged was quite a hefty cut, and of course many rivals were doing the same business for less. With Deak, however, the client could be assured the deal was backed by a solid company with liquidity, a company that would pay out the counter-value as agreed. We had a reputation we needed to protect.

More importantly, no-one outside of our tight circle would have knowledge of the transaction, so there was no risk of blackmail at a later date. Deak & Company was the Rolls Royce of money-laundering, the best in the business.

Upon agreement of the terms outlined in the example given, we would take a NT$1000 note and cut it in half. Half would be retained by the client and taken with him.

"Don't lose the damn thing," we would say, "or the deal is off."

We never collected the money from a third party unless the other half of the note was presented first. Otherwise, who knows, we could have been set up for a sting.

Once the money was ready, someone from our office would fly to Taipei to meet the client, who would hand over the cash to be transferred upon presentation of the other half of the banknote.

Our agents tended to be successful businessmen who were "dollar salting," which basically meant stashing away dollars overseas and not reporting this income to their own governments. They were happy to receive the local currency in cash at a rate over and above the official bank rate. It was a win-win situation for everyone.

Always on-call

A REQUIREMENT of the job was to have a good passport, and in those days, a US passport was the best. I kept a small travel bag in the corner of my office, and was ready to fly off at a moment's notice.

When I left home in the morning, in fact, I often never knew if I was going to be back home sleeping in my own bed that night or not. But hey, what the hell, this was a great life for a young fellow who loved to travel and who had a reasonably understanding Chinese wife.

Truly, it felt like the world was our oyster. Deak's operations spanned the seven continents, including the communist Soviet Union and the capitalist USA, and at Brink's behest I soon found myself flying more than an airline pilot, going through two 48-page US passports a year, with additional pages inserted so that when I opened it they fell out like an accordion. Hong Kong's Kai Tak Airport was like a second home. Sometimes the trips were back and forth on the same day; other times I was gone a week or more.

Another staple of the job was Brink's unpredictability. The master-mind of laundry methods was also constantly making spur-of-the-moment decisions — and when he did, there was no turning back.

Let me give you a one typical example. Bursting on the scene at the money exchange counter early one Friday morning, he seemed especially happy to see Helen Fennel, a delightful elderly American lady, sitting there. She was one of our regular clients and always cashed her US Social Security checks at Deak's.

"Helen, have you ever been to Manila?"

Brink had uttered the magic words: whenever he asked a question beginning with "have you ever been to…" it usually meant one of us was about to be packed off to the airport.

Before she could even exhale, Brink motioned to the Compass Travel staff.

"Give Helen a round-trip ticket to Manila for the weekend. She is a good and loyal customer. Book her into the Manila Intercontinental Hotel in Makati at our expense."

"Oh, Mr. Brink," she finally blurted. "Are you serious? You are so generous. Oh, my gracious, how can I ever thank you?"

"Oh, there is one thing," Brink replied. "My friend in Manila will drop by with an envelope Sunday morning. It's just documents. Put the envelope in the hotel safe, and check it in with your luggage when you fly back Monday morning. It's important that you remember this."

Brink was either a devil or a wizard. No customs agent would bother to check the luggage of a lovely old white-haired granny like Helen.

The weekend came and went. On the Monday morning, our driver, K.K., collected Helen from Kai Tak Airport in Deak's authentic black London taxi (an odd sight as it was the only one in Hong Kong to my knowledge) and brought her to the office. She could not thank Brink enough for the great weekend retreat. She had befriended a very nice local couple on the Sunday, she said, and they'd invited her to the ultra-exclusive Polo Club. She'd had a wonderful time — and, she giggled, a few too many gin and tonics. Brink was pleased.

Eyeing her check-in luggage, he asked her: "Oh, Helen, may I have the envelope with the documents?"

"What?"

You could hear a pin drop as the room went eerily silent. Helen paused and thought for a moment as her face turned crimson red and then pale as a ghost.

"Oh my God, I completely forgot about the envelope! It is still in the hotel safe."

Barely able to control himself, now Brink turned red, then suddenly pale.

"Bruce..." he said, turning his attention to me.

Damn it, Brink, you fool! I had just returned from Jakarta that morning.

"What time does the next flight leave for Manila?"

Two hours later, there we were, old Helen and I, on the Cathay Pacific flight back to Manila.

Returning to Hong Kong late that night, I handed the envelope to Brink. It contained $200,000 in cashier's checks. Brink, true to form, took it all in his stride, laughing heartily at the fiasco.

Behind the Iron Curtain

ONE day, Brink approached me with one of his gnomic questions: "Bruce, have you ever been to Leningrad?"

"No, not recently," I replied sarcastically.

Brink had already spoken to David Mok, the manager of Compass Travel. David was one hell of a nice bloke, very savvy and smart, and he carried money like the rest of us. Brink had a request that involved both David and me.

"Listen, Bruce, you know that we have been selling those damn worthless Aeroflot tickets for a couple of years now, and the Russkies never pay the travel agent commission. They owe us plenty for them."

He wanted me and David to go to Moscow, then Leningrad, and stay at the Intourist Hotel, a legendary Soviet hotel for foreigners. We would take some tours, meet the management of the airline and hotel, and ask for payment. "Teach them how capitalism works," he said. "We are not running a charity."

Looking at David, I wondered: what's the catch?

"Oh yes, one more thing." *Here comes the catch.* "When you get to Leningrad, you'll need this little black envelope. It is from Bankhaus Deak, Vienna."

My first thought was that the black envelope must be from Mr. Deak himself and that it probably contained a coded message. I knew that Deak was operating a "pickup and payment" facility on a select basis for a US intelligence agency out of Vienna. This felt like some real Cold War spy stuff, and gave me an uneasy feeling.

Brink told me to sew the envelope into the lining of my coat. He gave me clear instructions on what to do when I got to Moscow and Leningrad (as Saint Petersburg was known at the time). Of course, this was 1977 and Russia was *very* communist: they'd have KGB agents on every corner. Brink made it sound like child's play but this was my first time crossing the Iron Curtain to the Soviet Union.

As it happens, I had made a visit to Bankhaus Deak in Vienna just a few months earlier. Something that had stayed with me was that I'd had a very brief interaction with a visitor from Russia: the head cashier had made a point of introducing us. If I remember correctly, he said his name was Yuri and that he had been an exchange student at Harvard. I now wished I had paid more attention. I recalled Yuri's parting words: "Hope to meet you again one day."

After receiving Brink's instructions, the next night we found ourselves at Bangkok airport ready to board an aging Tupolev airplane for the ten-hour flight to Moscow. No one was going to Russia in those days and the plane carried only a few foreigners. After a couple of hours in the air and a few vodkas, the chap across the aisle leaned over with a smile.

"Hello. Your accent is American. Why are you going to Russia?" he asked, in a friendly voice.

The conversation continued, and when it began turning into more of an inquisition I told him a half-truth: that we were travel agents and going to Moscow for meetings with Aeroflot and the Intourist Hotel."

"Oh, I see. Be careful! Watch out for thieves and illegal money changers!"

Money changers? God forbid! I thanked him.

"Yes, do not change your dollars on the black market. You will be sent to prison for a long time." Given the gleam in his eye, I half-thought he was about to quote me a rate and offer to change the dollars for me himself.

At Moscow airport, customs was *totally* military-style. An official stamped my American passport with unusual fury. I had almost forgotten about the little black envelope I had simply placed in the back pocket of my jeans, but there was no body search, only a lot of suspicious glances. Outside, we were greeted by a driver from Intourist bearing a friendly sign with our names on it. The next morning, we began a series of meetings involving vodka breakfasts, vodka lunches and vodka dinners, of which I have almost no recollection.

Two days and dozens of bottles of vodka later, still under the influence, we bear-hugged Russian-style, said good-bye to our hosts — who'd cheerfully told us how all of their financial problems were caused by America — and took off from the domestic airport, bound for Leningrad. We'd totally forgotten to ask Aeroflot (or had been unable to bring ourselves to ask them) when they would pay the money they owed Compass Travel. But it was clear to me that chasing those payments was not our purpose anyway.

BY THE second night in Leningrad, I was sort of getting used to the place. What a beautiful city. At night, Moscow had been totally dark, with the exception of a few large red stars on the top of city landmarks. Leningrad was much more alive and cosmopolitan.

I had been instructed to go to the riverfront and find a boat called "Aurora" — supposedly the ship that fired the shots that began the Bolshevik Revolution in 1917. Turns out it was docked right in front of my hotel. Remembering Brink's instructions, I went down to the river precisely at 9pm, and spent half an hour walking around the vicinity. So far, so good.

Suddenly, a young Russian woman approached me and started speaking to me — in Russian. When I replied in English, she froze for a moment, and a look of shock and fear flashed across her face. She looked in all directions to see if anyone might be watching from the shadows, then did a pirouette and took off like a bat out of hell. I went back to my hotel.

My instructions for the second night were to hang out in the corner of the hotel bar and wait for a group of drunken Georgians to approach me, again at 9pm sharp. One of them would be wearing a Harvard sweatshirt and introduce himself as Alexander, and I was to slip the envelope to him.

The small bar was already full of people and cigarette smoke. There was a tennis exhibition in town — and there, just a few tables away, sat none other than the American tennis star Billie Jean King. I was about to walk over to her to ask for an autograph when a small group of men sat down near me. Sure enough, one of them was wearing a Harvard sweatshirt. He didn't say his name but he asked if I could speak English.

I could feel sweat on the back of my neck. Dealing in the currency black-market in Russia — if that's what we were here to do — was a very serious matter and not to be taken lightly. Brink assured me that Mr. Deak was operating a message delivery service for the CIA in Russia. I could feel KGB eyes everywhere and started to wonder if this was even the right guy. It was, in fact, the first — and only — transaction I would ever do absent the comfort of having a two-dollar bill to prove identity.

My brain was racing: What if the guy freaks out after I hand the envelope to him? Why hadn't I thought of these things before? The situation felt off-script, and did not follow normal procedure.

I made my decision, win or lose. I gave him the envelope. This was the split second that would reveal the truth. I could see his pupils dilate as he became aware of the envelope in his hand. My heart was racing. It was cold in the bar but suddenly I felt hot. Seemingly a bit drunk, he shook my hand and patted me on the back, offering to buy me a vodka. In that moment, such was my acute paranoia, I thought I could feel the eyes of everyone in the bar boring into me. We stayed another hour downing several more vodkas, until my new acquaintance and his fellow Georgians left. As they left, I felt a sudden moment of euphoria, and fantasized that this must be how "double 0" agents feel after a day's work.

I was later informed that this "Alexander" had also been in Vienna when I was introduced to the mysterious Russian there, and had been on the same flight David and I took from Moscow to Leningrad. I believe he observed me looking at the Aurora the night before. That told him the deal was on, although I was left completely in the dark.

Still, mission accomplished. I was looking forward to a visit to the Hermitage museum in the morning.

Looking back, it's hard to say for sure what we were doing in Russia. Brink later hinted to me that the US State Department and a US intelligence agency were our clients, with Deak facilitating various dollar and ruble transactions. If he knew who or what the payments were for, he never told me.

India calling

I STROLLED into the Shell House office just before opening time a couple of days after the drama in Leningrad: a sunny Friday morning. I had flown back from Moscow the night before and I felt exhausted, unwell, and seriously jet-lagged. It had been a tense and dangerous trip.

"Good morning," I said, anxious to tell Brink all about what had happened.

Brink and Ron Frame were arguing like hell. The door to Brink's office slammed and Frame, normally calm, cool, and collected, came out huffing. He lit up a cigarette.

"I'm off to London on home leave for two weeks starting tonight," he said to me. "And the bastard wants me to go to Bombay for a pickup."

"Have a good trip," I laughed.

"What the hell are you laughing at? You are the only one in the office with a valid Indonesian visa so guess where *you* will be going tonight?"

I felt instantly sick. I knew I should have stayed at the airport.

I remember struggling through the day and, worse, having to cancel a quiet, romantic dinner at home with my lovely wife. By 8pm, my bag was filled with $1 million, all in new $100 bills, and I was waiting for the call from our driver to take me from the office to the airport for the four-hour flight to Jakarta. I was chatting with Brink when the green phone rang — the one called by staff and agents when dialing from a public phone overseas.

"Bruce, pick that up would you?"

I picked up and turned to Brink. "Mr. Brink, it is Ron Frame."

"What!?" Brink exclaimed. "Where the hell has he been all day, I thought he was going on holiday?"

"Mr. Brink," I whispered. "Remember this morning? He is in Bombay."

"Where?"

"Bombay."

"Oh, shit!" he said loudly, and then "Oh, shit," again softly. "I forgot all about that. The deal fell through. You can't trust those Goddamn Indians."

"What about Ron?" I asked, handing Brink the phone.

"No, no, no, I can't take it. You tell him, Bruce."

"Tell him what?" I asked, finding it impossible not to laugh. Brink rolled his eyes and whispered it to me. I paused for a moment and took a deep breath.

"Ron, you there?"

"You bet I am here. What the hell did Brink say?"

"He said, 'Tell him to come right back.'"

"What! That's it, that's all? 'Come right back?'" The cursing on the other end of the phone continued until it was drowned out by Brink in a fit of uncontrollable laughter, then it stopped abruptly as Ron slammed down the receiver.

For my part, I was resigned to another stint of international nomadism. I would be met at the airport in Jakarta by our agent, who was to deliver the $1 million to our customer, Bank of Tokyo.

In Indonesia, oil companies' wages were paid in cash — in US dollars. And when their dollars dried up, we filled the demand. A cool $1m or $2m could be delivered instantly, in exchange for a one-percent fee. In this particular case, that amounted to an easy $10,000, which was simply transferred telegraphically to us by Bank of Tokyo.

I flew back to Hong Kong, utterly exhausted, the following day.

CHAPTER 5

Generals and monkeys

DESPITE DEAK'S and Brink's well-oiled operations, their years of experience and their safety protocols, uncertainty was always a factor in our business. More than once did we run into difficulties — sometimes minor hiccups, on other occasions mishaps that would have devastating consequences.

One of Brink's ongoing headaches was that he had so many deals going on at once that he couldn't find enough warm bodies to handle them. He sometimes became careless and would enlist anyone (such as good old Helen Fennel) who looked like they had a good passport or could do with a bit of cash or adventure.

One day, some time around 1979, a low-level CIA operative named Doug Smith (not his real name) came strolling through the lobby in Hong Kong. He came highly recommended by Barry Clark, a former marine and a close confidant of Brink's. Doug later went on to work for the Nugan Hand Bank — a corrupt investment bank whose downfall I was to witness in later years.

"Doug, so nice to meet you. Have you ever been to Nepal?" The familiar Brink rhetoric.

Doug was temporarily unemployed and looking to earn a few easy bucks.

"Here's the deal," said Brink. "There is nothing to it. Here is some money, go and buy yourself a good pair of Nike running shoes."

What we were doing was sending people to Kathmandu a couple of times a week wearing running shoes with the soles removed and stuffed with gold teals. There was a big margin to be had in smuggling gold into Nepal — once it had quickly found its way to India. You could hide a kilo of gold in two shoes.

Doug soon returned with his new shoes and was elated at the prospect of picking up an easy $500 and enjoying an all-expenses-paid trip to Nepal, one of the most beautiful and friendly countries in Asia.

Late the following evening, however, a frantic call came in from our friend and Doug's, Barry Clark. A sharp-eared customs officer at Kathmandu Airport had been walking among the passengers who had just arrived when he seemed to detect a faint clanking sound coming from the shoes of one of the passengers.

"Brink! Doug has been busted in Kathmandu with a kilo of gold in his shoes!" Barry yelled.

He may have had a few too many beers on the flight over, or perhaps he had just forgotten to wrap the taels so that they wouldn't clank on the hard floor of the arrival hall.

The gold was forfeited, and in lieu of a fine, Doug spent a couple of months in the slammer. So much for a free holiday in the Himalayas. We never saw him in the Hong Kong office again.

Deak & Company Taipei

TAIWAN was another location that yielded milk and honey for the Deak black-market machine. Its exchange controls were strictly enforced at the time and the place had a very serious aura about it.

We had about three dozen regular clients in Taiwan, many local and some expatriates who had plenty of New Taiwan dough to sell. Many locals were in the black market money changing business as well, probably with good connections and paying off the right bankers to turn a blind eye.

One of our favorite clients there was the happy fishmonger introduced in the last chapter: "Sam."

This Sam of ours had a tremendous business: Every day his agents would buy tons of fish and pay for it in New Taiwan Dollars, hard cash. The fish would be frozen and flown on a daily basis directly to Tokyo and Osaka, where it was consumed as sushi in the markets and restaurants.

We would collect NT dollars in huge suitcases from sellers in Taipei and then deliver them to Sam for him to buy his fish with. His Japanese buyers would send their payments back to his Hong Kong account with Deak in US dollars. A sweet deal for all concerned.

It was always wonderful to see Sam. Short and rotund, he was always smiling, and looked like a Buddha. He was the ultimate host, and I used almost any excuse *not* to avoid the Taiwan trips. For Sam and his trusted staff of eight, Deak & Company's bi-monthly visits were a cause for celebration. On the first night, we would all troop off to one of Taipei's finest Chinese restaurants. After being plied with endless food and beer, we'd finish the meal with a bottle of XO. By 9pm, I was usually passed out in my hotel room.

The night before I returned to Hong Kong was even more special. Sam and I would drive up to the city's red-light district, Pei To, to visit a beautiful Japanese-style villa operated by his friend, Yoshi. The place had to be experienced to be believed. In elegant surroundings, we were looked after by beautiful young kimono-clad Japanese ladies who would serve the food and pour the beer and saké. Smoking a Cuban cigar after dinner, you would hear the water running in the rooms next door in preparation for a bath and a massage, or anything else that struck your fancy.

Sam loved Deak & Company very much — a bit too much, we would later realize. Some time later, one of our customers in Hong Kong happened to casually mention that he had recently bought some US dollars at the Deak office in Taiwan.

"What?" we asked in disbelief. "We have no office in Taiwan."

Mr. Deak in New York was livid, and immediately asked Brink to check it out.

Sure enough, there it was — a small foreign exchange office on Nanjing East Road, in the heart of Taipei. The sign read "Deak & Company Taiwan," and it was staffed and run by none other than our dear friend Sam.

Confronted by Brink, Sam professed to be shocked. He said that he had simply opened the exchange as an official business in admiration and honor of his good friend Nicholas Deak. He offered to change its name immediately.

The Manila envelope fiasco

I BECAME fond of the Philippines during my first trip to Manila around 1971, when I was on R&R from Vietnam.

I was attracted to the people because they seemed to be good folks, always ready with a smile. It also occurred to me that they must all be musicians, because in every Officers' and NCO Club you went to in Vietnam, you always found a Filipino band playing on Friday and Saturday nights.

At Deak's offices in Guam, all of the employees were Filipino Americans, and there were many other Filipinos on the island who were contract workers in the construction business. And then of course there were our customers — the people who sent peso remittances, or *padala*, back home to the Philippines from all over the world. Filipinos would go to Deak offices in places like Hawaii, San Francisco and Los Angeles, to send peso remittances back home. Deak & Company Guam survived on peso remittances.

Every morning when I went to the office during my time in Guam, there would be a long ticker-tape payment list at least ten feet long overflowing from the telex machine onto the floor. The tape would list the names of the sender, the beneficiary, and the peso amount to be paid, either by hand delivery in metro Manila or by bank transfer to the provinces. We would use the same tape to send details to our agents.

To recap, here's how the whole thing worked…

Given the strict exchange controls that existed in the Philippines, there was always a lucrative and thriving black-market for dollars, or for dollar salting.

Those who had pesos stashed away but were unable to use them to buy dollars to credit their offshore accounts (which they were not even supposed to have), or those who needed dollars to pay bills outside the country, found it much more convenient to use the services provided by Deak, rather than going through the hassle of getting Central Bank approval, leaving a tax record, and getting a lousy rate.

Stockbrokers and bankers therefore provided Deak's agents with more pesos than they could handle — such was the demand for dollars. The remitters, meanwhile, would give us their dollars outside the Philippines, in exchange for pesos inside.

It really was that simple.

Another lucrative business involved US cash dollars. You could buy these in Manila, but you had to be able to get them out and into your offshore account. The old adage — "Where there is a will, there is a way" — is true, because many ingenious methods were used to accomplish this. And of course where there is demand, there will be supply — at a price.

One method was initiated by a leading Manila stockbroker, Arthur Gimenez, who simply sent sums of between $20,000 and $30,000 in so-called "Manila" envelopes looking like they contained travel brochures about Manila. He sent them to Deak Hawaii, Deak San Francisco and Deak Guam, and when the packages would arrive, we would immediately send him a telex confirmation of receipt. This method worked well as long as such transactions were infrequent, but soon others started copying it and packages started flooding into Deak's offices. One travel agent in Manila's Chinatown, "George," got particularly greedy, and soon increased his shipments of $20,000 weekly to one a day, and sometimes two or three a day. Needless to say, this caught the eye of the postal services. After all, how many travel brochures from Manila did Deak actually need?

Eventually, it all blew up in our faces.

The packages suddenly stopped arriving. George, the travel agent, was calling frantically from Manila every day on the hour in disbelief. After at least 20 packages had mysteriously disappeared, he went to the post office himself to inquire — and was promptly arrested. Fortunately for him, in the Philippines, if you have money — and he did — you were able to get off with a slap on the wrist and a big fine.

Deak & Company San Francisco was indicted for not reporting currency shipments in excess of $5,000, as required by law. The identity of Arthur was exposed and the discovery soon became a major problem for Deak, drawing the company and its operations squarely into the crosshairs as a target of the US government. Over $11 million had been received from Arthur alone but not reported.

(More about Arthur and Barry Clark — and their ingenious ways of smuggling cash — later. Some of their methods would become part of the *modus operandi* adopted by my colleagues and me.)

Meeting 'General Chul'

SOUTH Korea had a very protected economy in the '70s and '80s, and the government — still a dictatorship — wanted to know where all the money was and where it was going.

It was another country where you just would not want to get caught doing black market currency business — which in turn made such activities highly lucrative. Our agents in Seoul, two dapper brothers of Indian descent, Madan and Ram, operated a thriving trading company.

Transactions were also made cumbersome by the fact that the Korean currency, the won, was only printed in small denominations: you needed huge boxes of the stuff to add up to any interesting amount. Needless to say, we still had an excellent partner for making profitable pickups and payments. However, this business paled in comparison with the transactions we were asked to make, for reasons which stayed unknown to me, by the US government.

Sometimes they would amount to several hundred thousand dollars, usually payable to a man known as "General Chul," and it often fell to me to make the payments to this so-called General, because it was easy for an American passport holder to get visas for Korea and to travel there often.

According to Brink, the order once came from the US Embassy in Hong Kong — from an agent code-named "Bernie Blair." More often, they came from Mr. Deak himself.

I would contact our agent in Seoul and ask him to buy US dollars in the local market. From time to time he would be unwilling to risk the exposure, and I would have to smuggle the dollars in myself. A hundred thousand dollars was not a big package, so I'd spread it around my luggage in gift wrapping and simply check it in.

Upon arrival at my hotel in Seoul, I would call the number given to me by Mr. Brink or Mr. Deak. A very excited voice of anticipation always greeted me and soon the "General" and I would be having a sumptuous dinner, coupled with an offer to provide me with any-thing I wanted, such as the company of a beautiful girl for the evening.

After dinner, the General would hurry off, package in hand. What could it have been for? I would later become painfully aware of the US government's vast bribery operations in Asia, most particularly after news of the Lockheed scandal broke in Japan in 1975. More about that later.

New Zealand

"BRUCE, have you ever been to New Zealand?"

Guess who? Brink was at it again. It was a cool autumn morning when I checked into a little hotel Compass Travel had booked for me in Auckland. Our agent there operated out of an oriental antique shop in the heart of the city. New Zealand was a beautiful country.

There wasn't a whole lot of business to be done: I just had to review some account transactions and there would be a pickup, which Brink said would be small. He'd also told me just to check it inside my suitcase. I was booked on the following morning's flight back to Hong Kong.

The first trip of several, however, will always stand out in my mind. After feasting on a steak dinner, I was wide awake and looking for some excitement. New Zealanders are very friendly people and I met some nice fellows at a pub. Before I knew it, it was 3am and I was wasted. I asked the hotel for a 6am wake-up call and drifted off, thinking: "I only have NZ$50,000 to check with my luggage and I'll be able to sleep on the plane."

I vaguely remember getting my wake-up call, but when I finally rolled over and looked at my watch it was 8am. I'd missed my flight! I was supposed to be on the non-stop to Hong Kong and now I was in deep trouble. I had to be back in Hong Kong that night. My head and body ached from all the booze the night before.

A call to Air New Zealand revealed, thanks to God, that there was another flight leaving at 10am via Sydney. If I hurried, I could catch it. Nursing an almighty hangover and cursing myself for being a schlep, I made it to the airport just in time.

Another shock jolted me at customs as I realized they were being very strict and care-fully checking people's luggage. But I must have looked positively ill — because, to my surprise, I was passed over and waved straight through. Had I been sober, I thought, they would have likely checked my bag and found the money.

My relief didn't last long, however. Upon arrival in Sydney, I was whisked off to the awaiting Hong Kong-bound flight. As the door to the departing ANZ plane closed immediately behind me, I found myself facing an eight-hour flight in economy with a cabin full of passengers who seemed to be extremely irritated with me for causing a delay to their plans.

"Miss," I asked the stewardess, "what about my luggage?" I had told the airline I was in a rush, and that I had to get back to Hong Kong immediately. My luggage, however, wouldn't be coming until the next day. Oh, shit! I felt sick, and I knew I wouldn't be able to stop worrying for the next 24 hours. The following day, I was back at Kai Tak Airport in Hong Kong, praying as I went to collect the luggage. It had arrived, and I had learned a very big lesson.

Where the hell am I?

THE year I really started to tire of working for Deak was 1977. It had been a long time since I had been able to take a break and chill out in Orlando with the family, but finally it was time for a holiday, and I was looking forward to some home leave. I relished the thought of two glorious weeks in one place where I could completely relax and recharge mentally and physically.

Arriving in Orlando, I spent a few blissful days being pampered by my mom, peace be with her. I was relaxing like I hadn't done in years.

Just as I was beginning to feel good, chilling out with a cold beer in my hand and watching a New York Mets baseball game on TV, however, the phone rang. My mom answered it in her usual sweet voice, and I heard her say, "Hold on, Mr. Brink, he is right here."

"Bruce, how soon could you be leaving for Australia?"

"What the hell are you talking about?" I shouted. "I just arrived in Orlando."

"Please, we need someone to go to Sydney right away to do a series of pickups. It is a *huge* deal, and I'll pay you a big bonus."

He told me to leave as soon as I could. David Mok, the manager of Compass Travel, was already in Australia waiting for me. Brink said David would do the first pickup, then I'd put the cash in the bank and stay for a week. He'd be sending at least a half dozen more couriers in my wake.

As I made my way to Australia, I really was feeling like shit. I was sorry to leave Mom and cut my holiday short. The itinerary from Orlando to Los Angeles to Western Samoa, and then on to Sydney, was certainly not a stroll around the block.

David met me at the airport, and we went directly to a bank where Deak maintained a "very special" account, in which I surreptitiously made a deposit of A$500,000. (More about this special bank account anon.)

I met our client the same afternoon and received the balance of the Australian dollars that needed moving. It was over A$2 million. I bade David farewell, and as I slogged into the Hilton that night, it ran through my head that Brink could not pay me enough for this work.

Tony Pong arrived the next morning, and Ron Frame the day after that. The bank account was getting far too hot in my opinion, and Brink was clearly out of control. After three days, he called me and asked if I could go into the bank again.

"Don't worry. No problem." he said. "Just pretend you flew back to Hong Kong, then returned to Sydney. It's a piece of cake, Bruce."

My answer was: "Go to hell, Brink! Come do it yourself."

Three or four of our Chinese counter boys were sent over and the balance that hadn't yet been put in the bank was instead smuggled back to Hong Kong — using the time-honored method that you will learn about in due course. By this time, I was looking forward to getting back to Hong Kong myself. It had been three weeks since I had seen my wife.

I hesitated to pick up the hotel phone when it rang, but pick it up I did. It was Mrs. Alice Silva, Brink's trusted and super-loyal and efficient secretary, a short, fat little lady of Portuguese descent who always seemed to wear a cunning smile on her face.

With my ear to the receiver, I could hear her trademark giggle and imagine the twinkle in her eye that always telegraphed that Brink was up to no good.

"Hold on, Bruce. Hold for Mr. Brink."

I heard Brink on the other end, and I feared the worst.

"Bruce," he said, "I want you to meet me in a couple of days."

"No problem," I replied. "I am heading back to Hong Kong in the morning."

"No, not in Hong Kong. I am leaving for Zurich tonight to meet Mr. Deak, and then I'll be flying back to my farm in White River, South Africa. Meet me there. Compass Travel has already sent you a new ticket by DHL; it will arrive in the morning."

"But listen," he went on, "The routing is Sydney, Perth, Mauritius, and Nairobi, as in Kenya. You're booked into the Nairobi Hilton. There is a pickup, just a couple of hundred thousand US dollars. Coded details of the client have been sent with the ticket and he is already waiting for you at the hotel. It will take you an hour to collect the money and deliver it to Mr. Shah, our new agent. This is a big favor for Mr. Deak, and he asked me to personally thank you."

This last comment was probably another one of Brink's lies.

"After the pickup, enjoy the weekend in the bush with the Masai natives at the Hilton's Salt Lick Lodge; you'll love it. Then come and see me in White River, on the farm."

Needless to say, the ticket arrived, the pickup took place and I spent the weekend out in the bush, watching elephants come drink at a salt pond.

Nairobi was simply out of this world in terms of its exotic atmosphere, and I had to pinch myself to believe I was there. Mr. Shah was a gracious host: we walked from the Hilton to a restaurant across the street, and then enjoyed a night on the town in one of the local nightclubs.

By the time I arrived in Johannesburg and flew on to Pretoria and White River, I did not really care what happened next. I spent two days at Brink's farm waiting for him, until on the third night I heard the telex pattering away in his office. It was a most unusual office indeed, perched about 30 feet up in a tree house near the guest house. The mountain view looking towards Kruger National Park was stunning.

I carefully walked up the wood-and-rope spiral staircase that snaked its way around the tree a half dozen times. By the time I reached the top, I was dizzy. The message was short and to the point: "Trip home canceled. See you back in Hong Kong. Mr. Deak says thanks." I knew that last bit was bullshit, of course.

When I arrived in Hong Kong, I had been away for well over a month. But that didn't mean a thing: within 24 hours, I was back at Kai Tak Airport and boarding the red-eye Qantas flight for another deal waiting in Sydney. Sometimes, working for Brink was just simply too overwhelming.

It was then that I decided I may as well work this business on my own: one day, I resolved, I would opt out and become an independent agent, referring business to Deak & Company for the commissions. That way I'd spare myself working for Brink, who by this time seemed to me to be totally out of his mind — even though I knew I'd learned so much from him about people and about life. "Just do it and the authorities be damned," was kind of his mantra. His sense of adventure was contagious, but also dangerous.

It is said that the genius has no common sense. This statement truly applied to Mr. Brink, and it occurred to me that some of the outrageous stories I had heard about him may actually have been true. One that really takes the cake concerns a small monkey that Brink had sent from Jakarta all the way to South Africa in his German friend's hand-carry (people really will do anything for a free trip). The monkey was to mate with the one and only remaining healthy Indonesian female monkey living on Brink's farm. Somehow, a very important detail had been lost in translation, however: instead of a male they sent another female.

On another occasion, Brink had a valuable parrot sedated and hand-carried back to Hong Kong on a flight from Jakarta. Upon reaching his home in the Shouson Hill neighborhood, Brink excitedly opened the box to admire his parrot. Sensing its chance, and by now wide awake, the parrot bolted and flew straight for the only window that Brink had forgotten to close.

Knowing Brink, I never bothered to ask if these stories were true. In a sense, it didn't really matter. What's more, the fact that an extraordinarily large number of beautiful parrots are reputed to inhabit Shouson Hill to this day may be pure coincidence.

CHAPTER 6

A Game of deception

AUSTRALIA WAS A very important source of income for Deak & Company Far East —
and all the credit goes to Dirk Brink, who had devised a number of ingeniously simple
methods to move large sums of money from all of our major markets to Hong Kong, or
indeed anywhere in the world, often without the money leaving its country of origin. All
that was required was for someone to pull these methods off at first time of asking — and
in fact each and every time thereafter. There was a whole lot of deception involved.

Strange how one can rationalize things that go automatically against the conscience. I
never felt comfortable with deception, and dreaded it. I had to lie, or at least not let others
know the truth, while anticipating what they might be thinking about me. Nevertheless, I
learned to master the skill.

Flying to Australia for Deak & Company was always a pleasure — and an experience,
to say the least. I got to see much of the country, or at least the cities, and to meet a lot of
great folks.

In fact, I was going there so often during the late '70s and early '80s that I was beginning to develop an Aussie accent. "Good on ya, Bruce!" I thought to myself. I got to know
Sydney and the surrounding suburbs particularly well and I ended up taking a small flat
across the harbor, in Neutral Bay, and renting a car as soon as I arrived at the airport.

Here's how my trips typically worked:

Most involved visits to Melbourne, but they would always begin with me taking the
Boeing 707 CX overnight flight from Hong Kong to Sydney. From there, I would book the
Sydney to Melbourne leg under the name "Bruce Smith," paying cash. Back in those days,
one could fly domestically in many countries without showing ID, so no real record existed
of me leaving Sydney.

From Melbourne airport, I would take a taxi straight to Melton, a working-class suburb that was home to Abbie and Charlie, two Russian-Jewish immigrants who ran a slick money laundering operation from their spartan, completely unassuming little house. Abbie and Charlie's code name was "movado." I don't know why.

I vividly remember the first time we met, however. It was an unusually cold and dark winter's afternoon in July 1975. I walked up to the front door, pressed the buzzer and watched as a light went on in the foyer and another in the living room. I knew they were expecting me.

The door swung open quickly and there in front of me stood a large, massively overweight man: Abbie. I smiled; he frowned in return. When he spoke it was in a voice that made you think he was crying — Abby was constantly whining. His six-foot-tall frame carried what I guessed to be around 230 pounds of mostly fat.

"Come in, quick, come in. You must be Bruce." He stuttered, looking nervous.

Abbie wore a heavy wool coat, a white shirt that had turned yellow around the collar, crumpled baggy corduroy pants, and worn-out shoes. He looked like he didn't have a pot to piss in.

Right away he started yelling at Charlie in Hebrew or Yiddish, I don't know which. He squinted at me through beady, thick-lensed bespectacled eyes.

"Charlie, get Brink on the phone. This guy looks too young. How old are you anyway?"

"Thirty," I replied.

The inquisition in the foyer lasted several minutes, until Abbie's whining was interrupted by Charlie.

"Abbie, it's cold in the foyer, let him in."

Charlie offered to make hot tea, and turned on the heat in the extra room in case I needed to lie down for a while. Having been on the plane all night, I could not wait for a hot shower. I felt annoyed about the grilling I'd got from Abbie and I had actually come close to telling him to go to hell and find someone else to launder his fucking money. I could only marvel at his frugality. They only had heat in the living room, while the rest of the house was like the North Pole — which was weird because they had enough money stashed away to last them literally hundreds of years.

Abbie kept asking me — over and over — stuff like: "Are you, okay? Did anyone follow you? How is Dirk Brink? Please call him. You look far too young to carry half a million dollars in cash."

Over the course of the next several years, the tone never changed much.

Charlie, by way of contrast, was generous, relaxed, dapper — and a real ladies' man. He was half the size of Abbie, and dressed with exquisite taste: dark-brown flannel pants, a dark-yellow, long-sleeved shirt under a beautiful thick-knit dark-blue sweater, and a handsome dark-brown blazer. His leather shoes sparkled.

Charlie frequently told Abbie to sit down before he had a heart attack. "What is the big deal anyway?" he'd say.

We went through this routine *every month* for years. But once Charlie had made up his mind about me, he never hesitated to hand over the big bundle of cash.

That first night, after a shower and a bit of rest, Charlie made me boiling hot vegetable soup and a roast beef sandwich before we got down to the hard work, which was only interrupted by numerous phone calls to him from a bevy of ladies.

Hard work meant quickly bundling, while also counting, hard cash. Their money usually came in Australian fifty-dollar notes, the largest A$ denomination at the time, and would amount to somewhere between 400,000 and 500,000 in total. Bundles of 100 notes totaled A$5,000 — and I would have up to 100 such bundles to sort out on the overnight train back to Sydney.

Abbie and Charlie had no idea how the money was moved. To their credit, and unlike many others, they never asked. I always grew suspicious of the Deak clients who became overly friendly, trying to get me to reveal our secret methods, and I could be quite brusque if necessary. (I remember once firmly telling an overly-inquisitive client in Sydney, a Dr. Ted Krauss: "Now look, my dear friend, if I told you how we did it, then you wouldn't be needing to see me again, would you? And wouldn't that be a pity?")

I can still remember Abbie's face as I took Charlie's piles of ten bundles — each totaling A$50,000, and stacked them neatly into my Compass Travel bag: he'd stare, glassy-eyed at the bag, his gills turning green at the thought of never seeing his money again.

Finally, around 7pm, when it was pitch-black outside, it was time to take a taxi to the station to catch the overnight express train to Sydney. Having sat on a plane the entire night before, I never looked forward to the train ride, because I knew I would be working all night. But after being in Abbie's company, I tended to be sorely looking forward to being alone.

This was the life of a money launderer. Night after night of being on the move was part and parcel of my lifestyle in those days.

Once I'd settled in the train and the conductor had collected my ticket, I'd simply press the "Do not Disturb" button.

Armed with a copy of the *South China Morning Post* I'd picked up at Kai Tak airport the night before, I'd then begin to fold the money in the style practiced in Hong Kong — end over end, wrapped into squares, not elongated.

It was tedious and dirty work, made slightly easier by placing money-counting covers, those little rubber things that look like condoms or thimbles, over each of my thumbs and index fingers.

In between dozing off and packaging, I'd finally have all 100 bundles changed to look as if they had been wrapped in Hong Kong.

Next, after taking a break, I'd wrap the bundles in the newspaper, then wrap the whole package in clear plastic, and lastly brown paper. I always brought along the tools of the trade. Even though I was a non-smoker, I traveled in a smoking compartment, armed with a pack of Marlboro menthols and a little red lighter. Time to locate the metal seal and small bar of red wax I had hidden in the lining of my luggage.

After melting the wax, I'd make a puddle on all four corners of the package, and press the metal stamp into the wax, Chinese-style. Then I'd sit back to admire my handiwork. Our company seal completed the package perfectly: it looked exactly as if it had originated from *Deak & Company (Far East) Ltd., Hong Kong.*

My work would be finished by about 4am. All that was left was to put everything away. I'd let cold air in through the vent in order to eliminate the smell of the burning wax, and try to get a little sleep.

A $50 million deception

AS MY train pulled into Sydney just after 8:30am on one of these trips, I finished off my cup of some unforgivably vile concoction that no self-respecting connoisseur would call "coffee," and alighted.

From my favorite phone booth, I dialed the number for Cathay Pacific flight information, and got a recording: "Flight CX 101 nonstop from Hong Kong has arrived at 6:30am." The flight was scheduled to arrive at 5:30am, and the delay worried me somewhat.

I cursed Dirk Brink for not sending Tony Pong, our head foreign exchange trader, or one of the counter boys, ahead of me to do the preparation in Melbourne then meet me in Sydney and hand me the package as soon as I got off the plane. There was a lot more risk doing this solo.

Again, I suddenly thought: I must be crazy to keep doing this stuff. What kind of a job is this anyway? Let me think, let me think…shit, I'm tired! Decision time. OK, I'll finish the work before checking into the hotel. I'll go straight to the bank.

Downtown Sydney was a quick taxi ride from the train station, and I soon found myself a couple of blocks from the ANZ Bank at the corner of Pitt and Hunter. Unbeknown to just about everyone, it was Deak's number one money-laundering factory par excellence.

By this time it was a few minutes past 9am, and the bank had just opened. Walking in, I caught the eye of a familiar face — Richard Jenkins, the head cashier. The receptionist noticed me immediately, and an intense feeling of suspense permeated the lobby before I was whisked back toward the vault.

As we walked, I could hear whispering: "Deak & Company has arrived with another deposit of repatriated Aussie dollars collected from Aussie tourists and travelers." Yet another illusion created to avoid a world of Draconian foreign exchange controls.

Right away there was small talk — about the flight, what time I had arrived, whether or not I had encountered any problems with customs. All of this was, of course, part of the ruse, a clever ploy; so I quickly changed the subject to rugby, then asked where everyone liked to go to lunch and have a few beers.

Although the bank's management always asked, they understood we could never give advance notice of our trip for security reasons. But on this occasion, there seemed to be an added level of curiosity.

"Our Vice President, Adrian, asked to have a word," Richard Jenkins told me. "He asked to see you last month, but you had already left."

"Sure, no problem," I said, as a bead or two of sweat formed on my forehead. I tried to shake off the tiredness.

This was the worst and most dangerous time. While the A$500,000 was being counted, I watched as my handiwork from the night before on the train was destroyed and the Chinese-style bundles were converted right back to Aussie ones, in the same form as had been given to me by Abbie and Charlie.

This was the time when the questions would come. I'd always do my best not to answer, feigning a lack of sleep on the plane and a desire to get the counting done with. Then, presto, everything would be finished.

Since the money purportedly came from Hong Kong, Australia Reserve Bank gave approval for telegraphic transfer of the counter-value — in same-day US dollar value — to the account of Deak & Company Limited at Chartered Bank of London in San Francisco. What did Deak do with the money? We simply credited Abbie's account with Bank Leumi or Bank Leu in Zurich for the counter-value of A$475,000. The money was magically "laundered," and yet another cool five percent (A$25,000) went into our coffers.

Taking the lift to the third floor, I was greeted by Adrian. Suddenly, I had a throbbing headache.

"Mr. Brink never comes here himself anymore, and we just need to verify audit procedures — routine, you know," he said. "We have been doing business together for many years, and we realize Deak Hong Kong is the company's world collection point for overseas Aussie dollars you return here. You have deposited a lot of money with us over the years."

We went through the procedures, the questions about the flight and clearing customs. All of a sudden, I felt very glad of my insurance policy.

Brink always complained like hell, but I always insisted that if I were going to the bank solo I wanted a second dummy ticket from Compass Travel with the arrival date showing as the same as the deposit date. That's why I had checked the arriving flight from Hong Kong before heading to the bank. Fortunately, I'd also remembered to tear off the counterfoil on my dummy ticket. Checking off an audit form, he asked to see it.

Noticing that it was dated for arrival that morning, Adrian smiled, changed tacks completely, and proceeded to bend over backwards to say what an important account ours was and what a pleasure it was to do business with Deak. We'd passed again!

The deception always left me with a bad feeling and tainted my conscience. I just happened to be born with an honest-looking face, and over the years easily passed through customs at dozens of international airports while smuggling millions of dollars in my luggage. I overcame my anxiety by using my imagination.

Before facing Adrian, I had said to myself: *I have just come from Hong Kong, bringing A$500,000 which I have just deposited in the bank. How dare anyone question it!?* I went over this again and again, using my silent soliloquy to embolden myself. It worked.

Later, of course, I would say to myself: *What an insane way to make a living!* But truth be told, for the most part my chosen modus vivendi suited me to a tee. I loved the excitement and the glamor that went along with the turf of being a professional money launderer. How else could I travel the world all-expenses-paid, stay in five-star hotels and earn my keep for only a few hours of actual "work?" I also had time to read, take flying lessons, and meet wonderful, interesting people. For a poor boy from New Jersey, the choice was easily rationalized.

Tired, I checked into the Sydney Hilton, taking advantage of yet another deception. As a "member of staff" of Compass Travel, I would be instantly given a 50 percent travel agent's discount.

To my dismay, however, a message from Brink was already waiting for me; he wanted me to come back to our Hong Kong office immediately. I thought: *Give me a break!* I decided I'd call him later and let him know the deposit had been made. But from the shower, I heard the phone ringing.

"Hello, Brink," I said calmly. "What the hell is it?"

"Bruce, please get back here right away."

"What did you say?"

"You heard me. You are the only one with an Indonesian visa, and we have a big, urgent order. We need you to go to Jakarta tomorrow night."

Not again.

Over the years Deak maintained the ANZ deception, I would conservatively estimate we deposited well over A$50 million into the account, all sourced locally, and all disguised as coming from Hong Kong.

According to Brink, the whole scheme with the fake Hong Kong-style packages and the ANZ deception was the brainchild of his good friend Richard "Dick" Hughes, a Deak client who was an Australian war correspondent and is generally considered to have been a British spy, or even a double agent. Dick was the inspiration for the fictional character Dikko Henderson in Ian Fleming's James Bond novel *You Only Love Twice*, and for Old Craw in John le Carré's *The Honourable Schoolboy*, most of which was set in Hong Kong and Vietnam. Dick was a real-life "character," no mistake about that.

The $100m washing machine

ONE DAY in 1977, Brink struck on a new, even more ingenious way of smuggling money.

To check out the lie of the land, we first sent two big red Hong Kong phone books to Deak & Company in San Francisco, to see if such packages were routinely inspected or not. The package was about the same size as one that would contain $1 million in $100 bills.

Next, we ordered from Deak's USA offices a large supply of US one-dollar banknotes, spreading the order around so as not to attract suspicion from anyone. Our managers Otto Beusch in San Francisco, Tom Kelly in Los Angeles, and Robert Maier in Honolulu, were kept in the dark; perhaps they wondered what kind of a promotion or FX advertisement the eccentric Mr. Brink had cooked up this time.

We accumulated the one-dollar notes until we had exactly 10,000 pieces, which we then placed into 100 stacks of 100 pieces. If they had all been $100 bills instead of $1 bills, the package would be worth a cool $1 million, instead of a measly $10,000.

Next, we placed $100 bills, top and bottom, on each end of each stack. The total package at that point was worth $30,000 — but at a glance it looked for all the world like it was worth $1 million.

As per our usual practice, the package was vacuum-sealed in clear plastic, and stamped with red wax seals. It was then hand-carried on the flight to San Francisco and declared as $1 million upon arrival at customs. The package was addressed from Deak & Company (Far East) Ltd., Hong Kong to Chartered Bank of London, San Francisco, and marked as "Repatriated US currency for deposit."

When customs officials opened the brown paper wrapper on the package and saw the money, which certainly looked like $1 million, their first response was to ask if we had security waiting. "Yes, of course!" was our reply. "Security," as it turns out, was a taxi ride to the downtown Holiday Inn, where our staff were waiting to switch parcels, exchanging the package with the $1 bills for one that contained $100 bills — a real $1 million, wrapped and sealed exactly the same as if it had been brought from Hong Kong.

A quick taxi ride to Chartered Bank of London, San Francisco, and the deposit — with all the paperwork we needed from customs — was made. Just like that, another million laundered right there under everyone's noses. All in a day's work, and for the usual tidy five percent.

All that remained was for our staff to load the $1 bills into our smuggling devices of choice, fly them back to Hong Kong and stay standing by until it was time to go again.

It did not take long for Brink to turn the scheme into a gigantic "Mother of all Laundries," as we called it. Really, it made total sense. Since we were already shipping huge amounts of foreign currency all around the world — millions of Japanese yen, Philippine pesos, Swiss francs, Deutsche Marks, British pounds — by insured air freight, why should sending dollars back to America be different?

That said, Brink feared it was only a matter of time before US Customs would scrutinize one of the fake $1 million shipments. But we also had a laugh at the other potential snafu. The temptation for any given courier to disappear with a package of money on a flight to another country was ever-constant. In this scenario, any such capricious courier would have been shocked and disappointed when he discovered he had stolen a bunch of $1 bills. Brink laughed heartily when he envisioned such a scenario. Ha-ha! They would be easy to track down.

(Around this time, we also started using the services of an armored transport firm that had opened in Hong Kong: 'Brinks'. No connection to our own Mr. Brink, but we became a valued account for them: they would handle customs and other airport formalities for us, and offered a door-to-door service with full liability coverage.)

The last time I saw Dirk Brink, around 1984, he told me he had washed over $100 million by the method just described. Could that have been true? He was often prone to exaggeration, but I knew in this case he was cutting it pretty close to the mark.

On another occasion, we were sitting in his office one night, quite late on, when I noticed a file on his desk marked "Airway Bills—USA." It was so thick it could have choked a horse. We got to reminiscing about the very first shipment several years earlier and how, sitting in the same office, we'd admired our handiwork on the fake but very official-looking "million-dollar" package resting on his desk. "Ah yes," he had said, with unabashed admiration. "It looks good."

Indeed it did; and boy did that system serve Deak well.

CHAPTER 7

The Lockheed scandal

IT WAS NOT long after I had arrived back in Guam — where I'd gone to cover for the manager, Tony Evans, who was about to go on annual leave — that the telex in the Deak office there started tapping out messages in the middle of the night.

Things were afoot in Deak's world of Japanese yen pickups and payments — and the "special assignment" earlier alluded to by Mr. Deak in New York was about to come to fruition. He urgently needed yen in Japan, and he needed a warm body to deliver it. Drink Brink was on the case to find him one.

Guam was not my favorite place in the beginning. I felt so isolated there, although over time I began to relish the feeling and grew to like the place. When we worked, New York slept, and so it was with Hong Kong that we communicated daily.

It was a hot and steamy morning in January, 1973, and I was about an hour late arriving at work. The morning heat was getting to me: I wished I were in Hong Kong, which tends to be mild and dry at that time of year.

Tony startled me as I walked into the office. "Bruce, where have you been? Brink in Hong Kong has been calling every five minutes. Would you please get back to him and see what the hell he wants. And, by the way, ask him the rate for pesos today in Manila and what the hell to do with the 50,000,000 yen we bought over the weekend. Tell him I need a good rate or we'll sell it to our competitor, Bank of America!"

Suddenly, my spirits picked up. Dirk Brink calling? Maybe I'll be heading back to Hong Kong soon.

Straight on the phone, I heard the familiar, quick double ring of the Hong Kong telephone system, and then the friendly voice of the receptionist: "Deak & Company Far East Ltd, who's calling?"

"This is Bruce from the Guam office."

"Oh… hold on, hold on." Must be important if she's saying it twice, I thought. I wasn't even put on hold, so I could hear her as she yelled: "Mr. Brink, Mr. Brink, Guam on the line."

A split-second later, the calm voice of Brink came on.

"Bruce…" he said in his usual charming manner. "How would you like to come to Hong Kong for a couple of days?"

You must be joking. "Fine, how about today?"

"Yes, please come today; something important we need you to help us with."

"On my way!"

THE FOLLOWING day, back in the Hong Kong office, Brink approached me with an unusual question.

"Do you play golf?"

"What did you say?" I replied, a little startled.

He took me aside, and opened a closet door. To my surprise, I saw before me a dozen or so very nice-looking golf bags.

"To be clear, I don't want you to play golf. I just want you to take the golf clubs from Guam to Tokyo from time to time."

Naturally, this was yet another of Brink's unorthodox schemes to move money.

"OK," I said. "How much cash can you put in them?"

Brink smiled and proceeded to show me how to open the rivets on the bottom of the bag, then slide out a specially-made compartment lined with black cloth.

"Each bag can comfortably hold millions of Japanese yen in ten-thousand denominated banknotes," he proclaimed with extraordinary glee.

That was the equivalent of several hundred thousand US dollars.

"OK, I get the picture. Have you done this before?" I asked.

"Yes, of course, all the time… but never to Japan."

Tony Pong, the counter boys and all the staff at Compass Travel in Hong Kong had been to Japan too many times and we were attracting too much attention, Brink explained. New blood was badly needed, and that new blood was mine.

"Mr. Deak and I want you to make some trips for us, flying from Guam," he said.

Brink often cleverly referenced Mr. Deak, knowing that such authority would not be questioned and therefore making it nearly impossible to say no.

As with Compass Travel in Hong Kong, over in Guam we had the perfect cover: our subsidiary, Horizon Travel. The paradise island on which I'd cut my teeth as a Deak employee was known as "Honeymoon Island" in Japan, and 747 jumbo jets full of Japanese newlyweds descended on it each and every day, bringing huge amounts of yen notes. Furthermore, many of the male parties among these honeymooning couples were golfing obsessives — and Guam's ample courses meant large, heavy golf bags were a ubiquitous luggage item on flights from the Land of the Rising Sun.

Sensing I was about to be made a guinea pig, I asked Brink why we didn't just swap yen that was already in Japan for our clients and give them US dollars outside. "If I could do that, I wouldn't be asking you to take the yen to Japan now, would I?" he replied.

Japan's strict exchange controls made it dangerous to do unofficial business there and Brink explained that our agent in the country, code-named "Sanyo," was scared as all hell: he suspected his phone was tapped, that he was being followed and that somehow the authorities were on to him. "He has to lie low. He thinks the Japanese police are ready to pounce and says he can't supply me with any yen for now. We have these urgent payments piling up, and I'm getting calls every hour from..."

Brink suddenly hesitated, looking slightly nervous. "You don't want to know who from; I can't say who, but he is attached to your bloody consulate here in Hong Kong."

"The United States Consulate?"

"No, the New York Yankees!" he replied sarcastically.

It all made perfect sense. I had suspected it for a while in the wake of my visit to the Soviet Union and my deliveries to "General Chul" in South Korea, but now here was confirmation that we *were* making black-market payments for the US government. I pondered the thought almost with a tinge of patriotism.

I remembered Mr. Deak's past with the OSS — the Office of Strategic Services, today's CIA — and his contacts inside the intelligence community. It was generally assumed, though rarely discussed, that he was still deeply connected with that world.

(Incidentally, I would eventually meet the US Consulate contact referred to by Brink on numerous occasions. Standing about six and a half feet tall and weighing at least 250 pounds, he wasn't the kind of guy you forgot easily. His code name was Frank Price.)

The night of my conversation with Brink, I was on a plane back to Guam, arriving just after 2am. (Because of its location, out in the middle of the ocean where America's day begins, Guam flight schedules really suck.) From there, I was booked on the JAL flight to Tokyo in the afternoon. Clearing customs and collecting my golf bag, I suddenly felt uneasy. I could still hear Brink's parting words as I was leaving the office: "Don't worry, man… there is nothing to it. Remember, smuggling is a white man's privilege."

Reassuring words from a self-confessed racist Afrikaner. I reminded myself that, racist or not, however, Dirk Brink was a very clever man. He had a quick, razor-sharp mind — and a gift for thinking up ingenious ways to move money, ranging from the devilishly complex to the stunningly simple. And this was one of the simplest.

"When you get to Tokyo, check into the Okura Hotel, which is not far from the embassy, and wait for Father Jose to call."

Father Jose. I had heard about him and was looking forward to meeting him. Turns out he was Deak's other agent in Tokyo, and arguably the most important one in Japan. When Sanyo wasn't running scared from the cops, he would pick up yen from the Yakuza, members of Japan's notorious criminal syndicates — or even from our high-placed mole at American Express Bank, or Manufacturers Hanover Trust, or anyone who was selling — and give it to Father Jose, who would make our payments.

It was essential that those responsible for the pickups were kept separate from our payees. Otherwise an agent might quickly put two and two together, match up buyer and seller and decide to do the business himself — thereby eliminating Deak's commission.

Why the "father" in Father Jose? Well, it was because he was a bona fide Spanish Catholic priest. He would lug bags of money all over Tokyo to make payments for Deak, then send 100 percent of his hard-earned commission of half a percent back to a church he'd founded for former prostitutes in Mexico City. He was truly a wonderful man.

As I waited at the gate to board my flight to Tokyo, I took great comfort from knowing the deal came from the US Embassy, and that our agent was a man of God. I told myself it was good karma.

My thoughts were interrupted by a sudden observation, however. I had gone to the office in Guam early, filled the golf bag with JP¥50 million, and arrived at the airport at 2pm. I'd then waited for a couple of jam-packed tourist buses to arrive, and chosen a check-in line along with about a dozen other fellows with golf bags. Now, standing at boarding Gate 3, I noticed several of these looked almost identical to mine — white and red in color, and kind of heavy.

I got a little nervous. Shit, Brink, you are either an idiot or a genius — this must be the most popular color. I hope no one picks up my bag when we get to Tokyo. Suddenly, I did not feel so good, but what the hell could I do about it?

The attendant at the check-in counter stapled my luggage stub onto my ticket, and I watched the bag slide into the belly of the airport luggage system. Good-bye. Don't lose the luggage check-in stub, I told myself.

IT WAS close to 9pm when I touched down at the old Tokyo Haneda Airport, ready to make my way to my hotel. I had drunk a couple of beers during the last hour of the flight and felt quite relaxed. Japanese are always polite, even the immigration and customs officers. I lined up behind the other non-Japanese at our designated counter.

"Ah, sooo. Why you come to Japan?" an officer asked me in broken English. "How long you stay and where?"

A few short questions and off I went to the luggage carousel. I was beginning to feel the sweat on my palms as I searched three carousels, looking at all the red and white golf bags going round. One by one, they were picked up by others; my eyes watered, straining to look at the numbers on the check-in tags. I could feel stares coming from a nearby customs agent.

Suddenly, I saw mine. Thank God! I watched it come around the corner until it passed in front of me, flipped it onto a luggage cart, put my hand-carry on top and went to the nearest customs check — all the while looking for an Indian passenger to get behind.

Why an Indian? I'll let you in on a little smuggling secret. Brink used to say: *"Customs will tear the Indians apart because they are always trying to smuggle something. In the meantime, they'll just wave you right on through."*

Next best thing to standing behind an Indian was lining up behind a little old lady — even better, in fact, to strike up some small talk with her, as this left a favorable impression on anyone watching.

With not an Indian in sight, I managed to find an elderly couple to fall behind. They were from Guam and spoke no Japanese. It didn't matter. They were waved through, and then the customs agent who had been staring at me asked me to step up to his counter. He noted I had nothing to declare. "You play golf here in Japan?" he asked, taking a long hard look at the red and white bag I had just placed in front of him. It dawned on me that it must be very rare for non-Japanese to bring golf bags into Tokyo — especially in the winter!

So much for Brink's number-one theory — it didn't quite work here. I could feel a knot building in my stomach, and my palms beginning to sweat.

"Oh no," I replied truthfully. "I don't know anyone who will invite me to a club here and besides, the weather is too cold now. I plan to play a few rounds in Manila."

Luckily, as insurance, my ticket had been written Guam/ Tokyo/ Manila/ Guam.

He asked to see it, then hesitated for what seemed like an eternity. I stared him in the eyes, and my eyes told him I was beginning to become annoyed. Regaining my confidence, I asked quickly: "What is the problem?" He still paused. I lied, and told him I would be leaving the golf bag in the stored luggage locker at the airport until my flight to Manila. My demeanor reflected that I was in a hurry.

"OK, go ahead," he finally said.

Walking off, I let out a sigh of relief and cursed Brink for saying this would be "as easy as pumpkin pie."

When I arrived at the Okura hotel, there were already three messages waiting for me — all from a "Mr. Chan," calling from Hong Kong. This was "Charlie Chan," the fictional Honolulu police detective. Of course, it was actually Brink.

Once in my tiny hotel room — the Okura was a five-star hotel, but all hotel rooms in Japan are small — I transferred the yen to a Horizon Travel shoulder bag, and leaned the golf bag in the corner.

It was past midnight when the phone rang. It was Father Jose, calling to tell me he would contact me early the next morning. It was good that he did not want to meet in the hotel. We agreed to meet at a Spanish restaurant — Los Platos — this time. (On subsequent occasions we met at one called El Castellano.)

"Come at noon," he said. "And make sure you come alone."

I checked the map, took the underground, then a taxi, and almost got lost walking the last ten blocks or so, looking over my shoulder all the while. Shit! Everyone looked the same to me. How would I know if I had "company"?

After a bottle of Father Jose's favorite wine — shipped from Spain — and a great lunch, I was feeling fine. A couple of hours later, I put him into a taxi, bag of yen in hand, and returned to my hotel. Father Jose had given me some accounts and coded payment records to send back to Brink. I decided to telex the info when I returned to Guam.

Father Jose was worried, and would seem to be more worried each time I came to see him, which turned out to be more than a dozen times over the next two years. We decided to hold our future meetings closer to the US Embassy, hence the change of restaurant.

Back in Hong Kong, I saw the settlement accounts for the money I was delivering to Japan on behalf of the US consulate in Hong Kong. Our customer was none other than Lockheed Aircraft Corporation, the American aerospace manufacturer. Point of contact: John W. Clutter, Lockheed Tokyo Office Chief (and, we would later learn, a payment agent for the CIA, possibly even a CIA Station Chief).

Father Jose, Sanyo and I became good friends. Father Jose was anxious about security and asked me to watch his back. We never met in public or allowed ourselves to be seen together, except at El Castellano, and Father Jose knew everyone there.

As for Sanyo, I would watch him meet with several Japanese gentlemen over the course of time — sometimes in a hotel car park, sometimes at the British Embassy car park, other times at a residence, even a couple of times at a phone booth. Due to his paranoia, he liked to have someone looking on from a distance.

But what was it all about? Why was Lockheed Aircraft Corporation using the services of Deak & Company? I was to find out the answer to that question two years later, in 1975.

Red alert

BRINK's amazing secretary in Hong Kong, Mrs. Silva, really ran the place while Brink was away, which was quite often. Brink traveled every other month between Hong Kong and White River, his family residence in South Africa. As Assistant Manager I sat at his desk during the times he was away, and got to see first hand what was really going on.

During one such spell, Brink had just returned the night before, and we were waiting for the "master" to arrive when Mrs. Silva came running in, frantically waving her arms.

"Bruce, the *RED PHONE* has been ringing all morning."

"What?" I didn't believe it.

I had worked in Hong Kong for almost two years, and the red phone had *never* rung. It was never even *touched*.

There was a battery of phones on Brink's desk, each with a special purpose. One was only for calls in German, another only for French, and there was even one for Esperanto. Brink was a brilliant eccentric.

But the *RED PHONE* was a very special phone, with a number that only special agents around the Far East knew — and they had to memorize it. It was only to be used in case of dire emergencies.

"What are we to do, Mrs. Silva?" The words had barely left my mouth when the phone suddenly came to life again: *RING! RING! RING! RING!* I had never heard it ring and when it did, the sound was totally unexpected… fast and shrill, with a sense of urgency about it.

"Don't touch it!" Mrs. Silva said.

Brink had told me to answer all phone calls while he was away. I hesitated as long as I could, hoping the damn thing would stop.

It didn't. I picked up the receiver.

"Hello," I answered quietly and calmly, in a voice not at all like my own. To my shock, the voice on the other end recognized mine anyway.

"Bluse," it said, in a heavy Japanese accent. It was Sanyo calling from Tokyo. He never could pronounce my name. "Is Mr. Blink there?"

"Yes, on the way soon. What is it?"

"Big, big, very big problem! Oh, my God, oh, my God, it is on the TV, and in all Japanese newspapers! Father Jose has been arrested by Japanese internal police! Oh… it big news, you see! You watch TV. Good-bye! Sayonara! Tell Blink I go to hiding."

A loud click followed.

I felt sick. Father Jose was my dear friend. Brink arrived a few minutes later and turned slightly pale at the news, but then the adrenaline kicked in. His first thought: what about the money, the accounts? Only Father Jose would have this information — not written down, only in his head. Many millions of yen paid out in recent days and weeks had to be accounted for.

"We must inform Mr. Deak." Brink said.

"Yes, let's ask Mr. Deak what we should do," I said.

For the first time, I was *seriously* asking myself: What was all this money we'd paid out really for?

WE WERE about to find out what it was all for, because it became a story of immense interest and importance that would shake political and legislative systems to the core in America, Japan and a number of other countries.

In the late 1960s and early '70s, the airline business was booming and the market for wide-body planes was taking off. The Boeing 747 had changed the world and rivalry between airplane manufacturers and airlines was fierce. Up against the 747 and the McDonnell Douglas DC 10, Lockheed's TriStar airplane was by far the underdog.

To gain advantage against their competitors, therefore, top officers at Lockheed had inaugurated and directed a program of foreign bribery that involved payments of tens of millions of dollars to officials in several countries between 1970 and 1975.

In Japan, we would later discover, Lockheed had hired the underworld figure Yoshio Kodama — a right-wing ultranationalist and a prominent figure in the Yakuza — as a consultant in order to lean on Japanese parastatal airlines, including All Nippon Airways (ANA), to buy the Lockheed L-1011 TriStar. And the apex target of this pyramid of bribery was none other than Japan's sitting Prime Minister, Kakuel Tanaka, who would eventually be charged with taking $1.6 million from Lockheed, a considerable fraction of some vast amounts paid to an extended cast of Japanese officials and agents. It was the scandal of the decade, and Deak & Company was at the very heart of it.

On the evening of Sanyo's call, we were still in the office at around 9pm local time, which was 9am in New York, when the black phone began to ring.

The black phone was a direct hotline: it was reserved *only* for calls from Mr. Deak, and it was *only* to be answered by Mr. Brink. I thought it might have been Mr. Deak's way of checking to see when Brink was in Hong Kong or South Africa, but in fact, when he was not in the office it never rang once.

When the black phone rang, everyone normally fled Brink's office, leaving him to close the door and deal with the matter at hand. Strangely, this time Brink motioned for Ron Frame, Tony Pong, Mrs. Silva and myself to stay.

The conversation is etched in my mind. Much of it switched back and forth between English and German, which only Brink understood. But what I remember clearly was the solemn look on his face. He just kept nodding his head, listening, nodding his head again, and then continuing to listen in silence. Obviously, this was extremely serious. After about 20 minutes, he slowly hung up.

Everyone started to speak at once. "What did Mr. Deak say? What can we do? What about Father Jose?"

There was a long pause before Brink said anything. "What about Father Jose?"

"Yes," we all said in unison. "What about Father Jose? Damn it! What in Jesus' name did Mr. Deak say about Father Jose?"

After a long pause, Brink finally looked at us. With a sly grin, he repeated: "About Father Jose?"

"Yes, God damn you, Brink."

"Mr. Deak said, about Father Jose... He said to *pray for him.*"

"Shit! That's all he said? Pray for him?"

So praying was Plan A. The reality was much more serious.

PLAN B would be devised three weeks later, after Father Jose had been thoroughly interrogated by the police and let out on bail. We kept a close ear to the ground until one day Sanyo called and said he had seen on TV that Father Jose had been released. The news said Father Jose knew nothing, and was only delivering documents for Deak & Company.

Sanyo said the police had been watching Father Jose for a long time, that they knew it was Deak & Company that was delivering money — and also that the Deak and Compass Travel couriers were coming from Hong Kong.

(What they had no idea about, it transpired, was the golf bags coming from Guam. In fact, to this very day, they *never could* figure out where most of the money was coming from or determine its source.)

"Bruce, can you go to Tokyo right away?" Brink asked. "You know where to meet Father Jose."

I had been the only one besides Brink and Pong who had ever been to the little flat — in Shibuya-ku, not far from Tokyo University — from which Father Jose provided Spanish-Japanese translation services. He would be expecting someone, and that could only be me. I felt that big knot return to my stomach.

"This may give me an ulcer," I said out loud to myself.

I weighed the risks, and stupidly talked myself into believing there were none.

The next day, I was on the plane to Tokyo, having first flown from Hong Kong to Guam yet again. I was not relishing the thought of showing up at Father Jose's flat at two in the morning, but that is what the situation called for. I took the train and walked the last ten blocks, then circled around from across the street. I had a good vantage point, and could see 360 degrees; I saw no one.

The entrance to the building was partly obscured by bushes, and if anyone approached me, I could keep on going around the building towards the university.

Convincing myself I was helping my dear friend — and doing nothing wrong — I walked around the bushes and toward the lobby door. When I was less than ten yards away from the entrance, however, the door sprang open. My heart stopped for what seemed an eternity before, much to my relief, a young man in his twenties walked out, quickly crossed the road and disappeared into the metro, taking no notice of me.

Approaching the entrance, I glanced at the doorbells, found 8C, and rang the buzzer. Almost instantly, I heard a deep, familiar voice.

"Father Jose," I said.

Silence, for a split second, and then a loud buzzing that broke the tension. The front door opened. I walked in alone and took the lift, pressing the button for the fifth floor, then took the stairs up to the eighth.

Father Jose and I drank my duty-free bottle of Johnny Walker Black Label and talked non-stop for the next three hours. He gave me all the account balances, payments outstanding, deliveries pending — the works — to bring back to Brink. As he talked about the uncertainty of his situation, and as the whisky flowed, emotions tumbled out. Ultimately, he felt the prosecutor would be kind to him, given that he'd only played a small role in the scandal and had no direct knowledge of what it involved.

Interestingly, when I asked him if he liked being famous, to my amazement he said yes, and that since he had been on TV he had received many calls from young Japanese stewardesses from ANA, all of whom wanted to thank him for supporting ANA TriStar. In fact, they were knocking on his door day and night. When I had buzzed earlier that night, he'd thought I was another one! (Of course, there was never any question of sexual impropriety on Father Jose's part — he just found it all quite funny and liked the attention.)

I left Father Jose's flat before sunrise, making my way back to the train station, then to the airport for my flights to Guam and back to Hong Kong.

The police had been very thorough in monitoring airport arrivals, and had been watching employees of Deak & Company and Compass Travel for more than two years. They saw them come and they saw them go. Every time they entered Tokyo, an alarm went off. They had also seen them every time they'd met with Father Jose: all the meetings were photographed and documented.

I was very fortunate not to have been connected to Deak Hong Kong or Compass Travel by the Japanese authorities, and I thanked God for my good fortune in having made all my trips from Guam undetected.

WHEN word broke of the bribes that had been paid to their Prime Minister, dozens of Japanese reporters descended on our office in Hong Kong. "Ah sooo, where Mr. Blink? Mr. Blink please! Must see Mr. Blink?"

On the morning of my return to Hong Kong after seeing Father Jose, I went to the office at about 9am. It was a beautiful sunny day, and I was feeling pretty good: a nice weekend at home beckoned. When I pressed the lift button at Shell House, however, five Japanese men with cameras suddenly appeared behind me, all trying to squeeze into the same lift. I looked at them, and they looked at me. One of them pressed level four — our floor — and I thought to myself: this time the shit has really hit the fan.

When the lift stopped at level four, they looked at me again, hesitated, and when I went out first, they immediately yelled: "Ah sooo, you Mr. Blink?"

"What? Who?" I yelled back.

"Mr. Blink! Mr. Blink! Mr. Blink?"

"No! No! No!" I said truthfully, adding: "I don't know any Mr. Blink."

Pretending to be a customer, I walked over to the Compass Travel counter and called Mrs. Silva, who had just come running out of Brink's office.

"What's happening?"

"Oh!" she said, with a hearty laugh. "There are 20 Japanese journalists and photographers here, and all of them have been trying to squeeze into 'Mr. Blink's' office since early this morning."

All of a sudden, the Japanese chatter stopped, instantly quiet. Brink happened to be an avid non-smoker and had a big red and white "NO SMOKING" sign behind his desk. When he pressed a button on the floor with his shoe, the thing would light up and start flashing. It was flashing now, and in front of it Brink himself stood facing down a room full of men whose shirt pockets bulged with cigarette packets. They looked totally amazed as he pointed to the sign.

"You came to see 'Blink?' There, watch this 'No Smoking' sign blink! And by the way, I'm Dirk *Brink*. First, before we begin with your questions, please let me tell you a true story about my experience with the Japanese army."

The silence was broken only by the sound of shuffling feet.

"You see," he continued, "I was a soldier in the Indonesian Army, and when I was captured I spent four years as one of your prisoners of war in the jungles of Thailand. I was slave labor, forced to build a railroad through the jungle on the River Kwai."

The Japanese journalists looked at him in shock. The room by now was stark silent: they seemed to have forgotten about Lockheed. One by one, each of them got up and walked out with a downcast face. Brink went on about how he was treated as a POW, and continued doing so until the last one left. You could have heard a pin drop.

Guilty

PRIME MINISTER Kakuei Tanaka was eventually found guilty, along with a series of lesser figures who had been involved in the scenario — many of them businessmen from Lockheed, ANA and its trading partner Marubeni. Lockheed President Carl Kotchian had approved payments to Tanaka for the purpose of influencing ANA. Tanaka, for his part, had agreed to do Lockheed's bidding and had approached ANA Chairman Tokuji Wakasa, who also fell into line. A couple of months later, much to the surprise of Boeing and McDonnell Douglas, the contract was awarded to Lockheed for a fleet of TriStars costing US$30 million dollars per aircraft.

Put crudely, Lockheed Corporation got the contract, with Marubeni receiving a commission; ANA got 21 Tri-Stars at a cost of over $600 million; the Japanese public got good planes; and Prime Minister Tanaka and various other "agents" got a little pocket money.

The only problem was that it was all highly illegal — a minor detail the protagonists had failed to take seriously; at least not until the scandal blew up in their faces. And that's exactly what happened when a sub-committee of the US Senate led by Senator Frank Church started looking into the affair.

What followed was a complicated saga that would take years to unfold in the Japanese court system. As the heat from the story intensified, Tanaka quietly tried to return the money, but it was simply too late.

⎯⎯⎯⎯⎯⎯•◈•◈•⎯⎯⎯⎯⎯⎯

BY THE time matters finally came to a head, almost seven years had elapsed. There had been a total of 190 hearings, involving more than 100 witnesses; three of the 16 defendants had fallen ill, quite possibly to avoid testifying; and three witnesses and one judge had died. More than twenty 20 books concerning the trial had been published, with most of them becoming best-sellers.

Judgment day was set for October 12, 1983 — and when it arrived the whole of Japan reached fever pitch. Millions stayed bolted to their televisions and radio sets; 17 helicopters hovered in the skies to witness Tanaka's drive from his home in Mejiro to the courthouse; 450 members of a special police unit were deployed; 1,500 news personnel swarmed the two key locations; and thousands lined up to claim one of 52 available court-galley seats. Live coverage began at 7am.

Tanaka's Chrysler motorcade arrived at the courthouse shortly after 9:30am. The veteran politician had by this stage incurred legal fees estimated at $4 million, but the cost to the state was considerably more. Judge Okada delivered a 55,000-character ruling in which all of the defendants were found guilty. Okada admonished Tanaka for damaging the reputation of the nation and "forfeiting the people's trust in public offices" as he handed the fallen leader a four-year jail sentence and a fine of JPY500 million — almost $4.5 million..

The TriStar's selection in Japan over the McDonnell Douglas DC 10 and Boeing 727 could only be described as a miraculous, mind-boggling turn-around that reeked of impropriety and corruption. For many in Japan, the fallout left a feeling of shame and humiliation. Back in the US, meanwhile, there was widespread shock at how Lockheed had resorted to bribery to win the contract — probably with a tacit "nod" from the CIA. Was this really the typical modus operandi of US companies in foreign lands?

The Lockheed Bribery Scandal, with Deak and the CIA caught up in its tangled web, led directly to the passage of the 1977 Foreign Corrupt Practices Act, the first-ever law criminalizing bribery of foreign officials. Essentially, the act prohibited US citizens and entities from greasing the palms of foreign government officials to benefit their business interests.

The legislative response reflected the sense of shock at yet another Watergate-level scandal coming to light — America's dirty laundry being thrust into the open for all to see. Lockheed was really a great embarrassment to the US government, which in fact subsequently put a gag order on the scandal under the guise of protecting "national interests." Therefore, the truth about what we all knew — namely that the CIA was a Lockheed collaborator, or enabler — never really came out. What's more, several of the Japanese players who had been involved in the scandal suddenly — and rather conveniently, you might say — "passed away," taking their knowledge to the grave.

For Deak & Company, it was also a disaster. Having made all of the payments, amounting to at least $30 million, we were truly exposed. The ramifications of the affair for Deak & Company in Hong Kong, in America and for Mr. Deak himself were to be far-reaching and devastating.

In the immediate aftermath, though, the business continued merrily on its way as if nothing had really happened. All of the Deak and Compass Travel counter boys in Hong Kong were now known to the Japanese police, but we recruited new couriers to service our Japanese accounts.

Father Jose was defrocked — but happy. We continued to meet over the years whenever I was in Tokyo or whenever he passed through Hong Kong on his way to Macau to visit his sister, who was a nun.

As to what had really happened, so much remained unknown. Dirk Brink said to me one day in confidence: "Look to a man named Clutter for the truth. He was our contact." Clutter had been the bridge between Deak and the CIA.

"Did Clutter work for the CIA?" I asked. Brink's eyes darted around the room quickly in confirmation.

"Ask Mr. Deak," was his reply.

I've often wondered whether it was because of what Nicholas Deak knew about the Lockheed affair and the off-balance sheet transactions he'd orchestrated for Uncle Sam over the decades that he was murdered some years later. Perhaps Lockheed was the final straw — the reason he just had to be removed from the picture. More about that later.

As Brink once told me, sagely: "When you are dealing with clandestine government agents or agencies, you are dealing in a murky world. They are the real criminals, and they will stop at nothing."

⋅◈⋅

AS TO MY own involvement in the whole business, years later — after I had found myself "kidnapped" by the US government, incarcerated, and confronted with two major money-laundering indictments — I happened to be asked by my investigator, Steve Swanson, whether I had anything on the government as a result of Deak & Company being the CIA's purported "paymaster." I immediately thought of Lockheed and Clutter.

When I proffered certain information via Swanson to the prosecutor, suddenly the government was ready to deal, even though they tried to tell me: "That Lockheed scandal is ancient history." *Oh, really?*

Later still, another interesting footnote. In a chance meeting at the Hong Kong Foreign Correspondents' Club in the Fall of 2013, I met the Japanese author and investigative journalist Eiichiro Tokumoto.

Familiar with and intrigued by the Lockheed affair, he subsequently wrote about it in an article published in the influential *Bungei Shunju*, the same magazine that had originally broken the story wide open in 1975.

His article, published in May 2014, finally revealed for the first time how most of the payments were made.

CHAPTER 8

On My Own

IN HIS 2007 book *Reefer Men – The Rise and Fall of a Billionaire Drug Ring,* author Tony Thompson describes, in stark detail, the beginnings of my company:

"[The ring] became increasingly successful, so they began to amass increasing amounts of cash and needed a way to launder it. The solution was provided by Tim Milner who, while investing his own earnings in a Hong Kong-based finance house, Deak & Company, became particularly friendly with an American banker named Bruce Aitken, friendly enough to admit that the money he was investing came from the drug business.

"Unfazed by the revelation, Aitken calmly offered to launder Milner's cash, first moving it around the world's money markets and then ultimately into offshore accounts and tax havens, for a modest commission. So efficient was Aitken that he was soon performing a similar service for them and for others. Within a year Aitken had quit his job at Deak and set up his own company, First Financial Services Ltd. His work consisted almost entirely of moving money for marijuana traffickers."

In reality, several factors spurred me to take the plunge and go on my own. The whole Lockheed scandal had brought a question to the fore that had been bothering me since Doug — the CIA guy with the poorly-concealed gold in his Nike running shoes — had been nicked in Kathmandu: What if it happened to me? Similarly, what if it had been me instead of Father Jose who had been arrested in Japan? I knew what we were doing was more than slightly illegal; but in my mind, it wasn't on the same level as smuggling guns or drugs. You can call me naive, but I felt we were simply moving money around the world in a very off-the-radar way. It was all about privacy. It seemed a happy-go-lucky sort of profession and not a big deal. Moreover, we were very good at it. Experts, in fact.

Each time I flew somewhere, however, I was risking my freedom — because most countries held a decidedly different view of my chosen field. And the Lockheed scandal had brought that realization to a head.

In the wake of Lockheed, and gradually over time, the mental burden finally came to a boil. One day in early September, 1977, I walked into the Hong Kong office and sat down in front of Brink. He didn't look up but simply asked: "What is it?" He must have sensed that something was wrong.

"This whole Lockheed thing has got me thinking," I told him. "We sort of left Father Jose swimming in deep shit without even so much as a paddle to help him out, didn't we? So, what about me? Where does that leave me, exactly? How would you feel, may I ask, if you were in my shoes, after what happened to him?"

I continued: "Tony Pong just told me about a huge pickup in Taiwan tomorrow, and he is asking me to handle it. What would happen if I got caught in Taipei tomorrow? Please tell me. What is the position of Deak & Company?"

"What do you mean?" Brink lifted his head and looked directly at me, brows furrowed, almost angry. I was slightly taken aback.

"What do you mean, what do I mean? What I mean is this: What if I am arrested while on company business working for Deak? Will you guys back me up? Will the company back me up?"

Tony, the head trader who worked the counters exchanging money, had joined us at my request and watched as I sat waiting for an answer.

"You know I'd have to speak with Mr. Deak about that, Bruce," Brink said. "But in the meantime, you're scheduled for that pickup in Taipei tomorrow."

"You're going to call Mr. Deak today?" I questioned Brink.

"Of course, Bruce. I'll call him as soon as possible."

I went home that evening not feeling at all well.

Recalling my visits to meet Father Jose, I had come to feel that "they" — whoever they might be, were watching me. It was not simply my imagination. I could feel eyes on me. I also knew that if I should get caught with any large amount of money or with accounting records, the powers that be would not be as lenient with me as they were with a priest. They respected Father Jose because he was a man of God. Me? I would be nothing more than a dirty money launderer trying to steal taxes from their coffers.

I did not sleep well that night. For the very first time, I felt a strong fear of the unknown and a stark intimation of the risks I was taking. The Taiwan deal was big and involved a new client. The next morning, by the time I woke up, I had made up my mind. I didn't even bring an overnight suitcase with me to the office.

When I walked in before 9am, the usual motley chaos of people and deals were just starting to whirl around Brink and Tony.

"Hey, Bruce, you ready to go?" Brink asked.

"Any word from Mr. Deak?" I asked.

"Nothing yet, Bruce. You're booked on the early afternoon flight."

I stood there staring at Brink intensely while I gathered my resolve. "Well, in that case, screw it. I'm not going!"

"What? What do you mean you're not going? Someone has to pick up that money! The guy is waiting in the Taipei Grand Hotel, for Christ's sake!"

Tony chimed in — and in a tone I did not like — "Yeah, Bruce. Please just go over there and get that money; deliver it to our agent and come right back. No problem!" I ignored him.

No problem? I thought about that for a few seconds, remembering the look on Father Jose's face as we spoke about the Lockheed ordeal.

"Look, Brink. I'm not going unless I hear from Mr. Deak that I will be backed up by Deak & Company. I'm an employee. What if something goes wrong in the course of my employment? I have a wife to think about. Will the company continue to pay my salary if I'm in the slammer somewhere?"

"Nothing is going to go wrong," Brink said. "You've done it dozens of times."

Brink's eyes were piercing. His face was beginning to turn red. To my surprise, he was becoming very angry. I felt intimidated, but it served to strengthen my resolve.

Then Tony said: "Bruce, if you don't go then I'll have to go."

I hesitated for a split second and decided.

"Well then, get packing Tony, because I'm not going!"

He stormed back to his desk and slammed down some papers.

Brink tried to pacify me. "OK, OK Bruce. Let me speak to Mr. Deak. I am sure it will be alright. You'll see."

"Here's what I see," I retorted. "If I am not backed by the company, then I'm not going anywhere anymore, at any time, understand?"

I took a deep breath and looked Brink straight in the eyes. "You see, I'd want much more than your prayers to help me if anything unexpected happened."

I left the office with a sense of peace and relief. I did not go to Taiwan. To his credit, Tony made the Taiwan pickup and had no hard feelings afterwards. He was a pro, and in fact he too was anxious to know the company's position. We both already knew the answer.

Now I urgently needed a new game plan or a new job.

FORTUNATELY, it happened that Mr. Deak planned to visit Hong Kong in November 1977, and I had a chance to discuss my plans with him over dinner as we enjoyed a pleasant evening on a yacht moored beside Sai Kung, in the city's New Territories. Pan Am was still flying into Kai Tak Airport in those days, and the owner of the yacht was a Pan Am captain by the name of Steve Meuris. Steve and his wife were a great couple.

I remember the conversation with Mr. Deak clearly, because he saw the advantage to both the company and to me of my becoming a free agent and operating as a "Business Development Manager."

"Mr. Deak," I said, "I have been traveling to different countries doing pickups and payments on almost a weekly basis. As soon as I arrive I do the deal, and when it's finished, I barely have time to catch my breath before I fly back to Hong Kong to start the next transaction. But what if I had the time to stay in Australia, for example, a while longer, and ask our happy clients to introduce me to new clients? Then I could also service their businesses."

Mr. Deak thought it was a great idea and said Deak & Company would quote me a preferential rate. I would give my client my quotation, and keep the difference. A satisfactory arrangement for all concerned.

I'll always remember that night for another couple of reasons. Firstly, Jenny was there. Mr. Deak had given her a job in New York when I started with the company and was very fond of her.

The other reason was somewhat less pleasing. As we all chatted happily away, I remembered I needed to get something from my briefcase, and Steve's wife motioned that it was on the lower deck.

On the boat, all of our shoes were off, and in honor of Mr. Deak's visit it had been thoroughly cleaned and waxed from top to bottom. Suffice to say that as soon as I took my first step, in my socks, on the newly polished teak stairs, I found myself airborne, flying through the night like a *mis*-guided missile. I landed flat as a pancake on my back with such force that the whole boat shook, as if a bomb had just exploded.

Funny how you remember things. My father was a house painter, and sometimes he fell off the ladder. He told me that when you start to fall, you should relax, and then you will be alright. I tried to relax during that twisted, airborne fall, but the first thing I felt was *WHAM!* The breath was knocked out of my lungs and a shock wave ran across my entire body, emanating from the center of my back.

Everyone rushed to see if I were dead, looks of shock covering their faces. Being very embarrassed, and stubborn, I got up as fast as possible and brushed the whole thing off, insisting that I was perfectly fine. Mr. Deak observed me closely, looking me straight in the eye over dinner and realizing that I was in some kind of pain, but he said nothing, and neither did I.

By the time dinner ended, I had recovered and was feeling much better. I wasn't much worse for the wear, but I was sore as hell for about a week, and nursing a bruised ego too.

A few months after my meeting with Mr Deak, the company HQ in New York sent out an official information bulletin regarding my move:

DEAK – PERERA GROUP
(INTER-OFFICE INFORMATION BULLETIN)
No. 253   New York, February 1, 1978
Deak & Company (Far East) Ltd., Hong Kong:

"As of January 1, 1978, Mr. Bruce Aitken has opted to become a freelance agent for the Deak-Perera group with the title of Business Development Manager. He will continue to be closely in touch with the Far East office through which he can be contacted at any time. We wish him good luck."

Prior to the announcement, I had done a lot of soul-searching. It made sense to become an agent for Deak & Company, giving up the big salary and benefits as an employee in exchange for something better: commissions, my time and my life. At least, that's what I thought.

Hooked

SOON after I became a freelance agent, in November 1977, my first deal materialized — a pickup from a client in Sydney. The amount was $200,000, in US dollars, and my fee was 3 percent, an easy $6,000 for my efforts. This would be the acid test.

What were my efforts?

Having met the client, I packed 40 bundles of 50-dollar notes, each bundle totaling $5,000, into "Old Faithful," my favorite golf bag.

Doing deals for myself was totally different from doing deals for Deak. I felt a thrill, something like an adrenaline junkie might feel, as I prayed inwardly to myself at the airport check-in at Sydney, and then said another prayer — of thanksgiving — when I collected the money upon arrival at Hong Kong. It was an easy but satisfying job.

The next day happened to be a beautiful Sunday morning. I had slept well. Jenny and I had breakfast at Hong Kong's American Club, at St. George's Building in Central district, and I pondered the $6,000 I had just made. It was a lot of money at the time, and I savored an amazing feeling of being a good provider for my family — the man of the house. Smuggling money was so good it felt like a drug addiction. Breakfast at the club that morning never tasted so good. Suddenly, I felt alive.

I was hooked.

Truly I couldn't have felt better or more satisfied with life. The new arrangements with Deak were working well. Mr. Brink, ever the pragmatist, understood what I was trying to do, saw the advantages and was actually happy with what had been agreed. He even granted me full use of the office — no hard feelings.

Ahead of the official announcement of my new arrangement on January 1, I remember looking forward to just chilling out over the holidays. I was in the office on the last working day before Christmas and counting down the minutes when Mrs. Silva referred a caller to me.

A Sydney-based American chiropractor, Dr. Ted Krauss, was calling from the five-star Peninsula Hotel in Hong Kong. He wanted to see me. When? I could not believe it. *Christmas Day.*

The sources of Dr. Krauss's referral to me were impeccable, and as he was due to leave Hong Kong the day after Christmas I couldn't very well turn him down. With humble appreciation, he thanked me profusely for agreeing to meet him.

On Christmas afternoon, I pressed the buzzer of Room 806 at the Peninsula. I heard footsteps coming from behind the door and moments later Dr. Krauss appeared from behind it. Dapper would be a fitting word to describe the elegantly-attired, curly-haired gentleman before me. He was about five feet, nine inches tall, and in addition to an affable smile, he wore sharply creased designer jeans, matching dark-blue leather loafers, and a loosely-flowing white silk shirt.

He smoked a cigarette in a long holder, and offered me one. I declined. Five minutes later, he offered me a joint. *Now, this is one interesting fellow! Surely, he is up to something besides working as a chiropractor.* (Actually, he wasn't.)

Over the following years, Dr. Krauss would become a very good friend. I soon learned that he was an extremely sociable character, and an enthusiast for both weed and wine. More than anything in life, he wanted to be around people he saw as interesting, or who lived on the edge in some way.

Cito & Lynn

THE world in which I operated was a small one, and the souls who moved within it often turned out to be mysteriously connected.

One of Cito's close associates (and a Deak client) was a man from Cape Town, South Africa, named Tim Milner. Tim and I went back a few years, and were comfortable, good friends. We would meet in Sydney from time to time and do some quick business. As birds of a feather, you might say, we flocked together.

Six feet tall with a slim build, Tim was always casually dressed and wore a carefree smile that matched his personality. Brink once described him as a large catamaran twin-hulled vessel that would slowly sail along, until, at the slightest sign of trouble, a switch would be flipped, revealing two jet engines — and suddenly the boat would become a hydrofoil leaving the authorities in its wake as it slipped through the waves. Brink was a master of hyperbole but his description gives some idea of how Tim operated. Tim himself had a good chuckle some years later when I mentioned this to him.

Dr. Krauss, as it turned out, was also good friends with Lynn and Ray "Cito" Cessna — yet more birds of a feather.

Cito was an American who had found his way to Australia via rugged places such as Iran, Pakistan and Afghanistan, and had many interesting tales to tell.

I was first introduced to him and his wife when — on one of my trips to Sydney, around 1976-77 — Tim invited me to have dinner with them. They were strict vegetarians and knew some really excellent veggie restaurants around Sydney and in the suburb of Moseman, on the North Shore. (Until meeting them, I had no idea vegetarian food could be so delicious.) They also had a nice home in Lane Cove that was stuffed with beautiful Afghan, Persian, and Pakistani carpets, and as we got to know one another it was always a joy to get an invitation to theirs for dinner washed down with excellent Aussie wine.

Their place was well-guarded by two large Great Danes that growled at you as soon as you drove up to the house, which was located about 50 meters from the road. I always hired a rental car, and got into the habit of parking it in front of another house a couple of blocks away, then walking the rest of the way.

Initially, it wasn't just the dogs that were hostile, though. Cito seemed very uncomfortable when Tim first brought me into their circle — and into the sanctum of his home. He certainly wasn't friendly towards me, and I did not feel welcome. Even though I handled money for him, I think he wondered if I could be trusted.

After several trips and cash pickups, he must have decided he could, because the couple and I became the best of friends — so much so, in fact, that they insisted I go to their house every time I was in Sydney. Once he accepted you as a friend, he was loyal and true. I came to love just hanging out on Cito's stack of exotic carpets as he chain-smoked unfiltered Camels, and there was always one lit in his hand — his one bad habit.

Like Tim, Cito had an interesting extended circle of friends, which included some great connections through his gracious and lovely Australian wife, the aforementioned Lynn.

One of these was a top-class solicitor from Ireland — Morgan "the Magician" Ryan. Morgan and his mates were class acts. You had to admire both the way they lived their lives — with genuine gusto — and the way in which they operated in and out of the system.

I remember the first night I was invited to go along and meet Morgan at his home in Neutral Bay. By that time, I had already moved a lot of money for this circle of friends, and the magical service I'd provided in making money disappear in Sydney, only to reappear somewhere else, was opening lots of doors for me. Everyone, it seemed, had a need for such a service.

Likable from the outset, Morgan was both shrewd and sharp as a tack, a funny Irishman who had a great zest for life. Standing about five feet, eight inches tall, he was always impeccably dressed. He had a round, warm face and wore beautiful tweed sport jackets that mirrored his enjoyment of the good life. We hit it off the moment we met and I expected the introduction would result in some pretty good business outcomes in the future, provided everyone could keep their heads down.

As it happens, fate had some other ideas.

A tune for Mr. Piano

WITH dozens of successful deals now under my belt since "going it alone," March of 1979 began uneventfully. As I sat in my little office at Deak & Company in Hong Kong surveying my list of accounts, however, I realized that in spite of every effort to develop relationships and accounts with straight-arrow types, the greater part of my business operations had to do with money-laundering from the sale of marijuana.

The phone rang. It was Brink.

"Bruce, pick up line one from Australia."

At the end of line one was a man we'll call "Mr. Piano" for the purposes of this narration. He was calling from Perth.

I had actually met Mr. Piano, a lawyer, twice before: once in Hong Kong and then again in Melbourne. For some reason, I found myself in two minds as to whether to take the call or not. I wondered why Brink had decided to pass him along to me.

On first meeting Mr. Piano, I'd told him how we operated. Then, in Melbourne, I'd given him half a two-dollar bill… and forgotten about him. Sure enough, though, he wanted to proceed. Could I come to Perth immediately to take care of his first and only transaction? I quoted him my fee of five percent for a one-off deal, which he confirmed would involve picking up A$300,000.

My mind raced. Why had Brink just passed up on three percentage points for Deak & Company? I decided to speak to him, and he said he didn't want to use the Deak account at ANZ Bank in Sydney for Piano's business. This sounded a bit strange and it worried me slightly. Brink, however, advised me that this was indeed a one-time deal and that he had passed it to me for that reason.

You know when you have that feeling deep down in your gut, a *premonition* telling you not to do something, but you do it anyway? That was how I felt. I buzzed Compass Travel.

"Please book me a ticket on the CX non-stop flight to Perth, and get me a reservation at the Perth Hilton." I would bring the cash back with me in Old Faithful, and pocket the full five percent fee.

A big problem with Perth was that there were only two direct flights a week, so I would have to stay longer than I wanted to. I hoped Piano had his shit together and would be ready. He said he was. Armed with Old Faithful, I arrived on the morning of March 13.

I was tired, but I got right on the deal, phoning Piano as soon as business opened at 9am. By 10am he was at my hotel. He looked very nervous and was sweating profusely; it was clear that he was having second thoughts. It had been so much easier to agree to the deal over the phone than to actually go through with it.

As I watched this agitated lawyer figuratively shitting himself in front of me, the situation began to seriously piss me off. Finally, I gave him an ultimatum.

"Look, my friend," I said, as politely as possible. "Either bring me the cash within 24 hours, or no problem — we simply walk away from the deal as if nothing happened. However, you will have to forfeit my expenses and a fee for breaking the deal. Please bring me either A$300,000, or a fee of $5,000 for my time and expenses."

Frankly, I was fine either way. I honestly hoped he would just bail out and pay the penalty. He said he would get back to me in the afternoon.

I agreed to wait for his call and in the meantime welcomed a stroke of luck. The Hilton happened to be the registration point for a golf tournament happening nearby — meaning there were golf bags everywhere you looked. If the hotel lobby looked like a golf shop at the 19th hole, no-one would look askance at me as I headed out the door with a cash-filled Old Faithful.

When Piano rang my room, he said he had spoken to his advisor and was prepared to go ahead. I was shocked.

"Who is your advisor?"

"My banker, of course," was his curt and somewhat rude reply.

"You have violated a very important rule; you've broken the confidentiality of the deal and *substantially* increased the risk," I replied. I wanted to add "*You moron!*" but held my composure. I wasn't sure what to do. He then assured me his banker was a lifelong friend and trustworthy, and that he, Piano, would be delivering the goods to my hotel by 4pm, just after the bank closed.

I told him to come alone.

After hanging up, I called the airline to make a reservation on the March 14 early-morning flight to Sydney, hoping that I could get home sooner than planned. But there was a hitch: the onward flight to Hong Kong was fully booked, so the earliest I could get back there was on March 15. I resigned myself to having to spend a day in Sydney babysitting the golf bag, because I could never feel comfortable leaving it alone. I would be in Sydney for one night — but I wouldn't be able to meet up with either Cito or Dr. Krauss.

The doorbell rang at 4:30pm and in came Mr. Piano, alone but sweating. I did my best to reassure him. He said he had been referred to Deak by a well-known Perth businessman and handed me the money. I gave him a pat on the back. I told him I needed to act immediately and transfer the money without hesitation or delay, so he would have to excuse me. He understood and quickly left the room.

As soon as he had gone, I bolted and double-locked the door. I took out the golf bag, which had been out of sight in the closet, unscrewed the bottom and quickly packed the cash into the bag's specially-made sleeves. Now I was the one sweating. This was the time that I felt most vulnerable.

The whole operation was completed in ten minutes. I breathed a sigh of relief: it was so good to have the cash out of sight. I placed the golf bag back in the closet where I knew it was safe and sound.

About an hour later, the phone rang. It was Piano. "Is everything OK?" he inquired.

"Yes," I assured him. "As a matter of fact, not only is everything OK but the goods are already on their way."

He expressed shock, verging on panic. "What?" he stuttered and mumbled something incoherent.

"Yes, sir," I continued. "No turning back now. It will be deposited within 48 hours to your account in Switzerland, as per your instructions."

He didn't say anything.

"Are you alright? Hello? Hello??"

An ominous silence then followed. We were disconnected. I called him back. He did not pick up.

I was worried — paranoid, in fact. I decided I needed some fresh air.

Opening the door to my hotel room at the end of the corridor, I glanced all the way to the end where the lifts were located — and immediately noticed two men in black suits standing there. They could see me plain as daylight and were staring at me, as if I had startled them as much as they'd startled me. *Oh shit! They look like police. What the hell am I to do?* I was already halfway out the door. *Keep going, Bruce.*

I walked slowly down the corridor and approached them. One had a big ring of keys in his hands, which made him look like a member of the hotel security staff. I nodded. They nodded back. I waited for the lift, which seemed to take forever to arrive.

I could sense the two suits were becoming almost as uncomfortable as me. They started making their way slowly down the corridor, heading toward my room — and as they walked I stole glances out of the corner of my eye to see where they might stop. The lift bell rang too soon and the door opened. I let it pass. They would think I had taken it.

I looked for the door to the stairs, but first, stealing a last glance down the corridor, I saw them unlock the door to my room and enter. I felt a wave of heat on my forehead as my temperature rose and my heart rate shot up. I walked down one flight of stairs and pushed the elevator button for the lobby. I suddenly felt very sick. *What the hell should I do now?*

I waited for a short while in the lobby, but no-one appeared so I went out to the street for a walk to clear my head. A half hour passed, then an hour. It seemed like an eternity. If I returned to the room, what would I find? Would they be waiting for me? Would they have checked the golf bag? Would it be gone? If anything, my curiosity became even more overwhelming than my fear of what might happen next.

With my only option being to finally return to the hotel, I proceeded to my floor. The lift opened. I looked down the corridor — and saw no-one. I stopped in front of my door and listened. Silence. I took a deep breath. My heart was racing. I prayed. I approached the door and, turning the key in the lock, slowly opened it. The room was dark with just a reflection of light coming from outside the window. I turned on the light. There was no-one there.

Immediately looking towards the closet, I breathed a sigh of relief to find the golf bag still there. Bolting the door, I carefully opened the bottom of it. *The money was untouched.* I could not wait to get the hell out of there, and onto the morning flight to Sydney. Old Faithful had passed the test. If the men in black suits had come looking for A$300,000, they had clearly left disappointed.

The next morning, as I checked the golf bag in at Perth airport, I had a terrible feeling of eyes being upon me. Trying to take it all in calmly, I was happy to see the bag move along the conveyor belt on its way into the plane's belly. At least it was out of my hands. I shuddered for a second, imagining that a customs agent or the police might still tap me on the shoulder.

Arriving at Sydney in the afternoon, I proceeded to the Hilton, golf bag over my shoulder. I was happy just to stay in my room, order room service and enjoy a quiet dinner and a couple of beers. Inevitably, I was tempted, after the beers, to call Cito or Dr. Krauss, but I felt I had already had enough excitement for one day and needed some peace and quiet. The golden rule of money laundering is never to mix the business of babysitting cash with pleasure.

Late that night, my peace was shattered by the phone ringing. It was Jenny.

"Hi!" I said, "Do I have something very interesting to tell you when I get home." But she interrupted me. Her news was more devastating than I could ever have imagined.

"Bruce," she said, "Are you sitting down?" My stomach turned over as I waited for her to speak. Silence.

"What is it, Jenny?" Someone unknown had called from Sydney and left a shocking message on our home phone. Cito and Tim had both been arrested the day before in Lane Cove, having been found to be in possession of a huge stash of 100,000 Thai cannabis sticks.

As I would learn later, Tim — an expert yachtsman — had routinely sailed weed from Thailand, burying it on a remote beach on the coast of Western Australia. Cito would then recover it and drive a loaded truck 3,934 km back to Sydney.

The message for me, which came from Morgan Ryan, was to be "ultra-careful." They had no idea who'd tipped off the police or who they were now watching.

My first worry was about Cito and Tim. It had been over two months since my last trip to Sydney, and on that trip I had met them both downtown. They must be in very deep shit. I wanted to call Dr. Krauss but decided not to do so.

It suddenly occurred to me just how exposed *I* was right now. The flight back to Hong Kong was due to leave in a little over eight hours. Could I be taking a higher than usual risk by checking a golf bag full of money onto the plane? If I were stopped, I might be linked to the case against Tim and Cito. I wished I had never heard of Mr. fucking Piano in Perth — and that I had never become involved with his bloody transaction.

And then there was the other nagging question: Just who were those men who had entered my room at the hotel?

Decision time…

I checked out of the hotel early the next morning and took a taxi to the airport. Everything looked normal. Approaching the Cathay Pacific counter, I checked in a loaded Old Faithful. After that, it seemed to take forever until we were finally called to start boarding. I still feared anything could happen.

As the plane taxied onto the runway, I said one last prayer. The pilot gave it full throttle, the aircraft reached rotation speed, and I felt the lift on top of the wings as we finally became airborne. Take-off — at long last! I sank into my seat and pondered what in the world might happen next. I had a much more important deal coming up in Melbourne in April. I would have to be very careful indeed.

I was to read the following some time later, in a stinging report by an Australian Royal Commission (more of which to come):

"Early in 1979, New South Wales police tapped the telephone of a suspected drug dealer at Cronulla. This led them to Moseman and then to Drummoyne, which led to a tap on the phone of Dr. Theodore Frederick Krauss, a chiropractor. Krauss had conversations with an American, Roy Bowers Cessna, but was cautious in his remarks, so a tap was placed on Cessna's phone. Soon after, on Wednesday, 14 March 1979, the tap enabled police to arrest Cessna and an Englishman, Timothy Lycett Milner, in possession of 110 000 Buddha sticks weighing some 137 kilograms. This amount suggested an intention to supply the drug, so the offence would thus be indictable (i.e. go before a judge and jury), and carried a maximum penalty of either ten or fifteen years in prison, depending on the strength of Indian hemp in the material."

Back to Sydney

BACK in Hong Kong, I could not stop thinking about Cito and Tim being in the slammer and facing God only knew what — although for myself I was relieved to have flown out of the country with Mr. Piano's cash safely checked in the hold.

I knew there would be more news waiting for me in Hong Kong — and, sure enough, when I got to the office the next day there were several messages for me from Lynn, with instructions from Morgan. She'd been calling collect from a pay phone.

Later that day, Cito was bailed out. Things weren't looking good, but Morgan had assured Cito and Tim he would get to work on fixing the situation right away. Naturally, there would be expenses — namely Tim's bail and the grease to hopefully get a good result.

The task of bringing in "the bread" from their Deak accounts could only fall to one person — me. I hesitated to return to Sydney immediately, however. I decided I would wait a week and try to line up a seller of Australian dollars in Sydney, rather than carrying the cash from Hong Kong. The amount required for bail and solicitor fees would be somewhere between A$50,000 and A$70,000. Cito and I arranged for me to make the delivery to him in person at a little vegetarian restaurant in Mosman.

When we met there, no one seemed to have an appetite. I hugged Cito and Lynn, wished them well, and asked them to let Tim, who was in the notorious Long Bay prison, know that I would do as he instructed as regards payments. I would pray for him, I added.

CHAPTER 9

The Cessna-Milner Affair

THE SITUATION IN Australia seemed dire. The seized buddha sticks weighed some 137 kilograms — an amount that suggested intent to supply the drug, which carried a maximum penalty of up to 15 years in prison, depending on the strength of the hemp involved.

As matters played out, however, both men were given much lighter punishments. And that was all thanks to some extensive high-level bribes.

Tim Milner was given an 18-month sentence — and served only six months of it. Roy Cessna, meanwhile, received merely a A$1,000 fine. Amazing. Morgan Ryan and his pals were clever as foxes, and ingenious in the tricks they used to create favorable outcomes for their clients.

Having blown over so swiftly, the affair would later blow up in everybody's faces, though. Almost a decade later, in fact, it came to light that the arrests had been the result of a tap on Dr. Krauss's phone. And the revelations stemming from that tap, and others like it, created a scandal of the highest order in Australia — almost as big as the Lockheed scandal in Japan.

At stake would be the lives and livelihoods of not only Cito and Tim, but of numerous top solicitors, magistrates, judges, and the police commissioner himself — all Irishmen, I might add. In fact, the debacle would almost bring down the New South Wales government.

What became known as the "Cessna-Milner Affair" revealed links between organized crime and the highest levels of the police, the judiciary and politicians in Australia. Full details of how it all worked trickled out over several years and the shockwaves have continued to make headlines in the Aussie press up until recent times.

⟶⟨❦⟩⟵

THE truth of what had gone down began to emerge in 1984 when recordings of various conversations, including some between High Court Judge Lionel Murphy and a magistrate, were exposed by *The Age* newspaper. The material — obtained illegally by the New South Wales Police Force and the Australian Federal Police — hinted at a host of murky associations and improper conduct and led to the Royal Commission alluded to in the last chapter (and to the conviction of Justice Murphy on a charge of attempting to pervert the course of justice).

Three years after that, Tim would spill the beans, under significant duress from the Aussie police, about the part he and Ray had played in this whole shady nexus of corruption. (These admissions followed an ordeal in Thailand of a rather different nature — his own kidnapping. We'll come to this later.)

According to Tim's statement, as reported by the journalist Andrew Keenan in the *Sydney Morning Herald*: "I stayed on bail for two months until my case came up. I was told by Ray Cessna that if I paid money, things would be easier. He would say a figure, and then a different one, ranging from A$50-70,000. I went to court and was sentenced to 18 months. Then, when I was inside, my lawyer visited me, and I signed a letter to Deak & Company (Far East) for an unlisted order for A$30,000. I knew it had to do with my case, but I did not know who was getting paid, or how it was done. They also took my A$20,000 bail money."

Acting as Tim's and Cito's attorney, Morgan Ryan, with the aid of some "grease," had been able to convince certain key decision makers in the case that the amount of THC — the main psychoactive compound — in the hemp found in his clients' possession when they were arrested was of a very low quality and percentage, making this in reality a very minor drug bust. What's more, to top it all off, on the day of sentencing the case was magically transferred to a Magistrate's Court. That meant it was subject to a magistrate's decision instead of a jury's, and that there would be no recording equipment in the courtroom. Whether they knew what they had paid for or not, Tim and Cito certainly got good value for their money.

As Keenan described it in the *Herald*: "Timothy Milner has admitted that he paid at least A$50,000 so 'things could go easier' for him after he and Ray Cessna were charged with supplying Indian hemp in 1979. Although Milner said he does not know to whom the money was paid, he 'knew it was to do with my case.'"

Appraising the Cessna-Milner case following the Royal Commission investigation, Judge Donald Stewart concluded that, in addition to Tim and Cito, the leading figures in the scandal were Morgan Ryan, Chief Stipendiary Magistrate Mr. Murray Farquhar, and police chief Mr. Merv Wood. Judge Stewart found all of them to have been involved in a conspiracy to pervert the course of justice.

It would later emerge that the Cessna-Milner fix was plotted out over a now-famous dinner at Ryan's house in Neutral Bay on 10 May 1979. All of the characters mentioned above — Lionel Murphy, Morgan Ryan, Farquhar, Wood — were present, along with Magistrate Clarence Briese, who was about to replace Farquhar (Briese would later testify that he felt the purpose of the dinner was to determine if he would be as "flexible" as his predecessor. Rumors that Farquhar was bent were already rife in the judiciary, according to media reports.) Discussions at this dinner determined that the Cessna-Milner case would be heard by a Magistrate's Court, as explained above — no sound recordings and peanuts penalties.

The details of the deal were laid out starkly in a 2017 report for the *Sydney Morning Herald* by the investigative journalist Kate McClymont: "Five days after the dinner, the head of the police prosecution department was shocked to receive a call from the police commissioner himself instructing him that he had spoken to Farquhar and that the Cessna-Milner case was to be heard summarily rather than by way of indictment. This guaranteed a lesser sentence."

Mystery man

KEENAN'S *Herald* reports, following Tim's statements, correctly identified a sixth person involved: "Regarding the 'cast,' it was not five, as was always reported, but six." Guess who?

He continued: "Bruce Aitken would nicely fit the role of a 'sixth man' in the Cessna-Milner Affair. Aitken's involvement and background are less well-known than those of Messrs. Raymond Cessna, Timothy M., Morgan Ryan, Mervyn Wood and Murray Farquhar. Bruce Aitken was the 'mystery money mover.'

"According to Milner's statements describing several cannabis imports in which he was involved, dating from 1975: 'The money was taken out by a Deak Company representative on all the trips.' He later identified 'Aitken' or 'B. Aitken,' a sometime Deak employee or contract agent, as being the man to whom he gave money from drug sales in Australia to be sent back to Southeast Asia. A final specific reference to Aitken concerned Milner's A\$20,000 bail money, which he says: 'Cessna arranged for me via Aitken.'"

In short, I was exposed by the *Herald* on the back of the *Age* revelations and Tim's interview in Thailand.

The report went on: "According to the public records of the Stewart Royal Commission regarding the *Age* tapes, phone taps had been placed on various drug dealers, then moved to the phone of Dr. Theodore Krauss, the Sydney chiropractor. In early March, the taps were moved to the home phone of Raymond Cessna, one of the two Americans overheard speaking to Krauss. The other was Bruce Aitken.

"On March 21, 1979, two months before the Cessna-Milner case was finally disposed of, the NSW Police Crime Intelligence Unit sent a telex to Interpol in Hong Kong requesting certain 'discreet inquiries.' In particular, the CIU wanted to know the occupants of 406 Shell House, Queen's Road, Central, and whether 'Milner is in any way connected with the address, and also a man named Bruce Aitken.'"

Of course, the address was for Deak & Company, described as a "foreign currency specialist." The inquiry uncovered that I had been transferred to Deak's Hong Kong office from Guam in November 1975 at the direction of Deak's New York office, and by 1978 had become a general agent or commission agent.

In addition, a separate but inter-related Royal Commission — the Costigan Commission — noted that I had traveled a great deal in Australia and elsewhere: "During the three years up to 1981 Aitken was known to have visited Sydney more than 15 times, Manila and Tokyo more than ten times, Taipei more than eight, and Bangkok more than seven. He had also visited Singapore, San Francisco, Honolulu, Macau, Brunei, Kuala Lumpur, Jakarta and Melbourne, and several countries in Europe and Africa. Although his name might not have emerged publicly during the Cessna-Milner matter, by late April 1980, NSW police had him listed as being an 'associate of Ray Cessna and Ted Krauss.'"

Thus, some time after arriving in Sydney on April 16, 1980 — nearly a year after the original resolution of the Cessna-Milner case — I came under surveillance by the Criminal Investigation Unit of New South Wales, and was recorded in conversations on one of Morgan Ryan's tapped phones. According to summaries of the calls recorded, Morgan tells me: "We all have to be ultra-careful." That would be about right.

Again, from the *Herald*: "CIU surveillance running sheets noted that early that morning, April 30, Aitken drove from his apartment at McMahons Point to Ryan's Neutral Bay home. He was seen to walk down the steps to the front door, go to the letterbox, and then walk back to the front door before leaving."

The paper added: "That night Aitken drove to Double Bay…and later on in the evening was stopped by police in William Street. In the boot of his car was a canvas bag containing about A$60,000 wrapped in two brown paper packages. He was subsequently charged with 'goods in custody.'"

Yes, I was arrested by the police with packages in my trunk containing cash. Ironically, it wasn't connected to the Cessna-Milner affair, but it did increase tension in the camp.

Judging from the police phone taps, May 1 was a particularly busy day for Morgan Ryan. First, he learned of my arrest from Cito, who — according to police summaries of their exchanges — told him that I would not make a statement, and that I had said I was simply on company business.

Morgan later called Cito back and was told that I "had been picked up carrying company funds." Morgan was concerned that "they should not get any of the paperwork."

What paperwork? Morgan was known as "the Magician" for his skill in arranging Australian residency visas for Asians: crucially, he had some good Irish buddies high up in Immigration. Truth be told, the paperwork he was worried about was for the expeditious handling of a resident visa for an old friend of mine from the Philippines.

Next, Morgan called Mr. Abraham Saffron — a major figure in organized crime in Australia. He asked Saffron if he knew anyone high up in the Criminal Investigation Unit, and told him about my arrest. According to the summaries, Saffron later called back with a reassuring message: "Abe said he will think about it."

<hr />

BEING arrested in 1980 was a traumatic experience. Most of all, I dreaded telling Jenny: I knew she would be very disappointed in me.

I had foolishly gone out to a party the night it happened, having been invited by one of my very best mates, Peter King, also known as "The Duck" (as in "Peking Duck"). A lot of alcohol had been consumed, and there was a lot of hashish smoke floating in the air.

When the police picked me on my way home I was taken to a holding cell. It was 3am and I felt miserable. I cursed myself profusely, and wondered what had happened to my character.

Dr. Krauss — via his lady, Jinny — promptly posted my bail of A$10,000, and I was released from custody just minutes before I was due to be transferred to Long Bay.

The minute I was free, I called Jenny. Instead of adding to my torment, happily she comforted me. What a woman. I had to appear in court and then return to Sydney for a hearing the following month. I was sick with worry, but pacified by Morgan's assurances to me of the outcome.

The bundle of cash I'd been carrying actually belonged to a good friend of mine, a merchant banker named Warren Magi. I had been to Warren's house earlier the same morning to deliver the funds, unaware that the police had been following me. Warren's arrival in

Sydney had been delayed — and his wife refused to take the money. The irony was that this particular A$60,000 wasn't drug-related in the slightest.

Because I had indicated that I had brought the cash with me from Hong Kong, and that I could prove the fact in court, it was held as "goods in custody." Morgan said the money would have to be returned to me if I could prove that I had withdrawn it from my account in Hong Kong.

I hadn't, of course. But in any case I returned to Hong Kong and obtained from my good friends at Deak & Company the back-dated official A$60,000 withdrawal slip I would need to redeem the funds.

Police inquiries directed to the company prompted the reply that I had withdrawn the money from my own agency account with Deak before traveling to Sydney.

On May 10, 1980, a police inquiry to Interpol in Washington produced a different kind of response: "Subject is known to drug enforcement agency as a drug trafficker under particulars supplied."

All the same, the "goods in custody" charge against me was dismissed on June 4. According to the Stewart Royal Commission's confidential report, years later: "The magistrate did not accept the allegations of the prosecution that the money had been in Aitken's possession as a result of drug transactions, in the light of documentary evidence from Hong Kong as to the origin of the cash."

I'd dreaded having to return to Sydney for that court date, and agonized over the fact that I had taken such risks in spite of knowing how hot it had become in the kitchen.

Granted, Morgan's promises before I left Hong Kong that A$2,000 would cover my "expenses" and settle the case proved reliable. But I realized my days in Australia — a country full of people I considered friends, a country I had come to love — had reached an end.

There are times in life when although you see the approaching "tsunami," you cannot seem to get out of its way before disaster strikes. For me, it was as though some distracting noise rang in my ears, drowning out the whisper of common sense trying to tell me I was in grave peril. Against my better judgment, I did not heed that voice screaming "danger!"; more materialistic considerations prevailed.

I recall Morgan phoning me just before my departure for Sydney to attend the court case. The conversation was short and sweet: "Don't worry, Bruce, it is all done. After the decision, you'll be able to claim your money. Don't forget to bring the paperwork, and what was agreed."

I had a feeling, one that later proved to be correct, that the phone call was being taped. So I said "Thanks, Morgan, the truth always wins in the end!" and promptly hung up.

My main recollection of the court proceedings in Sydney is of the comment from the very old and frail clerk in the police evidence department who gave me back the A$60,000. Scratching his head, the old man said: "In all my years as custodian of evidence, over 40 years in fact, this is the very first time I have ever given back money!"

Hallelujah!

CHAPTER 10

First things first

DURING my time in Guam, I had had the pleasure of befriending a young fellow American, Tom O'Donnell. When I met him, Tom was 25, fit, of average height and build, with light brown hair and confident blue eyes. He had a happy and outgoing personality and I liked him instantly. At the time, he was a sharp, fun-loving bachelor and worked for Bank of America. He introduced me to Irene Cheng, a Chinese lady from Taiwan, who gave us both Mandarin lessons.

Over time, Tom went on to work as the representative of Philadelphia National Bank, living in the exclusive Manila neighborhood of Forbes Park.

He seemed to have it made in his career, but Tom was not really the type to work for just one company forever, and eventually he cast his fate to the wind — he joined me as a partner in First Financial Services Ltd., FFS for short, in Hong Kong.

The year was 1980 and I'd decided I wanted to step away from being a freelance agent for Deak. FFS was the result, and where Deak used the tagline "Have cash call Deak," we settled on "Have cash call Mr. Clean" — Mr. Clean being me.

For Tom, the excitement of the free market exchange business, the magical movement of money, the travel, the characters we'd meet — all were enticing. The deal was easily done.

Guam also produced another character who was to join us later.

Bill Thomasson was head of the Guam Savings and Loan Association, but resigned from that position around about the same time Tom and I were establishing FFS. Fatefully, we had a conversation one day and I confided in Bill, telling him about the nature of what FFS was about, how we'd be smuggling millions of dollars in and out of countries each day in suitcases, or golf bags, exercising amazing sleight-of-hand to out-smart customs officers and reporting requirements.

Being a straight-arrow type, I expected Bill to be shocked. But in fact I was the one who was shocked by his response.

"What a great business," he said. "Amazing! Like taking candy from babies! When can I start?"

Bill was six feet tall, wore horn-rimmed glasses and was prematurely gray — a distinguished looking gentleman. He was sociable, and had the executive air of a banker, say, or a professor. Customs officers would always wave him through without batting an eyelid.

Off to a flyer

IN THE FALL of 1980, *Mark Tier's World Money Analyst* organized a seminar in Hong Kong. *Mark Tier's* was one of the first investment newsletters to be published touting the desirability of two things: precious metals and privacy.

I had just finished giving a talk at the seminar when Tom and I were approached by an American attorney named Ed Seltzer. Dressed in a business suit with a light-blue shirt and dark-blue tie, he was about five feet nine inches tall and had the look of a typical lawyer — his tired face and droopy eyes suggested he never slept.

Ed told me he had listened with great interest to my speech, which I'd titled "Hong Kong and Your Financial Privacy" — and which in fact included a remarkable prophecy regarding the future loss of personal financial privacy, although I could not foresee the full extent of this loss at the time.

"Bruce," he said. "Can you help my client? He wants to buy gold here in Hong Kong, but his funds are in cash — and in Australian dollars, in Sydney."

He went on: "It's impossible to deposit this money into a bank in Australia or to remit it without the government having a look at it. You know how damn tough those Reserve Bank exchange controls are." *So much for privacy.*

"Well, Ed," I said, without skipping a beat. "You have come to the right place. This is not a problem we can't solve — that is, for a fee of five percent if you want us to get your cash out of Australia."

He smiled broadly. "That's a deal!"

Almost eight years later, the guy standing before me would play a very significant role in yet another huge money laundering disaster. But for now, the deal we'd just agreed made him First Financial Services' first client. The firm was about to launch into the murky world of international money-laundering.

Even in the wake of the Cessna-Milner fiasco, blocked funds in Australia were, to my mind, a piece of cake. Sure, we'd have to be careful, but being out of Deak's shadow conversely cultivated a feeling of business-as-usual with regard to moving money.

From my earliest days in Vietnam, through all my work for Deak & Company, to the establishment of FFS, it seemed almost like I was just destined to launder money. I often asked myself if my career would ever be based on anything else, but the reality was that I made a good living at it, and no one got hurt. And more than that, it seemed to me the people in this business had higher integrity, morality and ethics than any banker, lawyer or "straight" businessman I ever met. In spite of an occasional cringe of conscience, my rationalizations were easily made.

Cringe or no cringe, our first transaction with Ed was done just after the seminar. In the event, he arranged for his A$200,000 to reach Hong Kong himself. We then bought it at a good rate, which included our handling fee of two percent. FFS was off to a flying start.

Over the years with Deak, I had come to know the heads of the major banks' cash departments in Hong Kong, and no one ever raised an eyebrow when I walked in with large amounts of cash to deposit.

Hang Seng Bank was my favorite. Whether I called Rex Young, the head cashier, in advance — or simply showed up — I was generally given the VIP red-carpet treatment and served a nice cup of coffee in the lounge as the money was counted in the presence of my accountant, "Y.C." Ah, the good life! How the world has changed: today, Hang Seng Bank, or any bank for that matter, would instantly file a report to the monetary authorities or the police.

A helping hand

IN ADDITION to this, interest rates were sky high in the late '70s and early '80s and healthy deposits created a virtuous cycle of good banking relationships and good service.

In the early days, one little piece of luck helped to grow our balance somewhat out of the blue. By dint of what must have been sheer accident, not long after opening an FFS account at Hang Seng Bank our account was credited with US$100,000 — by the Federal Reserve Bank of New York.

I telexed them immediately, and followed up again after 30 days, asking for instructions about how to apply the funds. I didn't get a response for two years. Then, one day, they inquired. We gladly sent back the $100,000 and kept the interest, which had accrued at a rate of 20 percent per annum. A nice little earner.

Simple solutions

GOOD times lay ahead for us dealing with good, carefree, non-violent people whose word was their bond, and for whom a handshake was enough to establish trust.

After our first transaction, it was not long before Ed Seltzer referred one of his clients who had another nagging problem, having stashed away almost A$2 million in safety deposit boxes in Singapore. He was scared as hell to try and exchange it there, and so it was just sitting there collecting dust, instead of earning high interest.

Our modus operandi was the same as that of Deak & Company. If there was a deal to be done, the golden rule was to immediately say "Yes, no problem" — and then figure out how the hell to do what was required. We offered the client two options.

One was for him to bring the money to us. We would buy it and charge the usual two percent for going to the bank and depositing the money, no questions asked, and with us exposing ourselves in the client's place.

The second option was for him to give us the money in Singapore, then we would pay out the counter-value two days later, less a fee of five percent. This plan was based on our excellent contacts in Singapore who would launder the money without it ever leaving the country.

They chose option number two.

Tom, Bill and I said to ourselves: "OK, now that we have the deal, just how the hell are we going to carry it through?"

I did have good contacts in Singapore, especially with the Indian money changers, and one or two Chinese bankers, but I knew they would be expensive. So in the end, we decided the simplest and the only confidential way to proceed was to bring the money back to Hong Kong ourselves — in golf bags, of course.

How it worked was that I traveled to Singapore with Jenny and our baby son, Matt, and stayed in the Shangri-La Hotel. Every day, for seven or eight days, I would receive A$250,000 from the client. Bill, nicknamed "the Bull," loved to fly, so he would fly into Singapore, arriving late each morning, then take the evening flight, money in tow, back to Hong Kong.

The following morning, he would fly back to Singapore again, and we would repeat the process. Tom would meet him at night on arrival in Hong Kong, take the money and do the banking the next morning. By the time it was all over, Bill had flown to Singapore from Hong Kong, a four-hour flight each way, seven nights in a row.

Celebrating over dinner and champagne at the Mandarin Hotel back in Hong Kong, I reflected that life was pretty good. And that the best way to move money was always the most obvious way.

We developed a simple new slogan: "Just move it."

Enter Brian

SHORTLY BEFORE the advent of FFS, Tim Milner had introduced me to his good friend Brian Daniels. Over the years, we all three of us became close, sharing a life that was close to the edge — and sometimes dropped over it.

The philosophy ingrained in me by Deak was "Show me your money and no questions asked." As a result, some — sometimes all — of the money we handled was tainted. Rule number 1 was always "Know your client," but if you couldn't satisfy this rule, then you simply passed over it and followed your gut instinct. That got you to Rule number two: "Don't ask, just do it."

With Brian, we just did it — and no wonder. All told, he was the most generous, good-hearted person you could care to meet. He stood about six feet tall and had light-brown hair and a pleasant, gentle-but-firm disposition. He was also an accomplished sailor and yachtsman — and an all-round class act. What's more, we had a lot in common, both being the same age and coming from New Jersey.

Brian grew up on Staten Island, about 20 miles from my hometown, but he had traveled the world, married, and settled in Thailand, the "Land of Smiles." In fact, he spoke Thai like a native. If we had met earlier in New York instead of halfway round the world, it probably would have been at a peace rally in Greenwich Village during the Vietnam War.

Tim Milner, as we've already seen, became one of my best clients. Brian became another. Life was indeed good — and only getting better. The only "downside" was quite a bit of decadence: good beer and liquor, and partying into the night.

A family affair

FFS HAD all the trappings of a normal and respectable business — you might even say a "family" business.

We opened a nice little office in Central Hong Kong, on the 15th floor of the Connaught Centre. Jenny was my confidante and assistant, while her cousin, Patty, was our receptionist. We were also doing a bit of business with some clients back in the United States, and Jenny's sisters — Catherine and Maria — were occasionally sent on trips to meet me or my brother Jimmy over there. They would stay in a hotel and babysit hard cash (in US dollars) until either Jimmy or I could fly it to Hong Kong.

Risks were ever-present, but I always prayed to God that the suitcase or golf bag would show up, and it always did. Over the many years in which I moved cash, there was, in fact, only one incident where I thought the game was finally over.

In 1987, Maria met Jimmy in San Francisco and was given a suitcase full of dollars to check in on the Cathay Pacific non-stop flight to Hong Kong. I always hated using family members as couriers but sometimes we just needed people we could trust, especially when we had a client demanding the transaction take place pronto. Whenever I had family involved I couldn't eat or sleep until they arrived at the other end.

On this occasion, Maria arrived — but the suitcase, filled with a quarter of a million dollars, did not. We waited and waited for word from Cathay Pacific. In the meantime, the client was pressing me for his money, demanding it be sent by telegraphic transfer to his account.

I was so anxious and nervous that my arm muscles began twitching at random, and I woke up during the night in a cold sweat. Eventually, three days later, the airline called to inform Maria that the suitcase had been traveling around the world but was finally in Hong Kong. We breathed a big sigh of relief.

Maria went to the airport to collect the case. She still had to pass it through customs, of course — and, thank God, she was waved through without even a glance. There was nothing illegal about bringing any amount of money into Hong Kong, but we still preferred that no one ever knew about it.

The money was still in the suitcase.

———— ❧❦ ————

SPEAKING of my brother, his wife wasn't too happy when she found out he was moving money for me. Jimmy, ten years my senior, had settled into the family profession and become a house painter, just like Dad. When he was growing up, he did some work for one of the local mafia guys, Mike Weido, who lived in our hometown. By age 17, he was driving stolen commodities around the area in his brand-new Cadillac. He decided it would be a waste of time to finish high school.

When my "laundry" business began to flourish, I brought Jimmy into my confidence because I needed a hand in America — amongst other things, to deal with Raoul, the head FX dealer at Deak-Perera, on my behalf. He was in seventh heaven — painting houses, then taking a couple of days off to handle money. But his wife, Louise, had a fit when she found out.

From time to time, I would stop by and leave a big suitcase full of cash in their apartment in Hasbrouck Heights (our hometown in New Jersey). One day, Louise told Jimmy and I she did not believe us about the money, and asked to see it. Always careful with her budget as a good housewife, she almost had a heart attack when we opened the big suitcase. Right there in front of her was a couple hundred grand in cash.

It was a big mistake. After that, she began having nightmares.

A good run

AS MENTIONED previously, during my Guam sojourn the Philippines became one of my favorite countries. You always feel good arriving in Manila. The country's people blend a certain big-hearted native hospitality with a huge portion of Latin or Spanish fiesta spirit. And thanks to the legacy of years of American occupation, almost everyone speaks English.

While working out of the Deak Guam office, I was introduced to our Manila agent, Arthur Gimenez. Arthur — who came up with the scheme for making bundles of cash look like travel brochures, as described in chapter five — was well connected in banking and stock brokering circles; however, the backbone of his business was foreign exchange.

His customers were all the same — in need of dollars and of getting them "offshore" into their Hong Kong accounts, rather than in the Philippines where they would be subject to high taxes. Nobody in the Philippines, it seemed — certainly not the rich and well-to-do — wanted to pay taxes, and most of them did not.

It was actually Arthur and our friend Barry Clark — the guy whose friend Doug got busted in Kathmandu with a kilo of gold in his Nike shoes — who came up with the original iteration of the golf bag scheme some time before Brink introduced me to it.

Lined inside with black silk and a black plastic container to hold the cash, the golf bags were a beautiful thing to behold. The story goes that when Arthur prepared the first bag for a trial run, though, he almost had a heart attack. He'd accompanied the courier to see the bag placed on the airport conveyor belt, but just as it was passing through the X-ray, the technician was distracted by her colleague cracking a joke and wasn't looking at the screen. Arthur had to go back and test it another time. Of course, it passed.

At FFS, we took full advantage of the Philippines' golf obsession. There are 18 or more golf courses in metro Manila alone, and Arthur had a system up and running whereby a group of couriers — mostly American, Australian and Swiss — were prepared to fly to Hong Kong for the cost of their ticket and a couple hundred dollars in expenses.

Working with Arthur, within a month or two we became so busy I had to rent a small flat near my office and stock it with rivets and tools to open the bags, take out the money, reseal the bags, and give them back to the couriers for the return trip to Manila. We were going to the airport every day, sometimes two or three times, to meet golf bags. We had found a steady line of work — and of course, as I knew from years of experience, golf bags could be sent anywhere without raising suspicion. No one, and I mean no one, ever questioned their weight, which was often several kilos heavier than any normal golf bag, even after the shoes and all but three clubs were removed.

IN THE PHILIPPINES, we had a very good run, several years in fact; but all good things eventually come to an end.

We were operating during the Marcos era. Some people loved President Ferdinand Marcos because, however brutal and corrupt he was in reality, he projected strength, and confidence in Manila was high. The First Couple, Marcos and Imelda, were also glamorous, and a lot of everyday people loved that. Of course, plenty of others despised the guy.

What was unique in the Philippines was that in spite of being poor, people seemed to be happy. The weather was good, and you could pick fruit right off the trees and eat it. Filipino families tend to be close and help each other, and the Filipino people are strong in their faith, thanks to the church. But corruption was also rampant, and spread like a disease. Salaries were so low that most government employees in positions of any authority, and most of the police, were taking bribes.

It did not go unnoticed by the authorities that large volumes of cash were somehow being moved out of the country. But they didn't know how; no one could figure it out. They realized they needed to take action, so they did. By paying informants, and even moving money themselves, the military and Marcos's loyal police force were able to identify the six largest money movers and shakers in Manila. Five were Chinese syndicates from downtown Chinatown, and the sixth was my very good friend — Arthur.

Early one morning, some time in 1985, the doorbell rang at Arthur's office. When he opened the door, he found himself suddenly confronted by three military policemen and a one-star general.

"Please, you must come with us."

The general explained that his boss, General Fabian Ver, desired to meet with Arthur. The situation was serious. Fabian Ver was head of the military under Marcos and one of the country's most powerful men.

"He has some questions he wants to ask you, something to do with moving money. You wouldn't happen to know anything about that, would you?"

"Of course not," Arthur replied. "Not me!"

What occurred thereafter was a gentle shakedown — a series of accusations and denials, all conducted in a somewhat congenial atmosphere. Arthur was told it was time the military took over the money-laundering business, and all they wanted to know was how to do it. Until Arthur would tell them how he did it, he could stay under house arrest at Fort Bonifacio in Manila.

From that point on, our little business stopped. I was very concerned about Arthur, and after a couple of months was able to visit him and his wife, Baby.

"What happened?" I asked him.

"No choice," he replied. "After a couple of weeks, General Ver sent for me again, and I told him the truth about how to move money."

"Very good," the General had said. "You will be released soon."

About three months later, Arthur — still under house arrest in Ft. Bonificio — was able to get a message to the general to ask him when he might be released. Seemingly shocked and surprised, General Ver paid him a visit. "Arthur, my friend, are you still here?" He laughed heartily. "I will follow up on the paperwork. I thought you went home a long time ago!"

Putting the 'H' in DHL

IN THIS LINE of business, I tended to rub shoulders with the most singular of characters. One of these was a fellow named Larry Hillblom.

Our local agent in Manila, Guy Coombs, was a kind and generous friend of mine for many years, a colorful fellow in his own right. In appearance, he bore an uncanny resemblance to a large Buddha. Guy had been in the military in Guam when he'd first bumped into Larry Hillblom in a bar in Agana. It was a meeting that was to change his life.

Larry's story begins with him attending law school in San Francisco. He would do classes at night and work odd jobs to scrape together some money to pay for them — in fact, he was so poor that he was forced to live rough, sleeping in his car. Whenever I feel sorry for myself, I think of what Larry was able to accomplish rising out of the ashes.

Eventually, Larry got a part-time job with a law firm in San Francisco that had a branch office in Honolulu, and from time to time, important documents had to be urgently posted out there. One of the partners got the bright idea of flying Larry over to hand-deliver them.

Well, after a couple of trips, Larry had an even brighter idea: send the documents on the plane as cargo. That way a courier could take a multitude of documents for different clients — and charge a fee to all of them. He convinced two friends to join him, and they combined their initials to form DHL. And so was born what would become one of the world's largest courier, package delivery and express mail service companies. Larry was the "H" in DHL.

Soon he opened an office in San Francisco, then one in Hawaii, and one in Guam, where he met Guy and asked him to open a DHL office in Manila. On the side, meanwhile, Guy became Deak's agent as well. With a stable of delivery boys on motorcycles already going around metro Manila, why not deliver pesos, too?

Larry was an eccentric fellow, to say the least. He was an introvert, and unusually shy until you got to know him. He came to be worth many millions, but he refused to wear a jacket and tie, and hardly ever wore a proper shirt. Six-foot tall with a ruddy complexion and skinny build, he seemed to have only one set of clothes: jeans and a faded white t-shirt. It was said that he was once barred from entering the boardroom at a DHL meeting in Seoul because he was dressed like a slob. Story goes that Larry canceled the meeting and threatened to replace the board.

Larry also had a penchant for street food. DHL had a very nice executive dining room in the Manila office, and whenever Guy invited me there for lunch, I'd gladly accept. Larry would go out and buy food in a plastic bag from the street and bring it back to the dining room to eat.

The one thing he spared no expense on, though, was girls. He had his own *mama-san* in Manila who would procure very young girls who — *he always claimed* — had just reached the age of consent. Cost was not an issue. The only requirement was that each and every girl had to be a virgin. Larry was terrified of getting AIDS.

Another of his "interests" happened to be vintage aircraft, and sadly for Larry this latter hobby is what did him in some years later. That made me wonder about what we're all really striving for in life: I mean, here was a guy with all the money in the world, and he dies in a vintage seaplane crash.

The accident happened on May 21, 1995. The bodies of the pilot and a business partner of Larry's were found — but his own remains were never recovered. Nevertheless, his untimely demise would spark a lurid drama revolving around who would inherit his substantial estate.

That was after it came to light that he had fathered several children as a result of "sex safari" trips in Southeast Asian countries, where Larry reportedly procured prepubescent girls and teenaged virgins. DNA tests confirmed that one Vietnamese child, Lory Nguyen, two Filipino children, and a child from Palau, Larry Hillblom, Jr., were all fathered by him. In the final settlement, each of the four children received $90 million, while the remaining $240 million from his estate went to the Hillblom Foundation, which followed Larry's wishes and donated a part of the funds to the University of California for medical research.

'No problem'

I HAD A lot of time for one man in particular at Deak-Perera — the aforementioned head FX dealer, Raoul Del Cristo.

Hailing from Cuba, Raoul ran a tight operation. Similar to Tony Pong in Hong Kong, he relished any time out of the office entertaining clients and staff in luxury. Several nights a week were party time — and yet, miraculously, everyone was back in the office the next morning by 8am. You had to be sharp in this business.

Raoul understood the free market well. If you asked him to undertake any task, the response was the same as that of Dirk Brink in Hong Kong: "No problem!"

In 1984, an opportunity presented itself for me to transfer $200,000 from New York to Hong Kong. The money was in 100 bundles of $20 bills, and I remember having to leave the first "pickup" — at the New York Hilton — to go and buy a bigger bag to carry it all. It was going to be too cumbersome to pack into golf bags, so we needed a more secure way to move it.

The first person I thought of to help was Raoul, who readily agreed to take the cash from us and then make it appear in my account in Hong Kong. "No problem," he said.

The only snag was that it did not take a couple of days, or even a couple of weeks, as he had promised. In fact, two months later, it still hadn't arrived.

After many calls and promises to send the balance, I was flying back to America on business regarding another transaction in San Francisco, and decided to make a surprise visit to Raoul in NYC to see what the hell the problem was. I stayed at his office all day, until the balance was miraculously "discovered" in his account — and finally sent to mine. Maybe it was a simple case of "out of sight, out of mind." Or maybe Raoul just liked "earning the float" for a while on top of the two percent fee I was paying him.

— ❖ —

ANOTHER associate for whom "no problem" was something of a mantra was Rakesh Saxena, an Indian financier based in Bangkok who would become a close friend of mine.

Unfortunately for Rakesh, it certainly wasn't a case of "no problem" some years later when his actions pretty much single-handedly destroyed the Bangkok Bank of Commerce — an event that prompted the collapse of the entire Asian financial system in 1997. I often traveled to Bangkok in the years prior, and usually stopped by to see Rakesh and his lovely wife, Suvanna, at their house near the Ambassador Hotel. Rakesh would hold court nightly in the dining room, consuming bottles of Johnny Walker Black Label and Throng Tip cigarettes as all manner of high-flying financial wizards came and went throughout the evening.

Rakesh was later sentenced to prison in what was a massive embezzlement case. The scandal that engulfed the aforementioned Bangkok Bank of Commerce, a result of Rakesh's activities, caused a run on deposits and led to the bank's collapse, contributing to the devaluation of the baht and causing a financial contagion that prompted a regional crisis.

Rakesh was arrested in Canada in 1996 but was extradited to Thailand only in 2009. A Reuters report explained how he had set up 60 businesses in Thailand and used them to secure loans from the bank to cover debts and running costs, but instead channeled the money into personal accounts, mostly in Switzerland. Estimates of the money he stole from the bank vary from US$60 million to $82 million.

CHAPTER 11

More untold tales

MY BROTHER Jimmy and I relished every opportunity to smuggle US dollars back to Hong Kong in our respective Old Faithfuls. After one successful double trip, we were sipping shots of 20-year-old Scotch whisky at the Captain's Bar in the lobby of Hong Kong's Mandarin Hotel.

Observing Jimmy in some kind of ecstasy as he smoked his favorite *Cohiba* Cuban cigar, I said: "Hey, Jim, the embargo of Cuba is really a load of bullshit, isn't it?"

Jimmy nodded approval.

"Let's smuggle in some harmless cigars!" I said.

My brother beamed with approval.

From that day on and over many years to come, our golf bags never returned to America empty: We filled them with dozens of the finest Cuban cigars, pre-sold to waiting friends in New York City. This not only marked a major improvement in the former method of smuggling Cuban cigars, which involved switching Philippine-made cigars for Cuban ones in Philippine cigar boxes; it also enabled us to cover the expense of our trips and make a handsome profit. But we weren't really doing it for the money; we were doing it for the fun.

The Captain's Bar was also the location of a very brief encounter that I will never forget. Staggering out of the bar one night in a stupor, I literally bumped into two of the most famous people in the world.

There we were, just the three of us — the two of them and me, standing alone in the front of the Mandarin. My jaw dropped, and I blinked several times. I could only think to say: "Uh, hello, good evening."

She gave me a broad smile. He gave me a glance of understanding annoyance. A limo pulled up, they got in, and I waved good-bye to John Lennon and Yoko Ono.

Close call in Orlando

MY ELDER sister, Honey, always had a nose for money, and was curious about what was in the stuffed Compass Travel bag I sometimes left in a corner of the condo I had bought for Mom. On one trip — when I had about $100,000 in the bag, all in $20 notes, which I'd collected in California and taken with me to Orlando — she almost found it at the most inopportune of moments.

I had decided to hand-carry the bag instead of checking it — a gigantic mistake that almost ruined me.

Honey drove me to the airport, and lovely little Mom, with her beautiful white hair, came along for the ride. As my bag went through the X-ray, Mom was chatting with the female customs officer at the conveyor belt. The lady looked at the bag and froze. "This is very dense," she said. "I can't tell what it is. Please open it for me."

Just then, Mom gave the lady a big smile, as I announced: "Sure, it's only brochures for a conference, and they're all wrapped."

"Brochures?" asked Honey.

"Yes, that's right," I said. "Travel brochures from Compass Travel." I stared at her hard, pretty sure I had "don't ask me to show you" flashing across my eyes.

To my relief, the lady looked at my mom, smiled and said: "Oh, that's okay then, have a good day."

At that moment, I said a silent prayer. I had taken a big risk, foolishly pressing my luck again.

Another memorable trip involved our mom's 80th birthday celebration. Her lifelong dream was to see Hawaii, so my sisters in Orlando put her on a flight to Los Angeles, where she was met by our brother Jimmy (who just happened to have $300,000 in large notes checked in for the flight to Honolulu). I had arrived in Honolulu the day before with my family, and we were booked for several days at the Honolulu Hilton off Diamond Head. July 14, 1983, was one beautiful birthday for our mom.

I really wanted to stay longer, but the money was burning a hole in my golf bag, and I had to get it to Hong Kong as soon as possible. Jimmy took Mom to a show in Waikiki, and we said our farewells as I rushed to catch the daily non-stop flight on Singapore Airlines, with Old Faithful securely checked in as baggage.

The $6 million ride

IN THE LAUNDRY business, there was rarely a dull moment.

On one occasion, syndicate associates of my good friend "Hawaii Jimmy" asked us to move a considerable amount of money for them — $6 million to be precise. The stash was in California but by this time we had become wary of our deposits with Chartered Bank of London in San Francisco becoming exposed, and had discontinued them.

An alternative plan was therefore hatched to move the cash from San Diego to Toronto, where we had a nice system that involved depositing money with a friend's company. Canada was a *civilized* country — there was no reporting there.

Because it was Mother's Day, I was in Florida visiting my mom, and taking in the annual Bermuda investment conference sponsored by *The Bank Credit Analyst* of Montreal. (I remember it well: a fellow attendee was Norm Ornstein, a political thinker whom I'd met at a previous conference and who would go on to head a Washington think-tank named the American Enterprise Institute.) After the conference, I returned to Orlando and waited a couple of days for a phone call indicating the money had been moved to the expected starting point in Winnipeg, just inside Canada. The call came, and we were good to go. I had an open ticket, and the next day found myself happily flying from hot and sunny Orlando to pleasantly cold and beautiful Winnipeg.

The money had been faithfully transported by one of our good mates, Daryl, who had some excellent connections across North America. He transported it without a hitch through an "Indian" reservation on the US-Canada border. God bless Native Americans.

In Winnipeg, Hawaii Jimmy and I hired a van for the long drive, cautiously creeping toward Toronto. I enjoyed the scenery along the way — while always keeping an eye out for police or radar speed traps. For several days, we were conservative as hell with our driving, stopping every few hours for coffee and a stretch. We checked into motels on the freeway for two, maybe three nights on the bounce.

Hawaii Jimmy drove the last leg. Having been to Toronto many times, I was studying the map, trying to get our bearings, when suddenly, coming over a hill, the city's famous skyline came into view. *Hallelujah!* At the same time, I noted how Jimmy increased speed and suddenly drove at 140km/hour, way over the limit. "Jimmy, slow down!" I yelled as I wiped the sweat from my eyes. Thank God, we'd made it.

Upon arrival, we both breathed a big sigh of relief. Within a couple of days, the money would be cleaned — and transferred to Hong Kong.

No laughing matter

IN 1986, I had another close call.

I was looking forward to getting back to Hong Kong from the US, via Hawaii, with US$400,000 in cash safely secured in my golf bag. Waiting to board the SQ flight from San Francisco, I called Hawaii Jimmy in Honolulu. Since he was a night owl — and since my flight touched down just before midnight, leaving me with a two-hour layover — we agreed to meet.

Since it was a domestic flight, all I had to do was walk out of the airport and re-board in time for the departure to Hong Kong. With my briefcase, boarding pass and passport in hand, it was pleasant to stroll out into the beautiful Hawaiian night, smell the flowers, and be met by Jimmy in his convertible Mercedes. Off we went.

First thing Hawaii Jimmy offered me was a spliff that we gladly shared, with one eye on the highway and one eye on the clock.

"Maui Wowie" is very strong shit. But, anyway, we smoked another one. When I think of it now, that was a very stupid thing to do.

Eventually, we headed back to Honolulu airport, and without paying much attention to precisely where we were, we parked the car and walked up to the boarding gate together. Suddenly, a big sign caught our attention: WARNING! ARE YOU CARRYING OVER US $5,000 IN CASH? It is an offense unless you report it under U.S. Treasury Regulations. Failure to do so will result in confiscation, fine and imprisonment, or both." What nonsense, we thought; blah, blah blah.

I hadn't told Hawaii Jimmy I had checked a golf bag full of money on my trip, but for some reason we both found this sign rather amusing, and started to grin broadly as we stood staring at it. We probably looked like a pair of clowns. By and by, I became aware of a man standing a few meters away. He'd been staring at us looking at the sign — and seemed very interested in what he saw.

As I approached the counter with my boarding pass and passport, he rushed forward. He was clearly a typical government nerd, and looked at me with venom in his eyes. Flashing a US Treasury ID and Customs ID, he demanded to know if I was carrying over $5,000, and that I open my briefcase. His eyes were as cold as steel.

I became instantly sober and turned to Jimmy with a wave saying: "Thanks for the beer; see you next time I'm in America, or better still if you come to Hong Kong."

The agent fumed when he found nothing special in my briefcase. I calmly stared at him, but my heart was racing. He reluctantly returned my briefcase to me, and I breathed a huge sigh of relief when we finally began to board.

It was a foolish situation. He'd taken my name and passport details but he apparently was not willing to hold up the plane or take me and my luggage off it — thank God.

I would have to be more careful in the future, much more careful. But just not quite yet...

San Francisco Airport, 1985 (or was it '86?)

LATER THAT same year, I was on another trip back from the US. I'd had a great time and I was feeling pretty good. Before heading back to Hong Kong, I had stopped in San Francisco to visit a friend, and a real character at that: a lawyer named Creighton Churchill, who claimed to be a distant relative of Winston Churchil. Creighton always had some kind of a project going on that required funding, and we were looking at doing some business together.

The day after meeting him for dinner downtown, I don't know why but I was feeling a bit restless to get moving and decided to go to the airport to check in my "loaded" golf bag a few hours early, then spend a couple of hours at the bar. As ever, I watched out of the corner of my eye as the bag disappeared into the belly of the cargo system.

After a beer or two, I switched to Scotch, and with an hour to go before boarding, I was beginning to feel just fine. Before I knew it, an attractive young lady took a seat at the bar near me. We started a friendly conversation.

Turns out she was part Native American, and very spiritual in her outlook. She looked me in the eyes and told me they were bright and clear, which meant that I must be a good person. Next time I came to America I should call her, she said. It was all just conversation — until she mentioned that she had a couple of joints with her and that we should go outside and have a smoke. By that time, I'd had enough to drink that my guard was down. I could hardly say no. Off we went.

Returning to the bar, she offered me a pill that she said would help me sleep on the trip back home. I told her I wasn't a pill popper, but she explained it was a Quaalude, a popular recreational drug of the day.

"Oh yes," I said. "I've heard of those." With my judgment thoroughly impaired, I took one. What happened next was amazing.

I bade her thanks and good-bye, grateful as I was that she had chosen, so graciously, to spend her time with me. I suddenly found myself looking around for my gate, as an announcement blared that boarding was commencing. I began to feel extremely drowsy — and I could hardly move. Actually, I could barely keep my eyes open.

I found the plane, thank God. Where was my seat? I fought to keep my eyes open and function normally, just until I could find it, fasten my seat belt and close my eyes. I remember I was flying Singapore Airlines business class, on an aisle seat. I wished the nice lady sitting next to me in the window seat a pleasant flight.

The next thing I knew, and to my amazement, I woke up with a start as the plane experienced a hard landing in Honolulu. The lady by the window looked over and I could see she was quite worried for me.

"Young man," she said, "I have never seen anyone sleep so soundly!" The stewardess agreed. I apologized for snoring, had I done so.

Apparently, the plane had taken off from San Francisco twice: the first time, the pilot had detected a small electrical fault and decided to quickly land again to get it checked out. That had taken an hour. Then we had taken off for Honolulu a second time, and flown all the way without further problems. For my part, I slept soundly throughout the whole experience, completely oblivious to what was going on around me.

I was to find out later that my guardian angel must have been with me, because I learnt that mixing Quaaludes with alcohol was a potentially lethal combination, one from which many people have never awakened. I may have been close to never making it home; and for sure, I realized there must have been some underlying psychological reasons that had caused me to take such risks in the first place.

This illegal money-moving business was taking a serious toll on my brain and on my spirit. Waiting at the luggage carousel at Kai Tak Airport in Hong Kong 10 hours later, I shuddered to think what might have happened to me, and pictured Old Faithful, fully loaded with cash, going around and around without me. Lost in prayer, I waited to collect it and go home.

Head-shake deals

DIRK BRINK'S wisdom about getting behind an Indian when clearing customs worked so well that in certain places, such as Seoul, we would bring along one of our good Indian friends, a "token Indian" from Hong Kong, to create the diversion.

Truth is, we did a lot of business with very trusted and excellent Indian friends and partners — in particular our agents, the Shahs and the Melwanis — not only in Korea but also in Kenya and Nigeria. But in Hong Kong, Brink said to never trust an Indian if he does not know how to wag his head when bargaining with you. Head-wagging was Brink's litmus test.

On one occasion, we had big trouble with a transaction done through an agent in Kowloon, a Mr. Patel. He had been referred to me and FFS as someone who could reliably make payments in rupees in Bombay. I was always looking for a new source and had told him I would keep his services in mind.

One day, an English gentleman arrived in my office and said he had been referred to me by Howard Marks, aka *Mr. Nice* — about whom, more later. He needed some funds in Bombay, in rupees, as soon as possible. Contacting Patel, I asked if he could handle a payment equivalent to approximately $100,000.

The client gave me his cash, plus my fee, and flew off to Bombay. I gave Patel instructions concerning who to pay and which hotel to use, and was assured it would be done the next day. I am a very trusting soul, and Patel's references were good, but of course I had made efforts to check him out before putting any business his way — I'd visited his office in Kowloon and tested all his contact numbers.

The next day came and went. I happened to be preoccupied with my brother Jimmy arriving in Hong Kong with a loaded golf bag, and the Bombay payment almost slipped my mind. Jimmy and I were leaving the next day to go to Macau, and I was really looking forward to the break: my nerves were becoming shattered and, with two or more deals happening at once, I had a sense of disaster waiting to strike.

Jimmy arrived late that night and we dropped the golf bag at my office for safe-keeping until the next morning. I noticed the message light on my phone indicating I had over ten messages, and I wondered who the hell it could be. It was Bombay. The client had been sitting next to the phone the whole day waiting for a phone call that did not come. I was livid! Although late, I called Patel and left a message on his office phone, and called him at home as well. He didn't pick up. I did not sleep well that night.

The following morning, I followed up again after apologizing to the client and assuring him all would be well. Patel finally arrived at his office just before noon. He apologized, but I sensed that he was stalling. Jim and I were booked on the 6pm hydrofoil boat to Macau. I called Patel back every hour and felt I was getting the royal run-around.

Decision time.

"Jim," I said. "It's almost 3pm. Let's go to Patel's office right now and sit there until the payment is made. You pretend to be the client's partner, a Mafioso from New York, the tough guy."

Jim replied with relish: "I can do that!"

In 30 minutes, we were both sitting in front of Patel. He was completely taken by surprise and I don't think he noticed the resemblance between us. Jimmy just sat there and stared at him, then spoke the only four words that the situation required: "I'm from New York."

Patel immediately got his agent in Bombay and my client on the phone to one another. Within 20 minutes the agent arrived at my client's hotel and the payment was made. Jimmy and I made it to the hydrofoil with time to spare.

Sailing near the wind

I WAS IN desperate need of a break. Most of our Aussie golf-bag couriers — like Graham Shields and Kim Barnaby — were "yachties." To chill out, I joined Graham on a yacht delivery from Hong Kong to Sydney, meeting him when he stopped off in the Philippines — at Surigao Del Sur, in Mindanao. A 600-mile sail across the Philippine Sea to Palau, a US Trust Territory in the Western Carolina Islands, lay ahead of us.

Relishing the beauty of the wide-open sea, we neglected to check the weather carefully enough, however — and on the third day out, we ran smack into a major typhoon. Caught up in 30-foot waves, our pleasant journey quickly turned into a giant roller-coaster ride.

I found out later that Graham was very worried we were not going to make it. Navigating only by sextant, in heavy clouds and with nothing to get a fix on — there was no SAT NAV on board this particular yacht — we miraculously found the directional signal emitted by a beacon located on the airport at Koror, the capital of Palau.

The harbor master and customs officials could hardly believe their eyes when we sailed in through the storm on our 30-footer. Naturally, they were suspicious. In our ignorance, we had failed to apply for a permit and at the time there was another yacht in the harbor which had been confiscated in connection with arms smuggling.

Fortunately, I happened to know *personally* one of Palau's legislators, a fine man named Kaleb Udui, who was an attorney I had met in Saipan years before when I worked on Guam. After speaking with him on the phone, the authorities rolled out the red carpet.

It was great to be back on land, and Palau was one of the most beautiful places on the planet.

It was also renowned for growing some of the best weed known to man. Thus, we spent a pleasant few days lounging around with the locals until it was time to say our farewells. Graham had to continue the sail on to Australia — and our new Palauan friends gave him a big bag of weed to tide him over on the journey. For me, it was a case of taking the Continental Air Micronesia "Island Hopper" back to Manila, and then returning to Hong Kong.

Although my profession was sometimes enormously stressful, and certainly destroyed millions of my limited supply of brain cells, my blind faith, coupled with a happy-go-lucky lifestyle, ensured that these were also often the happiest of times.

CHAPTER 12

M.I.T. Financial Services

A PARTNERSHIP that starts in good faith but ends up in a vicious rivalry can be compared to a marriage that ends in divorce. I have often wondered, lamented even, how something like First Financial Services Ltd., which started with so much joy and enthusiasm, could succumb to the sad fate that it did.

Tom O'Donnell and I had been the best of friends, but after Bill Thomasson joined the partnership, by around 1983 the chemistry between us had changed, I believe due to Bill's domineering personality and ever-increasing demands.

While we were still partners, I happened to come upon the knowledge that Tom had opened another company for himself — M.I.T. Financial Services. Worse, he had done so with my trusted auditor of many years — Armando Chung.

One day, Tom and I had a heart-to-heart talk and he matter-of-factly told me he was moving on. We had been about to open a commodity futures trading division — Tom and I both kept close tabs on trades and trading techniques, charting the markets with our friend, Rakesh Saxena, although I myself had my hands full just looking after our money-moving business. Tom later started a commodity futures operation on his own, and made a great success of it. Bill Thomasson also moved on. It seemed I could not satisfy his demands for a bigger and bigger share in our profits. I was on my own again.

The hardest lesson I learned from these experiences was that, in business, you really do not have many friends.

After Tom's departure, I noticed a sudden sharp decline in my money-moving business as a whole. From the Philippines to Australia, in fact, it began to evaporate before my eyes. An added shocker was finding out that several of my long-time trusted agents and clients had actually traveled to Hong Kong specifically to meet with Tom, and returned home without even calling me.

When I found that out, I asked Arthur in Manila and Ben Garcia in Sydney what the hell was going on.

"Bruce," they said, "business is business. You taught Tom well and he learned well. He is offering your same services at a big discount."

I should not have been so shocked, but being trusting and naïve, I was, in fact, stunned. No loyalty after so many years? I myself had left Deak & Company — but not before discussing matters with Mr. Deak and creating a friendly working relationship between us.

Outwardly, I shrugged it off. Tongue in cheek, I wished everyone good luck. I licked my wounds.

Little did I realize at the time, however, that Tom's moving on would turn out to be a blessing in disguise. Tom soon got involved with some nasty characters — specifically, one really quite despicable individual named Jack Corman, more of whom presently.

Over the next couple of years, I moved on with a handful of trusted friends such as Brian Daniels, Tim Milner, and Robert Kimball, who also happened to be known as "Todd" and as "Nicholas Hardcastle" (Robert was a canny operator, who liked to move in different circles and juggle identities). These were all real friends, none of whom would think of jumping ship.

For a while, Tom O'Donnell prospered with his new company. From FFS, he had taken with him his good friend Mike Brennan, whom we had flown from California at Tom's request and given a job.

What happened two years after we parted ways, however, was so shocking and heart-breaking that I cried. The tragic circumstances were summarized in a note written by a DEA agent just after the October 1987 stock market meltdown:

"Former First Financial partner, Tom O'Donnell, who started his own firm, MIT Financial Management, lost millions in the 1987 Stock Market crash, and who was also under a sealed indictment in Washington DC for money laundering, committed suicide in his Manila hotel room. He was set up by informant, Jack Corman, who later was working together with another informant, Phil Christenson [sic]."

I was in London at the time I heard of Tom's apparent suicide. I had flown in from Canada after attending an investment conference in Quebec City, and was looking forward to dinner at the family home of Sal Petrancosta, a dear friend who was a financial analyst formerly based in Hong Kong.

On that dismal day, a rare hurricane hit London and the taxi I was traveling in slammed into a tree on the way to Sal's apartment in Kensington. My guardian angels must have been trying to warn me.

My only thought was that if Tom had come to me with his problems, financial or otherwise, I would have welcomed the opportunity to bury the hatchet and start over again. The person who bears a grudge is the one who suffers.

I had fortunately avoided the stock market and had plenty of liquidity. Tom was also a very good commodities trader. We could have managed the clients' losses and rebuilt the company.

What I did not know at that time was that — as alluded to in the note above — he had been indicted.

Thank you, Mike Brennan

FATE'S CHANCE meetings seem to call the unexpected shots in life, and this is how I found out what had happened with Tom.

My wife Jenny and I rarely went out late at night. However, one night in early 1988 we joined some young folks visiting Hong Kong, friends of friends from Florida. We had a few nightcaps at a disco in the nightlife haven known as Lan Kwai Fong. It was nearly 2am and I was very tired.

Just as I was motioning to Jenny that we should be going, I looked across the club. It was very dark, but there, thanks to the flashing of the strobe lights on the mirrors, I spotted the reflection of Mike Brennan — the friend Tom had taken with him to work at M.I.T. Financial Services.

Mike, who could have been Dustin Hoffman's twin in appearance, was normally a happy-go-lucky character, but his face looked ashen.

"Mike," I said pleasantly enough. "How the hell are you?"

Before he had time to answer, I added: "I am just leaving, but let me buy you one for the road."

In a state of surprise at having bumped into each other, we shared a drink and spoke of Tom and how badly he was missed. Then Mike, drunk, dropped the bombshell.

"Bruce," he said. "Do you know a fellow living in Bangkok by the name of Jack Corman?"

"Sure I do," I said, "and to tell you the truth I don't like him one bit. Why?"

"Why? Because he is DEA, and he set Tom up! Tom was recently indicted in a big money laundering case in Washington, DC. Corman had an account with M.I.T. and lost a lot of money in the crash. But never mind that. He was setting Tom up the whole time. That can be the only reason Tom committed suicide: he was aware of the indictment, and because of the sentencing guidelines he knew he would be sent to prison for a long time. He could not face it."

Then Mike paused, and added: "It wasn't suicide." He told me that Corman's actions had caused Tom to have a heart attack.

Stunned, I said: "Thank you very much for sharing what you know, Mike." But I was already wondering something else: Was it murder?

I must have looked as pale as a ghost as I thought of the numerous times I had met Corman, including the times he had come to my office. He had been first introduced by Andy Rogers, a Bangkok-based art dealer and client of mine.

I was also acutely anxious about the fact my good friend Brian Daniels was — at that precise moment — deeply involved in a sizable deal with Corman.

I sincerely hoped and prayed that what Mike had told me about Corman would prove to be unfounded. With a flash of horror, and a biting chill that ran down my spine, I recalled Jack forcing my office staff — a few months before — to take a half million dollar cash deposit, for transfer to Brian, just before Easter weekend. More about this later.

All I could think of was that I needed to tell Brian immediately.

I WOULD LATER read about the case against Tom O'Donnell from part of a sworn government affidavit against other defendants in his case.

It read, in part:

"In this case the evidence against the defendant is very strong and includes the testimony of two confidential informants (Christensen and Corman) who were initially planted at the Thailand end of the operation.

Throughout late 1983 and 1984, the defendant made several trips to Thailand and Hong Kong to arrange the importation of twenty to forty tons of marijuana. The informants told the defendant they would need two million dollars front money. The defendant told them the money should be laundered in Hong Kong through a money launderer, Tom O'Donnell, and over one million dollars was fronted.

In March 1987, the informants, who were now working for DEA, tape-recorded conversations in which the defendant discussed the shipment seized by the Coast Guard.

On May 12, 1987, Special Agent Ogilvie (DEA) was introduced to the defendant at a hotel room in San Francisco. A co-defendant counted out three hundred fifty thousand dollars cash that Special Agent Ogilvie was to take to Thailand.

(The name of Special Agent Chris Ogilvie would ring a bell for me a couple of years later when I had the "pleasure" to make his acquaintance at the Bangkok Immigration Detention Center one morning, at 4am to be precise. Again, more about this later.)

Tom had learned to launder well, and was unwittingly doing a good job of it for DEA informants Christensen and Corman as they set up various drug smugglers. Things were bad — but there was more. Tom O'Donnell's demise wasn't the only scandal simultaneously swirling around.

CHAPTER 13

'Nicholas Hardcastle'

ROBERT KIMBALL would become a good friend of mine, but the first time I met him he introduced himself as "Nicholas Hardcastle," and I knew him by that name for years. Turns out Nicholas Hardcastle was just one of several aliases he used to keep his real identity out of the spotlight. Other pseudonyms were "Robert Bland" and "Todd."

Robert was an alumni of Stanford University and a brilliant thinker who — as with so many other clients of mine, including one Howard Marks (see chapter 14) — had chosen weed smuggling as the most rewarding and direct way to secure riches and happiness. But after his arrest and conviction in Bangkok on a smuggling charge, in 1980, he found himself staring at a 45-year prison sentence instead. Only a miracle would save him.

It was some time around the mid to late '70s, when I was still an employee of Deak & Company, that I first met Robert, and he was introduced (as "Nick") by our mutual friend Bruce Miller, a Deak client in Hong Kong.

At that time, Bruce was living in Nepal and Bangkok, and traveled around the surrounding countries dealing in art — or whatever he could find to turn a buck. He had a sharp mind and a sharp wit, and was the kind of person you were always pleased to see in town. He always had something going on. What he, Robert and I all had in common was that we'd left America for greener pastures and never looked back.

I always enjoyed visiting Bruce's house when I was in Bangkok, especially with Jenny and our sons. The house felt like an art gallery wrapped around a fish pond. (One day my son Doug, then about four years old, reached in to try to catch one of the fish, but lost his balance. We heard a big splash, and all had a great laugh, especially Doug. Dripping wet and with the goldfish having slipped out of hands, he found it all quite hilarious.)

When I became a free agent, I had more time on my hands and was able to get to know what business my clients and friends were really in. These consisted basically of two groups: the dope dealers, who smuggled pot, and the art dealers, who smuggled art. The latter would often smuggle valuable antique Buddhist "thangka" textiles from Tibet, by sewing them into their winter jackets.

Both groups happened to smoke a lot of pot, and I assumed this is how they overlapped. Both needed to move money back and forth, and both needed ways of doing so without going through banks.

The best dealer in the Thai black market for baht was Deak's agent in Hong Kong, ATB Finance, a subsidiary of Asia Trust Bank, Bangkok. It was headed by its flexible and very likable Chairman, Mr. Waloob Tarnvernichol, as well as a delightful lady named Kun Nathaya, who ran a money exchange and antique shop near the Ambassador Hotel called Vasu Carving.

Thailand's black market in currencies — the changing of Thai baht into US dollars, essentially — was something that was pretty well accepted, and as long as you could maintain an account in baht at a bank in Thailand and another account offshore, preferably in Hong Kong, a lot of people tended to think "why not?"

In India and other parts of South Asia, the informal money transfer system, often involving swaps within the same family, is known as "hundi." In the Middle East and parts of Africa, a similar informal value transfer system is referred to as "hawala." Money is transferred based on trust, and often without any records.

Visiting Bruce or Robert was always a pleasure. Before figuring out what to do for the day, it was best to start off with a couple of strong cups of "mud" and half a dozen reefers. Hashish mixed with tobacco worked well in the mornings, but by late afternoon we'd graduate to Thai Buddha weed. Or was it vice versa? *Ah, the good life!*

I VISITED Bangkok quite a lot during that time, and on one visit in particular I remember there was a big party going on at Robert's house near Soi Pahoenyitin.

(Thai houses with their big gardens were such a pleasant change from urban Hong Kong. I also loved that you always remove your shoes before entering a house in Thailand — such a civilized custom.)

I had brought along two bottles of Glenfiddich Scotch to the party, which wasn't a great move as I had to get up early the next day and catch the plane back to Hong Kong. When I woke I had one hell of a ferocious hangover — and in fact I swore off Scotch from that day forward. (Sensibly or otherwise, I decided to move on to XO cognac instead.)

Chugging down cold water to cure my headache, I bade farewell to everyone with the parting words that we would soon meet again in Hong Kong and would carry on the party from there.

I was halfway back to Hong Kong before I looked down — and noticed that I was wearing someone else's shoes. Out of the dozen or so sets of shoes on Robert's front porch, I had picked up the wrong pair: mine had been brand new and these were pretty old. How stupid!

All's well that ends well, though. When Bruce arrived in Hong Kong a couple of days later, he let me know that I wasn't the only one who had taken the wrong shoes — as he had *mine*. When we met, we turned up wearing each other's shoes and did a different kind of "swap" from what I was used to. What goes around does come around, after all.

SOME TIME around 1982, I was experiencing a slow-down in my business just at the same moment as Bruce Miller happened to be looking for a way to cover his expenses. He was a clever man, and observed that you could buy gold bullion for five percent less in Bangkok — in bullion baht chains — than you could in Hong Kong. If you could absorb the exchange difference from dollars to baht, then back to dollars, you could make a tidy profit.

I could not resist the temptation in front of me — to a seasoned money launderer, the art of the scam has a compulsion of its own. But how to pull it off? We'd have to fly from Hong Kong to Bangkok, buy the bullion chains, then fly back to Hong Kong and sell them, all the while also hoping and praying that the gold price would go up that day.

After a little checking around, and a trip to the Bank of Thailand for a chat, one immediate concern was eased. It was not legal to take gold bullion out of Thailand, but it was perfectly legal to take bullion baht chains, because this was considered to be jewelry, not bullion.

All you had to do was buy the chains, then take the receipt to the bank and fill out a form. I believe it was called an "EC 63." After waiting a couple of hours, presto, you would be handed your Export Permit, which had to be presented to Thai customs upon departure. We had found an excellent little money earner and we had found a way to make it completely legal.

Armed with the paperwork, and holding a travel bag loaded with gold chains, we confidently approached customs at the airport on a test run. We'd arrived a bit early in case it took extra time. The customs officers were shocked! "What is this? You cannot export gold bullion without paying a big tax!"

"But this is not bullion," I replied. "It is jewelry and perfectly legal. Here is the paperwork."

Well, the paperwork won out, to the amazement of us all, including the customs agent. Apparently, this had never been done before. Since we were able to make a tidy three percent and were otherwise quite broke at the time, we decided that we should repeat the process every week. After a dozen trips in the span of a few months, however, they changed the rules, imposing a limit on the number of chains we could take at one time. This temporarily destroyed our little business.

We looked for solutions to get around this little legal obstacle, and Bruce came up with the answer.

He approached a goldsmith and placed an order. Could the goldsmith make chains for us? "Sure, no problem," came the reply. Bruce said he would never forget the look of amazement on the customs agent's face when he showed up for what was destined to be our final shipment.

"What the hell is that?" the agent asked as he stared at what was probably the biggest Thai baht gold chain ever made. The thing must have weighed a kilo! Wearing it around your neck for any significant period of time would have possibly resulted in a permanent and painful spinal injury (or worse!).

In a state of shock, and having no sense of humor, customs did not think it was funny. They actually let us through with the chain but flatly told us we better not ever try that trick again!

Game over.

Nicked

ROBERT KIMBALL is one of the most decent, intelligent and humble people I have ever had the pleasure to know. A whole book could be written about him and his adventures. Bright and kind-hearted, he lived life on the edge and seemed to thrive under stress and great pressure. At first, I did not know what was causing the stress, but I soon found out.

Rumors circulating among mutual friends connected Robert to Thai marijuana smuggling. Specifically, he transported it to North America and the UK, and by the quickest of means — air freight. Personally, I had no interest in knowing the truth of his business, except I often felt that, while visiting Bangkok, I should stay at a hotel rather than at his home.

Then it happened. Thank God I was not in Bangkok on October 20, 1980, when the Thai National Police seized approximately 3,200 kilos of marijuana and 20 kilos of hashish, and arrested eight people at Robert's residence.

The smuggling operation had come under scrutiny due to its size and sophistication, with the goods being flown from Northern Thailand by military aircraft to a base near Bangkok, and then transported by commercial aircraft onwards to their target markets.

Amazingly, Thai military and customs had been in on the deals. Organizing such an operation was a master-stroke of brilliance and guts. The air waybills, for example, would show the origin of the goods as Bahrain or Hong Kong so as not to arouse suspicion at Bangkok customs.

About a year later, on October 20, 1981, Robert and his colleagues were convicted and sentenced. That was when Robert got handed a 45-year jail term, the longest sentence applicable.

Don't be late

UPON LEARNING of Robert's arrest, I was both worried and saddened. His phone had been tapped, and many Americans and other associates had probably stayed at his house without realizing the danger. To have been there on the wrong day, at the wrong time, would surely have been a nightmare come true.

Over the next year or two, I was able to visit him at the notorious Bang Kwang Maximum Security Prison in Bangkok. He was resilient to the core.

Food was brought to him daily from his house outside. Visiting him in prison was a bit cumbersome, however. In Thailand prisoners, when receiving visitors, are shackled with a ball and chain. It was certainly no joke for poor Robert, scuffling along with a chain on one leg, attached to a heavy metal ball that he had to pull along with him like some hapless beast of burden.

There is, however, a very big difference in the way things are done in some Asian prisons compared to the way they are done in America or even in Hong Kong. In Thailand, for the right price, you can make "arrangements" for a little bit of luxury to enter your life. In America, all they want to do is punish you. (Some time after the "war on drugs" began, jail management was privatized, making it big business in the good ole USA.)

To give an example, for a certain sum of baht Robert could "take the day off." Carrying a ball and chain in his arms, he would be sneaked out of the prison from time to time in a car, accompanied by three or four guards.

At the house of a friend, such as Bruce for example, he could then enjoy the finer things in life — steak, champagne, a good smoke — and make a long-distance call to his father in New York.

But time flies and Bangkok's traffic is notorious. Roll call at the prison occurred every evening at 6pm sharp. One day when he was "out," the clouds opened up and it started raining like hell. The streets quickly flooded and traffic came to a standstill. Panic set in. With the guards driving zig zag over both sides of the road, up on the sidewalks and everywhere and in between, Robert, aka "Nick," made it back to the prison for the evening line-up just in the *nick* of time, with less than five minutes to spare.

Sick leave

A YEAR prior to his arrest, I had come to know that Robert was working through a group in New York that would collect money and hold it for him. However, he was not particularly keen to go to America to collect it, so he asked if I could help. Never one to say "no," I agreed to make a lightning trip to New York City, meet his contact at the Pierre Hotel in Central Park, collect $250,000 and bring it back to Hong Kong.

"Could you do it over the weekend!" he asked. "It's an emergency."

"No sweat. For expenses and three percent, you have a deal, my friend!" He never was the type to quibble over fees. "I'll depart Friday night and have the bread in your hands Monday night."

"Deal!"

I left Hong Kong that coming Friday on board a JAL flight, stopping in Tokyo to connect with the non-stop to JFK Airport in NYC. I arrived the same day and checked into my hotel.

All of a sudden, stricken by the food I had eaten during the flight, I was so ill I wanted to die. I called the contact and made an appointment to meet at the Pierre Hotel in the morning, at 11am. But I was up all night: in fact, I spent most of it sitting on the toilet with my head in the sink, puking up some kind of green bile. What a nightmare.

The next morning, I could feel every heartbeat pulsating in my head. Eleven o'clock was approaching, but I could barely move. Looking pale as a ghost, I showered, put on a suit and took a taxi to the Pierre.

When the lift opened on the 10th floor, I was shocked. There was a doorman standing there, acting like he was directing traffic. The lift operator gave me a good hard look and mumbled something like: "Here comes another one."

A man introducing himself as Pete opened the door to the suite, and I found myself in a room full of people dividing up boxes of money.

"Here you go, Bruce!" Pete said, as he tossed over a couple of bundles of banknotes. "This is for Robert. Give him my regards. By the way, there may be $50,000 more coming. Where are you staying?"

I hesitated, and had a very bad feeling when I blurted out my hotel and room number. I immediately knew it was a stupid mistake. *I must have been very sick!*

In ten minutes, I was out of the suite and waiting for the lift to arrive, $250,000 in large bills stashed away in my Compass Travel bag. Just as the lift door opened, one of Pete's associates, a rough-looking character, appeared unexpectedly and got in with me. He asked me if I needed any help.

"No thanks," I forcefully declined. Then I lied: "I have all the help I need waiting outside." He split.

Back at my hotel, feeling sick and paranoid as hell, I checked the time on the digital clock in my room: 1:30pm. First things first. I immediately took the cash out of the Compass Travel bag — and threw the bag away. Reaching for Old Faithful, I took it apart with the rivet wrench, packed in the money and sealed it tight. I was sweating profusely but I'd got it done. I felt relief — no worries now.

I confirmed my reservation to Hong Kong for the next morning: Sunday, the 9am flight. Then I collapsed on the bed, holding my throbbing head, and tried to sleep. The phone startled me awake. It was pitch dark in the room, and the clock read 11:30pm. "Hello," I answered.

"Hello. This is Pete's friend. Remember we met today at the hotel? I am here in your hotel, and I have something important to ask you. Can I come up?"

"Hell no!" I said. "Give me ten minutes, and I'll come down to the lobby," I replied quickly.

I was still getting dressed when there was a loud knock on the door. I looked through the peephole and there he was, along with a young lady. I opened the door, and he said it was better not to meet in the lobby as there were too many prying eyes there.

"OK," I said. "Listen, I'm tired. So what is it you want?"

"I want to *buy* the money, the $250,000 you were handed today. Do you still have it?"

By this time, I was very pissed off and very wary of the two individuals standing before me. "Sorry," I said. "It is long gone, and besides I would never bring it here. I am leaving in the morning. What the hell do you mean, you want to *buy* it?"

With a sorrowful voice, he proceeded to explain what a great deal he had for me. He was prepared to give me $2,000,000 in counterfeit notes for the $250,000 I had. *Why me, Lord, why am I so lucky?* I asked myself. Good-byes were said quickly as he glanced around the room, probably looking for the Compass Travel bag. The golf bag was not in sight.

The next morning, I felt much better, having recovered from the food poisoning, and settled in for the long trip to Hong Kong. About 20 hours later, I found myself once again standing in that most familiar place — staring down at the luggage conveyor belt at Kai Tak Airport as I waited for the appearance of my friend, Old Faithful.

Get stuffed!

WHAT WAS to happen over the course of Robert's detention was nothing short of a miracle. Imagine yourself facing 45 years in prison. Even though Thai sentencing gives cause for hope, just the thought of a jail sentence that long — tantamount to life — is extremely daunting.

But there's no keeping a good man down. Robert was out in less than five years. How? Well, let me tell you.

After some adjustment to the prison routine, he got to work. Convincing the prison system, which needed cash, that he could make some for them, he put his sharp mind to a project that is hopefully still active today. The idea was to make stuffed animals: that's right, stuffed animals, made in prison — using prison labor — and then sold in Bangkok department stores.

Before long, different varieties of the most beautiful furry and cuddly stuffed animals were coming off the prison production line, bringing joy not only to those who bought them but also to those who made them.

Each year at the time of his birthday, the Thai king selects deserving prisoners to be given reduced sentences. (It hardly needs stating, but *all countries should do this.*)

Soon, Robert had about 200 happy inmates working for him, all pumping out so many stuffed animals that the prison fund was in surplus, and he had caught the attention of the King. His Majesty issued Robert a special Royal Pardon and he was suddenly a free man.

The miracle had happened.

As the story goes, however, it all came quite suddenly — and Robert was not ready to go. Who would take up the baton to ensure that the business would continue?

"I can't leave now!" were his parting words as he bade an emotional farewell to all his inmate friends. The fairytale ending to what seemed like a ghastly nightmare had come true — at least for a little while.

A fateful introduction

WITH ROBERT out and about, it wasn't long before the question of 'what next?' reared its head.

In Bangkok, I knew Robert and I knew my good friend Brian Daniels. They knew a lot about each other, even though they had never met. Both were very experienced in their respective areas of expertise, and the bottom line was they were both good people.

The decision to introduce them properly was both inevitable and fateful. To me, it felt like good karma, but I also had a hard-edged business motive. I could sense the growing heat and really wanted First Financial Services to become legit — but I was prepared to make exceptions. If Robert and Brian hit it off, there would be a couple of substantial investment accounts for me to look after, and I wouldn't need a lot of other clients.

The road ahead would ultimately lead to Reno, Nevada.

CHAPTER 14

'Mr. Nice' Comes to Hong Kong

IN THE MONEY laundering business, relationships are everything.

Some time in 1985, when I was visiting Raoul Del Cristo, Vice President of Deak-Perera NYC, I met a friend of his named Patrick Alexander-Lane. We all got on well, and as fate would have it, we were all due to be in California in a few days. I was going to pay Brian in L.A. the same day that Raoul had an important meeting in Beverly Hills — so we decided to take a little holiday from our cares and drive up to wine country. Seemed like a great idea.

I remember Raoul was very excited about his meeting. As he told it, the Governor of Mexico's Central Bank was going to be secretly driving up with some valuable information — namely, the date when the Mexican peso would be devalued. Armed with such inside information, Raoul could make a bundle.

On the drive up the coast, we were all in high spirits, and Patrick and I had a chance to get acquainted. He told me that his brother-in-law often came to Hong Kong on business, and that he would ask him to call on me on his next visit. I told him I would be pleased to meet him and suggested we could also do some business together.

"Excellent!" Patrick said. "You'll hear from him on his next trip. His name is Howard Marks."

•⟨⊰•⊱⟩•

MUCH HAS been written about Howard Marks, the Welsh drug trafficker. At the height of his fame — or his notoriety, if you prefer — his face graced the front pages of several national newspapers in the UK, and all his books, about a life less ordinary, became international bestsellers. Up until his passing a few years ago, he was something of a cult figure in British life — and the country's best-known cannabis smuggler by far.

In brief, Howard began dealing small amounts of hashish while studying a postgraduate course in philosophy at Oxford University, but he was soon moving much larger quantities. At the peak of his career, he regularly smuggled large consignments of the drug from Pakistan and Thailand to North America and Europe and his activities intersected with those of organizations as diverse as MI6, the CIA, the IRA, and the Mafia.

After we became friends, I would be his confidential money mover in Asia for several years.

A MONTH or two after my trip to California, the phone rang at my Hong Kong office: "Hi Bruce! This is Howard."

We arranged to meet across the street from the office in a little wine bar in the upscale Landmark mall. I liked Howard instantly. He dressed casually, spoke in a soft Welsh accent, and told me, with a wink, about the various projects he was working on. I believe one such project — presumably a front of some description — involved an English school in Pakistan, of all places.

Howard needed to set up a Hong Kong limited company, so I pointed him in the right direction. He said he also expected to receive and to pay out sums of cash in US dollars from time to time.

Perfect. This was basically my business at FFS. I operated something like a private bank, catering to the needs of a few select friends, and I'd had the respected law firm of Baker & McKenzie review the way I operated to make sure I was not running afoul of any Hong Kong regulations, such as the Deposit Taking Ordinance or the Trustee Ordinance. Everything was held in trust, and I was registered as an "Investment Advisor."

I loved Hong Kong's way of doing business then. If you wanted to be an investment advisor, you simply filled out a one-page form at the government office and presto, you'd soon have your hands on a beautiful-looking official *Registered Investment Advisor* certificate. No qualifications required. After that, how you built your reputation in the market was everything.

A simple handshake

HOWARD AND I never specifically discussed the nature of the funds that were moving in and out of his account. I made judgment calls based on the character and personality of my clients, and Howard was obviously a very bright, very likable and articulate fellow — a graduate of Oxford, no less. I realized later on that we had some mutual friends in the business of smuggling weed and hashish in large quantities, but I never viewed it as my business to ask questions.

Apart from the first deposit, the quantities of cash I handled for Howard were intentionally never too large, and the transactions were infrequent. Sometimes he would simply "park" funds with me for safekeeping. On his occasional trips to Hong Kong, the nature of our meetings tended to be more social than business-focused — we'd typically make a quick trip to the bank, then share a couple of glasses of wine and a few good yarns.

I vividly recall that first deposit. Howard appeared unexpectedly at my office after banking hours one Friday afternoon, and once we'd exchanged pleasantries, the conversation turned to business.

"Bruce, I'd like to open an account with you here at First Financial. I may leave suddenly over the weekend, so would you mind holding on to this large briefcase for safekeeping, until you can deposit it?"

"With pleasure, Howard."

He pushed away the simple document I used for opening an account. Instead of signing it, he shook my hand — and we headed to the nearest bar.

Having just returned from a grueling four days in Sydney, I managed to hang out with Howard until almost 3am. With my eyelids drooping, I vaguely remember saying goodnight, and bidding farewell, at a place called "Bar City" in Kowloon.

The Sydney trip had been tense. With no choice but to "just move it," golf bags containing $250,000 each had been given to couriers Graham Smith, Kim Barnaby, and Ben Rego (or was it Greg Pozar?), all of whom arrived and departed on consecutive days.

I'd had to change hotels four days in a row as a precaution. After all, people notice things that are out of the ordinary — small things like tattoos or a particular hat. How about the guy who goes in and out all day with a golf bag wrapped around his shoulder?

Back in the office the following Monday morning, I was on my third cup of coffee when I remembered Howard's briefcase behind the door in the pantry. It was heavy. I entered the combination written on a bar napkin by Howard: "333." Bingo. There, in front of me, was a pleasant sight — a cool S$1 million, in circulated $100 bills. Howard's instructions were to credit $150,000 to his account and telegraph the balance (less my commission), using my facility for "hundi" payments through BCCI, to Malik in Karachi, Pakistan.

That's how things worked with Howard.

LITTLE did I anticipate that one day we would both be defendants fighting for survival in different prisons, connected by a web of intrigue and fellow defendants, even though the cases were separate.

Equally shocking would be the Royal Hong Kong police investigation that emerged on the scene at a time when I was really beginning to feel the heat from various scandals being exposed all around me.

In a police interview dated September 30, 1988, with my disgruntled former secretary, Bernadette Layfield, it is recorded that: "Layfield remembers [Howard] Marks because he was polite, and because his first transaction with the company was for one million US dollars cash."

This certainly did much to strengthen the suspicion that I was a major launderer of narcotics funds. At the time, however, I was completely unaware of the fact that I had been placed under a giant microscope.

(As for Bernadette, to her eternal credit, I did hear through the grapevine that she regretted making the statement to the police about me. She also regretted spilling the beans that Arthur Gimenez was my Manila agent, and that I kept a false passport in my safe belonging to a "Robert Bland", aka Robert Kimball. She told the police she would never willingly testify against me in person.)

In time, I heard that Howard had been incarcerated in Terre Haute Prison in Indiana. By then, almost everyone I knew had either been indicted or imprisoned, and all were trying to sort out their lives and gain back their freedom.

I did not actually see Howard again until many years later, after the success of his best-selling memoir *Mr. Nice*. I read his incredible account and considered it an honor that he'd chosen to mention me and First Financial Services Ltd whilst also keeping his first large deposit with me a secret. In 2003, I attended one of Howard's hilarious speaking gigs at the Crystal Palace in London, and Howard had prepared a VIP table for me and my guests, right in front of the stage.

I was deeply saddened when I learned that he had died from colorectal cancer in 2016, and will be forever grateful that he took the time to write the foreword to the book you're holding just months before he passed away.

Though Howard had up to 43 aliases, and a multitude of fake passports, he became known as "Mr. Nice" after buying a passport from the convicted murderer Donald Nice. In my own case, I acquired the nickname "Mr. Clean" from a Sydney friend known as Surfin John for whom I washed a bit of cash from his exclusive Italian restaurant in London's fashionable Paddington area. Surfin's first words to me were "I'm pleased to meet you, Mr.

Clean," and the name just stuck. But my adoption of it for the title of this book is my small way of showing my respect for Howard.

CHAPTER 15

Blondie and the cowboys

I CAME TO love all my mates from "down under." In his foreword to this book, Howard Marks writes about "the excitement, glamor and sheer fun that an international jet-setting life of crime inevitably imparts." For me, those things were certainly in evidence in Australia, as well as in the countries to its north, in Southeast Asia.

In the era in which I operated, westerners who'd discovered the pleasures of surfing safari and smoking weed all the way from Bali to the "hippie trail," which stretched from Kathmandu in Nepal to Kabul, Afghanistan, were happy to be known as "cowboys." They didn't have horses and guns, though — only surfboards and Persian carpets. Let me briefly introduce you to a few of these colorful cowboys, many of whom were smugglers.

Hanging out with this crowd of Yanks, Aussies and Kiwis, some of whom also lived in Thailand and the Philippines, was always a blast. Among those I knew best were the "two Gregs," Greg Richardson (aka "Young Greg") and Greg Timewell (aka "Blondie"), as well as Patrick Bowler (aka "Top Hat"). Then there was Peter King, aka the "Peking Duck," who I introduced briefly in chapter 9 and who spoke so fast, yet so quietly, that no one could understand a single word he said. And I'd also like to mention Bob McGregor, a real class act who made a fortune from his daily telex newsletter, *Bob McGregor's Gold Alert!*

Lots of these guys had interesting lives, to say the least. Like birds of a feather, they flocked together in the famous nightlife district of Patpong, in Bangkok, as well as on Mabini Street and Del Pilar Street in Manila. The Mississippi Queen, Roxy Bar, Pink Panther, and the Sugar Shack were all bars owned by Aussies in conjunction with Thai partners. Everyone lived on a puff of smoke and enjoyed being on cloud 9, a place of well-being and elation.

No mistake, the times were good. During one trip, on which Jenny joined me, we went to a great party on Shark Island, right in the middle of Sydney Harbor. It was a birthday party for someone in a band — either John Paul Young or Rockwell T James or Piggy Morgan, I can't remember which. The party featured a barge with a piano, played by Piggy, plus an organized cream-pie fight on the beach during which the girls' bikini tops all seemed to fall off effortlessly and at random. I also always had a blast going to Palm Beach, up on the Peninsula, where another group of smugglers lived. I enjoyed the space, the beautiful drive over the Spit Bridge, and driving up the coast past Avalon Beach and Whale Beach.

Things could easily turn ugly in the cloud 9 heavens, however.

"Young Greg," an Aussie bloke I'd met in Sydney, helped me out quite a few times by picking up cash from some of my clients. When we were introduced, his disarming smile and confident swagger won me over immediately. When he later moved to Hong Kong, in the early '80s, we spent many afternoons together at the gym, getting fit, and afterwards sipping on some good wine at Greg's flat. One day (when I was not there) the police unfortunately came knocking and searched the place. Miraculously they did not find his little stash of "Bob Hope" because they never looked under the sofa cushion on which the Chief Inspector had chosen to ensconce himself. Greg had been indicted in Australia, however, and he was arrested in Hong Kong pending his extradition. It was a sad time. I did not enjoy visits to see him at Lai Chi Kok Correctional Institute in Kowloon.

It would be the other Greg — Timewell — who had to face the music hardest, though.

"Blondie" had an account with me, probably totaling a few hundred grand, for a time up until about 1987. I picked up cash from him on multiple occasions in Toronto and New York City. His partner, "Top Hat," was more of a social friend. Both were from New Zealand and belonged to the Hari Krishna religious sect. Neither, you felt, would swat a fly.

I knew they were big players in their field, but the magnitude of their operations would not be known to me until later, when I learned that both had been arrested as kingpins for a smuggling ring. Blondie was arrested in a sting operation in 1995 during an attempt to import 25 tons of hashish from Pakistan through Long Island to upstate New York and Canada.

To avoid life prison sentences in the US, Blondie cut a deal with the prosecutor and turned snitch. In fact, he gave up his mate, Top Hat, and hundreds of others involved in the drug trade. His testimony led to more than 180 convictions and tens of millions of dollars in drug proceeds being seized.

Reportedly, Top Hat was arrested in Switzerland in 1997 — after jumping out of a window and breaking both his legs when the authorities came to find him. He would also turn federal witnesses.

The pair would later plead guilty to conspiring to import hundreds of tons of marijuana and hashish into the US, and to leading a criminal enterprise that, in the words of a sentencing judge, was "mind-boggling" in its scale. It turned out they and their co-conspirators had controlled one of the world's most lucrative drug operations, reportedly earning in excess of a billion dollars from it during the 1980s and 90s. They'd had dealings with everyone from Taliban-connected drug dealers to shipping magnates and Irish gangsters.

"They were close to the biggest in the world at the time, they were tremendously active and with organizations all over the world," assistant US Attorney Burton Ryan told the Star-Times newspaper in Auckland, in 2015.

According to Tony Thompson's book Reefer Men, the operation led by Blondie and Top Hat— known as The Ring — operated on such a vast scale that just one shipment was enough to lower the price of pot along the entire West Coast of America.

Both men were released from prison in 2010. As quoted by the Star-Times, the US District Attorney who appeared at Blondie's final sentencing hearing claimed the only reason the latter avoided spending the rest of his life locked up was because he'd told the government all he knew about the global network of smugglers and dealers.

Some years after being released, Top Hat explained to the Star-Times that he and his fellow dealers had had a code of honor, in that they were never involved in the violence that follows most drug crime. "What angers me is the hypocrisy of a society that imprisons people for selling and smoking weed, yet in 14 states of the USA it is now legal to sell marijuana and governments and people in those States are making millions of dollars from it," he added.

As to whether Blondie or Top Hat ever gave information on me, I don't know.

What always seemed remarkable to me was that Blondie, despite giving up $100m and a worldwide network of associates, had the book thrown at him all because he forgot about one small account in Switzerland. Even the flabbergasted prosecutor objected, stating that the government had never had such a co-operative witness. Blondie was sentenced to an additional five years over this. Just thinking about it reminds of the jeopardy I myself faced up against a certain demented Seattle prosecutor when the noose was being fitted around my own neck. But more of this in due course.

CHAPTER 16

Nugan Hand

IN THE LATE 1970s, a sense of doom pervaded the offices of Deak & Company in Hong Kong. Little by little, the company's world had started falling apart. The business was experiencing severe liquidity problems — and was effectively being cannibalized by a high-profile group of lunatics who ran a new Hong Kong-based bank for the CIA.

Enter Nugan Hand, the creation of founding partners Mike Hand and Frank Nugan.

With Deak & Company employees already beginning to abandon ship, Mike — sensing blood — scooped up many of its best and most experienced foreigners, including Ron Pulgar-Frame and Jill Lovatt. Their appeal was that they knew how to manage customers "Deak-style." One day, Ron called me and set up a meeting with Mike and Frank. "Bruce," he said. "You should come and join us; this operation is better than Deak. For one thing, it pays double the commission."

At the time I was just launching FFS and doing fine, so I happily resisted the lure of Nugan Hand. But there was also just something about the organization that spooked me. They had opened an office in Chiang Mai, at the heart of Southeast Asia's infamous, drug-infested "Golden Triangle," and one sensed that whatever they were up to it was probably no good. What's more, the ridiculously high interest rates they were paying on deposits — always several percent above the market rates — was starting to attract a lot of attention from the authorities.

THERE IS some fascinating background information to know about Michael (Mike) Hand, much of it now in the public domain.

Mike joined the US Army in May 1963, and won the Distinguished Service Cross (DSC) in Vietnam. His DSC citation describes how he almost single-handedly held off a 14-hour Vietcong attack on the Special Forces compound at Dong Xaoi.

According to later investigative reports, in 1966 he left the army to work "directly for the US government," and was seemingly employed on undercover missions by the CIA in Vietnam and Laos. It is on record that he worked closely with the clandestine Air America crews and for the CIA's William Colby.

After moving to Australia in September, 1967, Mike made contact with a fellow named Bernie Houghton, who — according to testimony by Alexander Butterfield, a man famed for having exposed the White House taping system connected to the Watergate scandal — had previously worked with Hand as an intelligence officer in Vietnam, and was also connected to General John K. Singlaub, who ran covert air operations throughout Southeast Asia, especially in Vietnam, Laos and Thailand, during the war.

In short, Mike could not be said to lack connections in the American intelligence and defense community.

Francis (Frank) Nugan, meanwhile, was an Australian lawyer and worked as a solicitor and as a director in a mineral exploration company before linking up with Hand. His company had a lucrative contract to supply goods to the United States Navy Base at Subic Bay in the Philippines. (Another key figure in this venture was Houghton, who was closely connected to CIA officials Ted Shackley and Thomas G. Clines.)

The two men established the Nugan Hand Bank in 1973, with Bernie Houghton again also involved in the venture. (Houghton, incidentally, had also established the Bourbon and Beefsteak Bar in Sydney, a place that became notorious as a hang-out for all types of shady characters.)

Nugan ran operations in Sydney, while Hand took charge of establishing a branch in Hong Kong. This, of course, enabled Australian depositors to access a money laundering facility for illegal transfers of Australian money to Hong Kong — often using Deak & Company's currency swap services.

The partnership between Hand and Houghton, meanwhile, led the bank's international division into new fields: namely drug finance, arms trading, and support work for CIA covert operations.

According to reports, Hand told junior colleagues it was always his ambition "that Nugan Hand become banker for the CIA."

Some years later, an investigation by the Australia/New South Wales Joint Task Force on Drug Trafficking discovered that clients of Nugan Hand included several people who had criminal convictions relating to drug offenses — including the former policeman and Olympic athlete turned criminal kingpin, Murray Stewart Riley.

It is a small world. I had the genuine pleasure of meeting Murray Riley — a charming and intelligent fellow — even before I met Frank and Mike. I happened to know his girlfriend, a lovely Aussie girl named Maggie Davies.

Maggie ran a popular and delightful pub called Maggie's Revenge, in the Roppongi section of Tokyo. As an alternative venue to the Spanish restaurants where we had previously met, this pub became the favored drop-box location for Father Jose and I to leave secret messages for each other as the Lockheed scandal unraveled.

Quite the coincidence, then. Maggie's Revenge was also a regular haunt of the Bangkok-based DEA agent James Conklin when he happened to be in Tokyo. More about him later.

Them good ole boys

WHEN RON Pulgar-Frame, Nugan Hand manager Les Collings and Mike Hand himself told me about Nugan Hand Bank's interest rates on deposits, always several points higher than the going market rates, and about its 22 percent charge on getting clients' money out of Australia, I was shocked, to say the least. Deak had charged Nugan Hand five percent out of Australia, but they were charging *their* customers 22 percent!

Kevin Mulcahy, who was a CIA agent at the time, later told Australia's *National Times* newspaper about "the Agency's use of Nugan Hand for shifting money for various covert operations around the globe."

In hindsight, it is fairly obvious that the bank was exclusively laundering CIA funds and drug profits. An IRS investigation into Nugan Hand was said to have been dropped because of "legal problems." According to a subsequent *Wall Street Journal* investigation, the real reason for this was "pressure from the Central Intelligence Agency." And the *Sydney Morning Herald* later summed the bank up as follows: "Over the years, the two words Nugan Hand became shorthand for drug-dealing, gun-running, organized crime and clandestine intelligence activities."

During the years I worked as a free agent for Deak & Company, I had many conversations about Nugan Hand with Dirk Brink at Deak's Shell House office. Moreover,

Mike Hand invited me to several Friday night cocktail receptions for "visiting dignitaries" at the Nugan Hand Bank's own offices in the Connaught Centre. These occasions reminded me of my experiences with the military in the years I worked for American Express Bank, particularly at MACV Headquarters in Saigon. You could feel the "good ole boy" network in action, and it was mighty tempting to join it. And yet, by far the stronger pull was from my inner voice screaming at me that if I ever became too deeply involved with these folks, there would be no way out.

For Brink's part, he was furious about the long-serving, highly experienced staff who had jumped the Deak ship and moved over to Nugan Hand just for higher commissions.

Subsequently, after years of it serving the company well, Brink closed down Deak's "laundry bank account" at ANZ bank in Sydney, and discontinued any deals originating either from the US Consulate in Hong Kong or from the likes of Nugan Hand Bank. By then, Mr. Deak was experiencing a difficult time under the Carter administration regarding the company's business in South America (and would continue to do so under the Reagan administration). The bad vibes from that were spreading around the globe.

'Self-inflicted'

WHEN THE Nugan Hand Bank eventually collapsed, in sensational circumstances, the rumors about its connections to the CIA and organized crime could no longer be ignored.

On January 27, 1980, Frank Nugan was found shot dead in his Mercedes Benz on a dirt track near Bowenfels, in New South Wales. Along with his body was a list of prominent personalities in Australian politics, sports and business, along with a Bible that included a piece of paper on which were written the names "Bob Wilson" and "Bill Colby." Wilson was a senior member of the US House of Representatives Armed Services Committee, and Colby was a former director of the CIA who had been replaced by George H.W. Bush in 1975.

After Nugan's death, Wilson resigned from Congress.

A few months later, the official inquest into his murder, in June 1980, made front-page news amid testimony from Mike Hand that Nugan Hand Bank was insolvent, owing at least A$50 million and up to hundreds of millions. By then, the Australian government had already uncovered some of the extent of Nugan Hand's involvement in drug-dealing and covert money-laundering operations. (A November 1977 report by the Australian Narcotics Bureau linked Nugan Hand to a network that "exported" some A$3 billion worth of heroin from Bangkok prior to June 1975.)

The coroner concluded that the wound to Frank's head was self-inflicted — this despite police evidence that the scene of the incident had been disturbed, including by many footprints around the body.

Mike Hand subsequently fled Australia under a false identity, boarding a flight to Vancouver after giving testimony and then destroying Nugan Hand Bank's remaining records. Amid growing revelations of CIA and organized crime involvement, he went into hiding

— and in fact managed to stay in hiding until he was discovered living in Idaho in 2015. It is probable that, as a CIA operative, he had re-entered the US having been given a new identity.

Long before that came another mind-boggling twist in the tale, however. In a 1983 interview with *The Age* newspaper, Perth businessman Murray Quartermaine claimed to have evidence that Frank Nugan's death had not been a suicide. He also testified in a 1983 public inquiry into drug trafficking, the Stewart Royal Commission, that Mike Hand was living in Pretoria, South Africa under the name of "Hahn."

Years later, in 2011, Quartermaine was killed at his apartment by an insane 24-year-old French-Australian woman who had been diagnosed as a paranoid schizophrenic. In a chilling echo of how Nicholas Deak was murdered, in 1985, the woman later told a court that in the moments leading up to the crime she had "heard voices" in her head telling her to kill Quartermaine. The injuries she inflicted on him were horrific: she stabbed him to death with a pair of scissors, also severing his toes and genitals. Both Deak and Quartermaine suffered violent deaths at the hands of deranged women who were said to have been "mentally pre-programmed" to do the dastardly deed. I wonder who, or what agency, could possibly be capable of such abominable crimes?

CHAPTER 17

'He told me to do it'

NOTHING that had happened in my life until that time was more shocking to me personally than the death of Mr. Deak — a man I considered to be truly extraordinary in intellect and charisma, and a personal friend — in such a cloak-and-dagger manner. I remember the day I heard the news as if it were yesterday.

I was in my office early on the morning of November 19, 1985, when Tony Pong called to tell me what had happened. I was stunned, in a state of pure shock. Vivid memories of Mr. Deak flashed through my mind, along with the words spoken many times by Dirk Brink: "When you are dealing with clandestine government agents or agencies, you are dealing in a murky world. They are the real criminals and they will stop at nothing."

Deak & Company was for decades the unofficial paymaster of the CIA. Like Nugan Hand Bank in its wake, it was key to greasing the palms of those the government asked it to grease, no questions asked. Nicholas Deak was referred to as the "James Bond of Money." But something had gone terribly wrong.

The company had been under scrutiny ever since Senator Frank Church's 1975 hearings on CIA activity, which revealed Deak's involvement in the Lockheed scandal. The beginning of the end came in 1983, however, when a Federal informant accused the firm of laundering hundreds of millions of dollars in Colombian cartel cash. By the following year, a Federal investigation into its ties to organized crime syndicates around the world — from Buenos Aires to Manila — was in full swing, and not even Deak's close friendship with the Reagan-era CIA director William Casey, whom he had known since his OSS days during World War II, could save him.

The company declared bankruptcy in December 1984, but you might as well say Casey — who we now know was simultaneously working with Nicaragua's contra rebels, a group whose arms purchases were funded through sales of cocaine in the United States — hung Deak out to dry. (Whether or not Deak knew about what the CIA was up to in Nicaragua, he stoically responded to public questioning about the business activities of his clients with an economic libertarian's classic counter-punch, telling the Feds it was the job of law enforcement, not banks, to track drug money.)

The story given about his cold-blooded murder a year later was simply bizarre beyond all belief. Mr. Deak's killer, a homeless woman named Lois Lang, had apparently just appeared out of the woodwork, flown from Seattle to Miami, picked up a pistol in Orlando, then traveled on to New York City, where she walked into his office at 29 Broadway and shot him, along with his secretary, Frances Lauder. And all of this because a "voice" in her head told her to do so. I mean, were we born yesterday?

Lang was eventually convicted and institutionalized under the assumption that she was mad. A wealth of circumstantial evidence has been uncovered, however, that points to a CIA-directed brain-washing program having been at play.

After the murder, Lang took pictures of the dying Mr. Deak. Proof for someone perhaps? And upon being arrested as she left the office, she immediately cowered in the fetal position and said something to the effect that "He told me to do it."

Who is the "he" that told her to do it?

As uncovered by journalistic inquiries, Lang reportedly had come under the dominion of psychologists and institutions involved in conducting CIA-sponsored research into mind control techniques. In other words, she may well have been subjected to drug-induced attempts to alter her personality and behavior – and turn her into an assassin.

Mr. Deak was a truly brilliant man — and one whose abilities were matched by his knowledge and connections. Even today, speculation abounds that his despicable murder was a way of truly silencing him. Could it really be that he was "taken out" simply to ensure that the truth — not only about the whole sordid Lockheed affair but also regarding a host of other off-balance sheet transactions carried out for and on behalf of Uncle Sam over several decades — would quite literally be buried? No-one on the planet really believes that a deranged woman just happened to appear in his office and shoot him.

Arkadi Kuhlmann became CEO of Deak-Perera after Deak's death. As he explained in a 2012 interview with two journalists, Mark Ames and Alexander Zaitchik, for the news website *Salon*, he and his colleagues became aware that many criminal account holders had lost millions when the firm went bankrupt in 1984. Deak's murder, he felt, was no coincidence.

"I never believed that the whole thing was random," said Kuhlmann. "We were the CIA's paymaster, and that got to be a little bit embarrassing for them. Our time had passed and the usefulness of doing things our way had vanished. The world was changing in the '80s; you couldn't just accept bags of cash. Deak was slow at making those changes. And when you lose your sponsorship, you're out of the game."

He added: "The question is: Who was actually able to put the hit on?"

Intriguingly, on a trip to Macau in the wake of Deak's murder, Kuhlmann discovered that the manager there had vanished without a trace after the company's collapse. But the manager's girlfriend showed Kuhlmann a photo she'd found in his desk — a grainy snapshot of a dying Nicholas Deak that could only have come from Lang's camera and which was not in the public domain. In their piece, Ames and Zaitchik quote a couple of sources who corroborate the idea that Mr. Deak may have run afoul of the Macau mafia.

Kuhlmann reorganized Deak International's operations and relaunched the company in 1986. However, the name of Deak-Perera would never glitter again as it had in its heyday under the helm of its founding Hungarian-born war hero. (Kuhlmann would later found ING Direct Canada and ING Direct USA, both of which are now part of a multinational banking and financial services conglomerate.)

The remarkably similar circumstances surrounding the murders of Murray Quartermaine, as detailed in the last chapter, and Mr. Nicholas Deak — both of whom died violent deaths at the hands of deranged women who seem to have been "mentally preprogrammed" to kill — have never been satisfactorily explained.

To re-state the question I asked a few pages ago, who — or what agency — could possibly be capable of such abominable crimes?

The murder of Mr. Deak, a great man and a good friend, may have given the CIA "closure" on certain episodes they would rather like to remain unknown. On a personal level, it cast a shadow over my life that would affect me for years.

CHAPTER 18

'The World's Sleaziest Bank'

DEAK-PERERA was far from being the only player involved in the shady world of fast-moving cash to become a victim of changing times and feel the heat of government pressure in the 1980s.

With Nugan Hand history, and Deak & Company on its knees, looming larger than life on a horizon full of scandals was Pakistan's Bank of Credit and Commerce International (BCCI). And again, I would be caught up in the midst of the fall-out.

BCCI had purchased the Hong Kong Metropolitan Bank (HKMB), and my company, FFS, operated a gold counter at the HKMB's Hilton Branch. The bankers from Pakistan were smart, calm, very capable — and highly underrated. But there was definitely something strange going on with them. You could sense it, even if you couldn't quite put your finger on it.

Until one fine day.

———————⟨⟩•⟨⟩•———————

IN THE FALL of 1985, I realized I had a problem that I was struggling to find a way around. The conundrum I faced was one of logistics: namely, what to do with volumes of banknotes that simply took up too much space? I had huge piles of $10 and $20 notes "under management," so to speak, and I didn't know what to do with them.

Up until then, the Philippines had been my saving grace, of sorts. Armed with a list of names photocopied from pages of the Manila telephone directory, I would spend hours going from bank to bank, in San Francisco, and other cities, purchasing small money orders in the names of people on my list. I would send these orders back to Hong Kong by DHL, and we would endorse and deposit them to our account at Hang Seng Bank, for immediate credit. But oh, what unnecessary exposure it involved. And what tedious work.

The first place to look to for help was naturally my Chinese family. As it happened, my father-in-law, Mr. Cheung Ting On, was a merchant seaman. He was the chief steward on a ship owned by Swire — one of Hong Kong's old "Hongs" that had made their initial fortunes, so it is told, smuggling opium.

The first time I met Ting was in 1971 when I was working in Saigon and dating Jenny during my visits to Hong Kong. They lived in a small fourth-floor flat located at 933 King's Road, North Point, on Hong Kong Island.

Once, after a dinner date with Jenny, I was outside her home saying goodnight when the door suddenly sprang open. Ting screamed something in Cantonese that sounded quite vulgar to my ears, snatched his daughter away, and slammed the door in my face.

After Jenny and I were married, Ting and I laughed about it, and he and I became the best of friends (although I never did discover what exactly he'd shouted at me that night).

Ting traveled the seas between Hong Kong, New Zealand and French Polynesia, with occasional stops in San Francisco. When he returned to Hong Kong, we would often stop for a few beers at the Two Dragons, a "girlie bar" in the red light district of Wanchai that was owned by one of his friends. In these ways, my father-in-law and I became good mates.

Ting was a likable character who supplemented his income with some harmless smuggling whenever possible. One day, over a bowl of wonton soup, I confided in him that it would be great if I could find a "Chinese laundry" in San Francisco, one that could "wash" some money for me from time to time.

I vividly recall the day I stumbled into the "Hong Kong House," a tiny dim sum cafe just down a side street in San Francisco's Chinatown. I must have thought I was back in Hong Kong, because I automatically ordered in very basic Cantonese, saying something like: *"Yut booi won ton meen, m-goy"* or "One bowl of wonton soup, please."

The cook and owner, Mr. Wong, laughed and said: "You must be Bruce!" He had been expecting me. We became instant friends.

Little had I imagined that Chinese restaurants all over San Francisco not only needed a laundry to launder their tablecloths, but one to launder their money too. Consequently, for several years after that first bowl of soup, either my brother Jim or I would stop by from time to time for a bowl of noodles and to pick up a couple of hundred grand in small bills.

At the same time, my friend Peter Cavanaugh, ran a sharp investment company, Cavanaugh Capital Management, in Toronto, dealing mainly in managed gold trading accounts.

We had much in common, both having been employed by Deak & Company prior to striking out on our own.

Peter was Swiss, and an excellent skier. In fact, as I recall, he was a member of the Swiss National Ski Team and one of the skiers in the opening sequence of the James Bond film, *Dr. No.*

Peter's company managed quite a few of my clients' investment accounts and did very well for them. He also assisted me with processing cash deposits from the San Francisco restaurant business, which was perfectly legal in Canada. I was blessed to know Peter, a person of the highest integrity, ethics and ability.

All it took was some teamwork and a trusted crew. First, I had to get the funds to Vancouver — which was done by simply driving across the Canadian border. (Our modus operandi in those days was very simple.)

In northern California we knew lots of laid-back folks — old Chinese friends of Mr. Wong who were looking to supplement their retirement pot or help send their grandchildren to college. What better way than to create a neat little compartment under the back seats of their cars, enough to hold a couple of hundred grand, and occasionally drive to Vancouver for the weekend?

Either my brother Jimmy or I would meet them and fly the cash from Vancouver to Toronto on a routine domestic flight. Then it would be deposited with Peter's investment company.

The system worked like clockwork, allowing us to launder millions in restaurant money back home to Hong Kong, tax-free. However, the fact remained that small bills simply took up too much space. I kept thinking that *surely* there must be a better way. It would take the luck of the Irish to solve the problem.

What paperwork?

I COULD NOT believe my luck! Or was it fate?

It was a Friday afternoon in downtown San Francisco. Strolling around as the lunchtime crowds were beginning to swarm the streets, I felt the wonder of the place. What a great town! If I ever returned to America, SF would surely be a great choice. Suddenly, while waiting in the crowd at the corner of Union Street, directly in front of me I saw a banking friend from Hong Kong.

"Louis!" I yelled.

"Bruce, how nice to see you! Let's have a coffee."

Louis had been a well-known banker in Hong Kong, where he'd been the representative of Bank of America in the city. We first met in the late '70s when, amongst other things, I was the Hong Kong representative for Bankhaus Deak of Vienna. Representative Offices cannot do business as such, and actually Reps don't do much more than meet once a month for lunch and build personal relationships.

Louis was now working for BCCI in San Francisco. BCCI had purchased Hong Kong Metropolitan Bank, as I mentioned earlier. I explained my problem.

"Call this number and ask for Mr. Butt, our head cashier," said Louis. "He may be able to help you."

Well, to make a long story short, I did call and Mr. Amid Butt did help. He could *not* accept my large cash deposits and credit my account in Hong Kong without reporting them to the government, because BCCI had already been placed under a microscope by the US Treasury. However, he stated: "What I can do is to change your bills from 'small' to 'large.'" Excellent!

Subsequently, on quite a few occasions, we'd hand Mr. Butt a large suitcase of small notes, and a couple of days later, at the price of his small fee, receive a small suitcase of circulated $100 notes in return.

Later, when BCCI folded, all of its transactions came under scrutiny. We held our breaths, but we were never contacted, approached or questioned in relation to our dealings with BCCI after its collapse — because no-one ever knew. There was no paperwork!

Headlines and stories about BCCI trickled out of the woodwork regarding the bank, the US government and the CIA, until the bank was forced to close in 1991. Details of the debacle made for sensational reading.

In a nutshell, the CIA and other intelligence agencies had used BCCI to control and manipulate criminals and terrorists worldwide. The Pakistani bank was involved in some of the most sensitive intelligence operations of the Reagan-Bush years, including the notorious secret sales of arms to Iran. As recorded in official documents, investigators in the US and the UK determined that BCCI had been "set up deliberately to avoid centralized regulatory review, and operated extensively in bank secrecy jurisdictions. Its affairs were extraordinarily complex. Its officers were sophisticated international bankers whose apparent objective was to keep their affairs secret, to commit fraud on a massive scale, and to avoid detection."

In March 1991, Senator John Kerry's investigation into the bank heard about a secret CIA report on BCCI that had been given to the US customs service. Kerry's office asked the CIA for a copy but was told the report did not exist. After months of wrangling, with more and more information about the CIA's ties to BCCI coming out, the CIA eventually gave Kerry the report, and many others relating to BCCI. What it didn't do was share any documents relating to its own operations using the bank.

Kerry's public report concluded: "Key questions about the relationship between US intelligence and BCCI cannot be answered at this time, and may never be."

It is believed, although never proven, that the CIA's desperation to hide its relationship with the Pakistani merchant bank came from the knowledge that it solicited business from terrorists, rebels and shady underground organizations around the world. In July 1991, a *Time* magazine cover story branded BCCI "The World's Sleaziest Bank." And *Foreign Affairs* reflected, in 2020, that: "BCCI was a kleptocratic institution whose influence reached the White House — and a model for today's global crooks."

For me, it was yet again a close call. I had been lucky operating as a "one-man band" and not becoming embroiled in any tempting deals in Pakistan.

Incidentally, I always enjoyed traveling to Pakistan, most of all to visit my good friend Illyas Butt, in Lahore. He was my initial connection to BCCI, and facilitated many "hundi" payments for me, such as those made on behalf of Howard Marks. Illyas was also well-known in Hong Kong as the "King of carpets," thanks to his having cornered the market on imported carpets from Iran, Afghanistan and Pakistan.

Arriving in Karachi, we would always be met on the tarmac by Illyas' friend, the Karachi Chief of Police. Our passports summarily stamped, and armed with as many bottles of Johnnie Walker Black Label as we could carry from the duty-free store, we'd be bustled into a limo and soon find ourselves arriving at the residence of the Minister of Finance for a huge party.

By the mid to late '80s, however, even as my company rolled along like a well-oiled machine, I realized the party could not go on forever. Our dealings with BCCI had been one of several close calls, and I was very lucky there had been no paper trails leading back to me. Now, my gut feeling told me Kenny Rogers had it right: "*You gotta know when to hold 'em, and you gotta know when to fold 'em.*"

I held 'em too long.

CHAPTER 19

A hostage situation

AUGUST of 1986 was an eventful time on Phuket Island, Thailand.

The drama that unfolded was reported widely in Asia, especially in Hong Kong's *South China Morning Post*, the *Bangkok Post*, and the *Sydney Morning Herald*. And given all of the scandals that were unraveling around us at the time, the publicity was more than my clients and I really wanted. It seemed that everywhere I turned there was more trouble.

August is the last hot and humid month in Hong Kong before the beautiful fall and mild winter. On August 18, as I sat somewhat listlessly at my desk, the telex suddenly came to life. (We still used telex in those days, and I liked it because it was a secure and easy way to communicate.)

It was just after 9am, and I was on my second cup of mud. Patti, Jenny's cousin who served as our receptionist, brought the telex to me right away because it was from a coded account. I naturally assumed it was a payment instruction.

I glanced at it, and immediately recognized it had come from my friend, Tim Milner. Jenny read it at the same time. We both deemed it very strange because Tim was sending instructions to close his account and transfer the entire balance, as soon as possible, to an account with BCCI in Hong Kong under the name "Goldcore Ventures Limited."

My first thought, soon dismissed, was that as it was his money, he could spend it as he pleased. Moreover, it was quite possible that he had found a good investment opportunity.

My *gut* feeling was quite different. Obviously, something was not right. Our friendship and our business relationship went back many years and had been tried and tested. There had been the "Cessna-Milner Affair" just for starters.

Tim was comfortable with his account with us and I knew he would not be taking out the entire balance in one whack without at least having a conversation with us first and confirming. YC, our accountant, agreed with this assessment, but was perplexed because the code word and test key were correct.

That meant the message had to have come from Tim, and only Tim. The account balance was about $1 million, made up in the form of 220,000 in US dollars, 272,000 in German marks, and 69 million in Japanese yen.

Suddenly, I was very worried. I replied and asked for verbal instructions direct from the horse's mouth, so to speak.

Three days later, on August 21, we received a second follow-up telex from Thailand.

"Patti," I said. "Please send a reply as follows: 'Tim, confirm receipt of your cable instructions just now. Please follow up with direct telephone call to my private line for reconfirmation. Thanks and best regards, FFS Ltd.'"

I told Patti to send the telex to the address on the Thai number. The telex answerback confirmed it was registered to a Bangkok travel agency. Then we waited for Tim's call.

The phone rang at 3:30pm. For some reason, I made a point to jot down the exact time. It was Tim. He said he was calling IDD (international direct dial), meaning he'd placed the call directly rather than going via an operator.

"Hello, Bruce?"

"Hey, Tim! How are you, mate?"

"Bruce, I am in Pattaya and I sent you the telex. Please send the balance of my account."

His slurred speech was a bit of a concern.

"Right, Tim. Are you okay? I thought I better ask you to call because…"

"Bruce, I gotta go now. See you later."

"OK, Tim, first thing tomorrow morning."

"Thanks." He quickly hung up.

Jenny had heard the call. "Was that Tim?" she asked.

"Yes."

"But you spoke for less than a minute!" She was very uncomfortable about the conversation.

"Something is really wrong, Bruce!"

YC said: "Let me have the instructions, because if we are going to credit the account at BCCI in the morning, I'll have to notify Hang Seng Bank right away to remit the money overnight from our call account in New York."

I immediately thought of Tim's best mate, Brian Daniels.

"Get Brian on the phone right away!"

We made several attempts to reach Brian at his office in Bangkok. Then, around 4pm, we called again and he picked up:

"Hi Bruce, what's happening?"

"Brian, have you heard from Tim?" I filled him in, and his instant reaction was that Tim was in some kind of very serious trouble.

He said: "Do not send the money!"

"What should we do?"

Brian, thinking quickly, sprang into action. On checking, he discovered that there was no direct dial from Pattaya — which only served to further heighten our suspicions.

What happened next was a most amazing sequence of events.

Tim had clearly been kidnapped, but we needed to work out how. Brian and I spent the rest of the day frantically calling each other to piece together the details and figure out what to do.

We reached out to contacts and anyone who might have a lead. I looked into Goldcore Ventures Limited, the company Tim had told us to transfer his cash to, and discovered the names of two Germans — a Mr. Wolfgang and a Mr. Michael — who were connected to it.

Here's how Brian described what happened next in an interview transcribed by the Thai police:

"*Late that afternoon between 3:00-4:00 p.m., I received phone call from Mr. Karo Brown* [a low-level CIA operative attached to the US Consulate]. *He wanted to meet me about 5:00 p.m.*

"*Mr. Karo Brown told me that phone number of the phone which Mr. Tim called to Hong Kong. He had checked this with the previous information I had given him. The address where the phone number is registered is: 66/2 Soi 39, Sukhumvit Road, Klong Toey, Bangkok.*

"*Later about 6:00 p.m. August 22, 1986, I went to Thonglor Police Station to make a report that I believed something very dangerous was happening to Mr. Tim at the above address. The police questioned me until 10:00 p.m.*

"*The police said they would send men to the address as a precaution that night and would go into the house to investigate the next day. Police General Montri and I went to the address the same night.*

"*The next day at 6:30 am, I went to Thonglor Police Station as per my appointment, and met Major General Montri. Later, many policemen and I went to the address.*

"*When the police knocked on the door, it was answered by one of the Germans who said, 'Why do you come in here, who are you?' He shut the door and went inside.*

"I shouted at the house to let Mr. Tim out! We could not open the front door. Later on Mr. Tim was thrown out of the house. Strapped to a chair, he was tossed out of the second floor window, into a tree that broke his fall! Mr. Tim's physical condition was such that he could not speak coherently.

"I took some clothes from my car to give to Mr. Tim. Mr. Tim asked me to call Mr. Bruce to stop the telex transfer of the money! Later I went to Thonglor Police Station and I saw the suspects handcuffed there."

Exposed

AS MENTIONED, the publicity regarding Tim's kidnapping for ransom was not welcome. Much to our amazement, the Cessna-Milner Affair of 1979 was now thrown back into the spotlight in Australia, and it connected Tim, Brian and myself, along with a lot of other dots.

After the kidnapping, two members of the police force investigating team from the Stewart Royal Commission flew to Bangkok to interview Tim. It is understood that he was tentatively offered immunity from further prosecution if he would return to Australia and give evidence. They were fishing, since he had already served his time. Tim declined, although the police did not rule out the possibility that he might reconsider his decision.

Indeed, several months later, the Chairman of the Royal Commission, Mr. Bill Job, also flew to Bangkok to interview Tim.

Out of those interviews, the entire history of our relations emerged, and ended up being reported — as mentioned in chapter 9 — in a 1987 *Sydney Morning Herald* article headlined "Milner's claims of torture and drugged meals."

The article related: "As a result of his investments with Deak & Co, Milner came to know one of the company's employees, Bruce Aitken, from about 1977. Judging from the statements and records of the interview, Milner became involved in smuggling marijuana to Australia during the late 1970s, although he made no reference to this in court. These activities culminated in his arrest with Ray Cessna in 1979. He served a short term and was deported in January 1980.

"Later that year, Aitken established his own firm, First Financial Services, and Milner became a valued customer. Brian [Daniels] also became a client. Milner confirmed that he had referred Brian, whom he described as being involved in the gemstone business in Thailand, to Aitken's company. Milner also told the court that he did not realize that Aitken had been arrested in Australia in 1980 with $60,000 in his possession. The charge was eventually dismissed."

When I read this, I had a terrible sinking feeling in my stomach. My company and I were now totally exposed. I felt that life was about to change dramatically. Little did I know just how dramatically.

Revenge

THE ENTIRE experience of the kidnapping was harrowing, and one I would talk with Tim and Brian about later over a few beers.

The Germans, who had come from Manila, were tried and sentenced to long prison terms. Sadly, they had wives and young children whom they would not be seeing for some time. One was a medical doctor. Who had put them up to this kidnapping? We had our suspicions. We speculated. Could it possibly have been Australian intelligence?

No. Surely that was too far-fetched.

Thank God Brian had been able to locate Tim. What if we had sent the money? Perhaps we would never again have seen Tim alive.

One year after the Germans' sentencing, an anonymous letter arrived at an office of the DEA in Tokyo regarding my business. The details of my operation that were included made it clear that it was from someone who knew us all well — and on reflection it most probably came from the brains behind Tim's kidnapping, someone who was pissed off that we had foiled it and had not paid the ransom.

The letter — sent from Perth, Australia, in December 1987 — was later included in a cache of evidence sent to my defense lawyers in the US by the DEA. The DEA's report on the file notes that "the typewritten letter clearly indicates that English is not the writer's first language or a clever disguise to make it appear so."

The letter begins:

"aitkens of foirst financial hong kong is the banker for daniels and milner and many others aitkins gets a % for intruoducing other clients to other clients plus the banking business any dealing the clients do generally not less thsan 12% Vancouver is also a place he picks up and delivers monety deak connection from the past he also udses members of his chinese wife family to travel to countries to act on his behalf..."

Suddenly, the nature of the game had turned nasty, and the handwriting on the wall was not just screaming at me, but hitting me over the head.

You may be asking: What's the big deal with this report from the DEA? The answer: a NADDIS number. As the DEA file notes: "It appears that Bruce Emil Aitken, NADDIS 1066623 is the subject of the letter. Since Aitken is of interest to many offices, the letter is being distributed to offices mentioned in the file reference section of Aitken's NADDIS printout."

The Narcotics And Dangerous Drugs Information System (NADDIS) is a data index and collection system operated by the DEA, and comprises millions of reports and records on individuals. NADDIS is a tool in drug law enforcement that allows personal information about 'subjects of interest' — many of whom have no criminal history — to be quickly accessed and reviewed.

Basically, if you are in their system, they assign you a NADDIS number. The big deal was: I had one.

Chain reaction

THE KIDNAPPING of Tim Milner and the resulting publicity thrown on Brian and me was devastating. Pandora's Box had been opened. Sure, we'd had concerns as it was all happening, but we always assumed we would be able to deal with the fallout later. Now, much to our shock and amazement, it hit us that the Cessna-Milner Affair of 1979 was still alive and kicking. It connected the three of us and most of the dots.

Cito (Ray Cessna) flew in from Sydney. He too was shocked by the resurrection of the Cessna-Milner investigations, and in a private conversation over a couple of bottles of Aussie red, confided in me for the first time that the money I'd delivered to him in Sydney just before Tim's trial was given to Morgan Ryan so that "people could be looked after." So we reminisced first, then decided what to do next.

Funny how the story gets told, but the best part of it all was that we never lost our sense of humor and general good spirits. Brian used to retell the scene when Tim was unceremoniously thrown out of the second floor window, and after clearing his blurred eyes, the first words he spoke were: "Did Bruce send the money!?"

None of us really felt that we were in any kind of business that would cause us to lose sleep at night — that is, so long as the government did not get a whiff of our maneuvers. We actually thanked the government for making "weed" illegal, because it provided golden opportunities for good-natured people to supply it to those who wanted to smoke it — just like in the "Roaring 20s" when nobody really cared what was going on. In our minds, it was identical to Prohibition — the nationwide ban on the sale of alcoholic beverages in the US that turned much of the population into criminals from 1920-1933.

Of course, the money to be made inevitably attracted real criminal elements that brought violence to the equation. And then, of course, there were the *snitches*, that part of humanity that lurks in the underbelly of every deal.

Brian, Robert Kimball, Howard Marks and others like them were still very busy spreading joy in the form of Thai sticks going to America and Canada via sophisticated networks.

For my part, I was happy to be involved along the periphery by helping a few good friends who needed to have their bread laundered. I never wanted to meet anyone involved other than those friends who had already become clients of my company. I knew I could make a decent living just by servicing them from time to time.

I realized, however, that the time had come to retire from carrying money around in golf bags or using other methods of deception to clean it — it was time to get out before I got caught. There had already been too many close calls, and the nerds in the government were definitely not stupid. Certainly, there were a lot of people out there who were talking too much. Why else was I now getting a third-degree interrogation and search (they never found anything) every time I went through US Customs and Immigration?

"That's it, Jenny," I told my wife. "The shit *has* hit the fan!"

We struggled with the decision to wind down First Financial Services Ltd. FFS, a mini Deak & Company, had served me well, and there was a tinge of sadness because we had worked very hard for years to develop a legitimate parallel financial services business with "boring" clients. However, the real breadwinner, the foundation of the business, had continued to be "the laundry." I had made up my mind that this was now too risky.

I informed my clients and customers that First Financial would be closing down with almost immediate effect. I gave them a month or two to give me instructions concerning where to send the balance of their accounts, and I raised my fees so they would not delay. Trouble was, almost all of my best clients were in the smuggling profession, so I had to wait until they came to Hong Kong to pick up their cash in person.

(As part of the cleansing of First Financial, I had many loose ends to wrap up. One of these included picking up $250,000 in Vancouver — the very last money laundering transaction I planned to touch. I visited the client at his home, just south of Newport Beach, and my jaw almost dropped when he told me that he was an indicted fugitive on the run! I felt sick to my stomach and I had to steel myself, expecting there would be a sudden knock at the door at any moment. As we spoke, two lady friends of his were busy driving the cash up to Vancouver. The following day, I checked into the hotel we had agreed on and collected the car keys they had left for me. Sweating profusely, I had a hell of a time removing the carpet on the back left-hand side, unscrewing the floorboard and removing the cash.)

Closing down fully was actually easier said than done, though. For me, I suppose, the temptation was just too great. Sometimes you compromise with yourself and go half-way, and that's what I did. Why not have the best of both worlds?

I had decided to close down the ticking time bomb, First Financial, with pronouncements and fanfare. Secretly and confidentially, however, I would keep one very big toe in the water by creating a parallel banking and laundry system just to handle the business of a handful of my biggest and best smuggling clients who were still in need. And to do that, I opened an account with a major Swiss bank in the name of my elderly Chinese mother-in-law, peace be upon her.

From time to time, one makes a decision that has a major impact not only on one's own life, but on the lives of many others. Call it the knock-on effect, a chain reaction, or such. I don't know any better terms. I do, however, know that the cumulative effect of a string of several incorrect decisions made by me and by others was about to unravel years of hard work in the noble profession of smuggling and laundering.

Calm before the storm

BACK IN Hong Kong, I had no idea that the peace I was experiencing was the calm before the big storm. I prayed, and fantasized that all my problems would blow over.

I decided to take a well-earned break with my family. Jenny and I took our sons to Orlando to spend some time with their doting grandma, my mom, and my two sisters and their families.

We flew business class on a Northwest Orient 747 to Honolulu, and spent a few glorious days at the Honolulu Hilton on Diamond Head. On the way over, we had the whole upper deck of the plane to ourselves.

Later, sitting around the hotel pool, I reflected on the fact that despite everything that had happened life was incredibly good. Matt and Doug were seven and five years old, and Jenny and I could not have been happier in our family life.

Arriving in Honolulu had been an unusually disturbing experience, however. In front of my family, I was pulled aside and placed in a room for questioning. I was tired from the flight. It was all very strange.

Sitting alone in the room, I suspected there was a hidden camera. After a while, an agent came in and placed an open file on the desk directly across from me. I was very curious to have a look at it, but resisted the urge. After 20 minutes, I was told I could go, and I did. I headed straight downtown to lodge a complaint at the US Customs head office.

After a wonderful stay at home in Orlando, I went on to New York to see my brother Jimmy and some other friends, including Matthew Wallace, who was a close friend of Bruce Miller (the guy I'd been exporting gold chains out of Thailand with). As a family, we then hired a plane at Teterboro Airport — right next door to Hasbrouck Heights, in New Jersey — and flew to the Hamptons for the day. That evening I was back in Jersey for dinner with another friend, Steve Deutsch.

Ah, the good life.

Robert Kimball calling

TO END the holiday happily, we went to Montreal. We had tickets for an ice hockey match and were biding our time in the hotel beforehand when the phone rang. It was business: Robert Kimball calling from a hotel in Vancouver to request my services. It sounded like a promising deal, but I was already agonizing over another unexpected, and very tempting, transaction of $1 million in Toronto.

I'd been undecided as to whether or not I should do the transaction while on holiday with my family. It was a matter of meeting "Bill" from New York in Toronto, then delivering the cash to my agent. Bill always had perfectly organized $100 notes. I never saw his ID. I believe his surname could have been "Lamorte," another major smuggler who ended up being done in by the same two super-snitches.

In the end, I rationalized that the three percent fee of $30,000 would more than pay for our whole holiday. Easy money.

By the time we arrived in Vancouver several days later, Robert had already checked out of the Granville Hotel and returned to America — just 24 hours before his whole team was busted in that same hotel. They had been under surveillance based on information from Corman and Christensen. For the whole two days we stayed at the Granville, I couldn't escape the feeling I was also being watched.

Before heading back to Hong Kong, I rented a car and we went up the coast to go salmon fishing. The skipper of the boat noted we were novices, so decided we shouldn't go out too far.

The day before, he'd taken out two Cathay Pacific pilots who had caught nothing, so he thought we'd try the other side of the bay, toward the north. It turned out a school of whales had most likely come by the night before, prompting all the salmon to head north — because in less than an hour we had caught the legal limit and were back at the shore, giving salmon to a group of old ladies on a picnic. We packed or froze the rest, and checked some of it in my luggage, along with the $30,000, for the flight home to Hong Kong.

CHAPTER 20

Reno the casino

NOVEMBER 5, 1987 was a beautiful fall day in Hong Kong and I was feeling good about life. Although the future was uncertain, I felt "retired" from the profession of money laundering. It was a future most pleasing to contemplate. The day would, however, turn out to be one I would forever love to forget.

On a personal level, many trials had been caused by my constant travels and by my propensity to live life as a "dreamer." In spite of having started with nothing and accumulated a decent level of savings, and in spite of having a lovely wife and two beautiful young sons, I was always dreaming about doing something else or being somewhere else.

The root cause of my dreaming was probably a deep sense that I should have been a professional baseball player. I never found anything quite like baseball, so I found excitement in alternative ways, like making a profession of traveling and smuggling cash.

On that fall day, I dropped Matt off at school and headed to the office with Doug in my new BMW. To all intents and purposes, I had closed down the "laundry," even while establishing the temporary "parallel laundry" to service my small group of friends.

All seemed well.

"Good morning, Y.C.," I said to my accountant, as I entered my office.

"Bruce," he said. "Good morning, but there is something very urgent!"

"Oh?" My interest was piqued.

"Bob Seltzer, Ed Seltzer's brother, has been calling every ten minutes for the past hour. He asked that you call him as soon as you come in."

My heart sank straight to the floor. This did not sound good.

As part of my ambitions to wind down and de-risk my operations, I had approached my old buddy Ed (the American attorney mentioned in chapter 9 who was First Financial Services' first client, in 1980) concerning a potentially large cash pickup deal in the States.

A few weeks earlier, Robert Kimball had asked me to help him launder a total of $30 million that was stuck in the US. I had advised him to do a so-called "reverse smuggle": put the cash on a sea-worthy yacht in California and have the vessel sailed to Hong Kong, where the money would be cleaned over time through a series of bank deposits. It would have been my only deal for '87. It made good sense, actually: weed sailing east and cash sailing west. What a great idea! However, considering the high level of risk and the long timeframe that would have been involved, it was rejected. An alternative solution was to approach the only contact I still had in America who I could trust with such a deal — my old buddy, Ed Seltzer.

Ed was indeed by this time a very trusted and wise friend and very savvy about our business. A plan was hatched for Robert to be introduced to him, with the important caveat that I have no knowledge of their dealings. Should they come to an agreement, I did not want to know about it.

I had spoken with Ed personally to get things rolling, and he was keen. There was a good fee to be earned.

Unfortunately, this was to prove a fateful move that would have disastrous implications. It was a decision I would forever regret.

I DIALED the California number Y.C. had written down and Bob picked up on the first ring.

"Bruce, Ed asked me to call you right away! He said you would need to know immediately. Ed was arrested last night in Reno in an FBI sting as he was attempting to launder over $8million. It was a set-up. Ed told me you don't know anything about it, but you know the people involved."

Pangs of fear raced through my gut as I thanked Bob for the call and asked him to tell Ed I was deeply concerned. I did not know what would happen next. I had hardly given any thought to the introductions I had arranged for. What could have happened? Bob told me it had to do with a fake casino sting in Reno. The news was devastating.

Reno.

A dense black cloud descended over what had been a beautiful day. All I felt was fear.

But when Bob read the list of names of those arrested, my fear turned to deep depression and a feeling of sickness in my heart. Besides Ed and Robert, the list included Tommy Tuttle and David Bose (aka "Benji"), both colleagues of Robert's, a young employee of Brian's who went by the alias "Steve," and William Harris, a supposedly excellent associate of Ed's whom I had never met. And then there was the money that had been seized — Brian's,

Robert's, and who knew who else's! (David Bose, for what it's worth, was a fugitive from the US due to an old case he was wanted for in Texas, and traveled on a fake passport supplied to him by a diplomatic contact of theirs in Chicago.)

All I could say was: "Oh, no, oh, no, OH, NO!" This was bad. I had an instantaneous throbbing headache. However you looked at it, there was no escaping the fact that I had made the introductions.

The Knights of Malta

ED SELTZER had previously told me about his good friend William Harris, aka Sir William. Apparently, they knew each other from the Knights of Malta, an ancient "sovereign order" that even issues its own passports. It's officially called The Sovereign Military Order of Malta and was originally established in 1099.

Unfortunately, it was through this organization that Harris carelessly broadcast his desire for help to launder a large amount of money. A character with a nefarious past took the bite: a fellow "knight" named Joseph Stedino.

Ed's decision to bring Harris into the picture to clean the money for Robert turned out to be one we would all regret. For it so happened that this Stedino was an informant — a snitch for the FBI.

(We would later learn via a private investigation that Stedino's rap sheet included a conviction in 1969 for so-called "white slavery," a line of work associated with prostitution but which Stedino referred to eupemistically as his "real estate" business, as he was dealing with a "patch." For his trouble, he received a $1,000 fine and three years' incarceration.)

The plan cooked up by Ed, Harris and Stedino was to take all the cash to Reno, Nevada, and wash it in a casino. There were several problems with this plan, however. For one, the total volume of cash weighed a ton and had to be counted by hand.

Worse than that, in Reno more FBI spooks were waiting. According to the agency's reports:

"On October 13, 1987, Harris was called by Stedino concerning a legitimate business opportunity. Harris and Stedino had never met before but had mutual acquaintances through the 'Knights.'

"Approximately half an hour after Stedino's initial conversation, Harris called Stedino again and inquired if Stedino had any contacts with Nevada casinos in which to launder up to fifty million dollars in United States currency. Stedino told Harris that he was familiar with a casino executive who could handle such a transaction.

"During this and subsequent conversations, Harris told Stedino that an individual by the name of Ed, later identified as Edward Seltzer, an attorney from Los Angeles, had clients who wished to launder the cash funds. Harris also indicated another person was involved by the name of Bruce, who was from Hong Kong.

"On October 22, Harris and Seltzer traveled to Reno, Nevada, from Los Angeles via PSA Airlines Flight 1627. Stedino introduced them to an FBI agent named Daniel Camillo, who was acting in an undercover capacity and represented himself as a casino executive.

"...Camillo agreed to accept the cash, hiding it among the cash flow of his casino and then using his business accounts to wire it to Europe and Hong Kong.

"As a result of this meeting, it was agreed that the initial transaction would involve the sum of ten million dollars.

"When Harris and Seltzer arrived in Reno and met with Robert and David "B", they delivered what must have weighed in as a ton of cash. The money was taken to Room 352 at the Airport Plaza Hotel where Stedino and Camillo were waiting.

"Upon arrival in the hotel room... and more than 8 hours of solid counting, they decided they had a total of $7,618,570 in US currency. It was 4:00 am, time to stop for a well-earned break. Camillo began to order drinks, but before he was half way to the door, it burst open. Twenty men, some in suits and some in body armor rushed in, guns drawn."

FBI! Everybody's under arrest! Get on the floor!

The 'Kingpin'

THE NEWS of the casino fiasco was devastating, and I knew the ramifications would be terrible. Robert Kimball and Ed Seltzer were in jail in Reno, while Brian had lost a bundle of money and was in great danger.

I was in shock. I could not eat or sleep. I felt sick, and deeply responsible for introducing Seltzer to Kimball. However, I did not know Ed's friend William Harris, and thankfully we had never spoken.

Within a few days, the newspapers were reporting on agent Camillo's success as a phony casino owner. He told them Harris had "cracked like a dried twig" *in his first interview* and given up everything he thought he knew. According to Camillo, Harris told the Feds: "Well, Seltzer, the lawyer guy, he knows this guy by the name of Bruce, in Hong Kong. He used to launder money, but he doesn't do it anymore because he has a bunch of problems in the Far East. He's retired. You know, I think this guy Bruce, he must be the Kingpin."

Meanwhile, a DEA report on the sting stated: "Ever since the Cessna-Milner scandal and Tim's subsequent kidnapping, Brian's name had always been associated with that of Aitken, and the fact that his friend's name was now tied to the money seized in Reno was a massive cause for concern."

That report would later be included in the so-called "discovery" of evidence sent to me in connection with my own indictments. The discovery also included transcripts of taped conversations with informants and co-conspirator "hearsay statements." To wit:

Harris: And Ed, your Chinese guy (in Hong Kong), he's the guy who has done all this stuff before, tell him it's gonna cost him if he is getting anything out of it at all, I don't know.

Stedino: He's not.

Harris: Yeah, that was original talk from the Chinese, from Bruce in China. Obviously, he does not have control of this thing either and is not interested. He's retired from the business.

Stedino: Must be Wednesday, and the delay so far, it's not your fault, Bill, it's Ed's fault. You have done everything you can.

Harris: Well, it wasn't, in a nice way, there wasn't a deal. You know, there was a deal, but it wasn't a deal. The big situation was that somebody from China said, 'I used to do this business, and now our guy is over there who would still like to do it. But I'm not gonna touch it.'

And here's another transcript from Reno, of a conversation involving Ed Seltzer, Stedino and undercover agent Dan Camillo — again about me:

Seltzer: There is a reason because most of these guys have one person handling all their stuff. And that guy is not doing it now. It's a whole new ball game. He's out of business. See for years and years there was one guy that handled all this kind of business. Real funky and he catered to them. And he'd do it a lot cheaper. Uh, not real sophisticated... He could never handle this amount. But he would do one million dollars. For years and years, I would give him money and he wouldn't give me an accounting. Real private banker! And it was worth it. It was great for me. I used him for years, and now he is out of business. I never got an accounting from him. Some guys would keep millions and millions of dollars with him!

Camillo: I don't understand. Where did you meet Bruce?

Seltzer: You won't believe it. I met Bruce when I was running around Hong Kong, Singapore, trying to figure out how to float a bunch of bread out of Australia, at a time when they had restrictions. I had an appointment with these guys. So, I had appointments with three different people. Some were in Hong Kong, some in Singapore, to float this bread out. I went in there one day, had an appointment, and Bruce was not even there. He had an office in the Wan Chai District — that was built during the war as a whorehouse district, so it's real funky! So I talked to one of his employees, an American guy named Tom. It's like a feeling. I had a quarter of a million in a bag. I said okay, he walks me over to his accountant to set up a company. Everything was just spot on!

Seltzer: It's really hard starting out and I gave them $10 million bucks …about 10 years ago. That's $50 million today. That was Australia money. I gave him all of that money and it really gave him the kind of credit he needed to become substantial. He did very well. And now, he is going out of business and I don't want to see this go by the wayside, this particular deal. So, I said please don't! You know I can find a way!

Stedino: So he is the one who controls Robert — and Robert is all right?

Seltzer: Well, he did, but he's out of the business now.

Stedino: I think I can tell you, I have no greed. Let me ask you a question… if Bruce retired someday?

Seltzer: No, no.

Stedino: He'll always be in it?

Seltzer: Yeah, but he, well…he's got to get his. I have to make sure he gets his. That's my friend. It's like buying his business. [...] I'm getting wacky counting this damn money! Oh boy, I'm getting tired.

Stedino: I counted $2 million in 45 minutes; I'm faster than a fart!

Seltzer: I'm getting slap happy. Need some coffee… run the count!

Hunters and hunted

THE STING in Reno had highlighted the unpleasant fact that snitches were always lurking somewhere in the shadows, ready to rat out anyone for a few gold coins.

These individuals, who were about to make life extremely difficult for lots of us, were at the time also laying their baits in the red-light districts of Bangkok, right among the crème de la crème of my clients and the region's most active weed dealers.

Remember rule number one in Nicholas Deak's Blue Book, the "bible" of our operation, and of the free market money exchange business? Yes: "know your client!" But that's with the corollary that in some cases it is best not to know too much. This was precisely the situation that existed in regard to the Reno disaster, and indeed through much of the swinging '80s.

At the time of the Reno saga, even though I had started winding FFS down, there were over 200 accounts held in the company, all based on trust and with signed confidentiality agreements. I was looking after other people's money to the tune of $30–40 million on deposit at any one time. That was a heck of a lot of money in the early '80s. And the six or seven largest accounts were in the "know your clients but best not to know too much" category.

Simultaneously, the situation for my trade was being transformed rapidly under new American regulations that would have global ramifications. Cash reporting requirements — especially the Money Laundering Control Act of 1986 — changed the game completely. Once the US enacted laws requiring banks and financial institutions to report cash transactions over $5,000, money laundering became the focal point of criminal investigations everywhere. I never thought such a law would pass in America, but was I wrong!

In one swift stroke, a very important freedom of the individual — that of financial privacy — was completely trashed in the name of the government's sudden War on Drugs.

Of course, this law did not apply to other countries. And in a place like Hong Kong, the effect was in fact just the opposite — it magnified the city's status as the ideal place to deposit cash and park your money.

I knew my clientele. I liked them all, I knew the business activities they were engaged in , and I continued to feel no hesitation in looking after their affairs. No question, however, the heat around them was growing.

As I explained before, Bangkok was a hotbed of risqué bars and massage parlors and a place filled with both hunters and hunted. And this was especially true of a place called the Club Superstar, in Patpong. The hunted were composed of life-loving characters from all corners of the world, all looking to make their fortunes from smuggling weed. Many of these people would become well-known to the DEA, including my friend Brian (who — next to Howard Marks and some other characters — was by this time becoming one of the most powerful figures in weed smuggling globally and had done much to revolutionize the industry in terms of growing, harvesting and packaging the stuff), an American named Robert Lietzman, the Shaffer brothers (William and Chris), Englishman Michael Forwell, a jovial local supplier known as Tony the Thai, and various others who were my good friends and clients, all the cream of the crop.

But even among friends, scumbags were lurking. A partner of Brian's named Phil Christensen, whose name I introduced in chapter 12 and again in chapter 19, alongside Jack Corman (who I introduced as a DEA informant in chapter 11), had succumbed or would succumb — and flip to the other side. They became super-snitches. Yes, these were the same guys who were responsible for the sad demise of my former employee Tom O'Donnell, as related earlier.

(Chalk one up to the smugglers, though. While I was desperately trying to chill out in the wake of everything I'd learned about the Reno disaster, two separate shipments at sea were being compromised by the incessant stream of information now leaking to the DEA — but the knowledge of that stream allowed the ring to outsmart its hunters. In an amazing "reverse sting," they were able to seed out false information, via the snitches, about a smuggling vessel at sea, the *Stormbird*. When the DEA tried to seize that ship, they discovered its cargo was gone: it had been off-loaded to a local fishing vessel and landed right under the noses of the Vancouver authorities. The ring had lived up to all expectations and the only way ahead was up, up, up!)

As for myself, I had no more appetite for excitement. But trouble was always waiting like a cat ready to pounce. I had an unbidden sense of foreboding. A lot of cash was about to be generated that would need to be washed by someone, but not by me.

CHAPTER 21

Grievous encounters

BRIAN STAYED 100% true to his values, providing the best legal assistance to his people who had been busted in Reno. At the same time, he was pressuring Tom Sherrett — a partner so careful and professional that he had remained off the DEA radar until now — for a cash injection, on account of money that Tom owed him. He was confident that Robert Kimball would also do the best he could to raise cash, in spite of the fact that he was incarcerated. Robert was as honest as they come and would ensure Brian received any money he had been promised.

Meanwhile, a huge new scheme was brewing. Brian had teamed up with a group of other successful weed dealers in Bangkok — the Colflesh brothers, Sam and Robert, and their partner, Michael Forwell, who we met in the last chapter — to do "the big one." The plan was to make one big smuggling run on a ship called *Encounter Bay*.

In fact, this turned out to be a key moment in the history of Thai weed smuggling, with successful and experienced smugglers teaming up for the first time to handle the "mother of all loads" from Southeast Asia to America. This was the load that was supposed to clear everyone's slates and allow them to retire.

Michael Forwell happened to be sitting on heaps of cash, and therefore bought *Encounter Bay,* a large and powerful oil rig server, for $3.5 million. Brian was to purchase the weed from Laos, then pack and transport it across Vietnam for loading near Danang, where small boats would meet *Encounter Bay*. By these means, the biggest import in history, valued at about $100 million, was about to get under way. Tom Sherrett was invited to participate, but declined, saying it was crazy. Of course it was crazy.

Super-snitches Jack Corman and Phil Christensen were also very busy at this juncture. Brian had been friends with them for many years, and had no reason not to trust and confide in them. But the nature of betrayal involves stopping at nothing to save one's own skin. Maybe it all stems from a fear of spending time in prison. To me, it speaks of a supreme form of weakness that can be summed up in one word: cowardice.

Corman had gotten himself caught in a minor case of smuggling cocaine into Florida years earlier. To save himself he instantly repented and decided to devote the rest of his life to setting up and entrapping colleagues and friends, for and on behalf of the government. To be a good snitch, a person has to be willing to "do the crime but not the time." The DEA realized they had a pit bull on their team: wired, frothing at the mouth, always ready to prove his worth. Poor Jack.

Christensen, for his part, would brag in interviews about his military experience and daring raids behind the lines in Vietnam, Laos and Cambodia, although by his own admission his actual duties were clerical rather than heroic. He denied that he began snitching to the government because of pending criminal charges. "I realized it was time to get out of the business." More likely, since he was Corman's partner, he had no choice — otherwise Corman would have soon been snitching on *him*.

Brian really needed to recover the funds that had been seized during the Reno fiasco, and his attempts to do so were what allowed the snitches to rope him in. On January 26, 1988, Corman met with Brian at the Beer House German Restaurant in Bangkok to discuss the traffic of Thai marijuana. According to agency records, Brian brought up the seizure of $7.5 million dollars in Reno. He said he was presently trying to retrieve up to $22 million from US operations, and also expressed interest in developing a new laundering system. For the past two or three years, he said, he had shipped all his marijuana out of Danang, and that he presently had 100 tons of it under his management. Brian would also be interested in a joint deal with Corman. Christensen, Corman said, had just the right fellows waiting and willing to help Brian collect his funds in America, two pit bull collectors. These fellows, Jim Robertson and Bill Bartelucci, were in fact both agents from the Miami DEA office.

According to a DEA report from February 1988:

"Corman and Christensen met with Brian on numerous occasions. During the course of these meetings, Brian related that he presently had $15-22 million dollars in cash in the US that he wanted to collect and move to Hong Kong to be under the control of Bruce Aitken.

"He stated that transportation of the marijuana will be provided by Bob and Sam Colflesh, two brothers who own the Superstar Bar, Soi Patpong, Bangkok.

"He also stated that he provided 42 tons of marijuana sent to the US which he split with Christopher and William Shaffer. Robert Kimball was to collect the money and arrange to send the money to Bruce Aitken in Hong Kong. He stated that he presently has at least $15 million US dollars in the US he is unable to move to Hong Kong. He requested Corman to bring his financial experts to Bangkok for a meeting to explain the methods of money transfer to Hong Kong.

"On February 11th, both informants met with Brian and Tom Sherrett. Sherrett related that two of the defendants in the Reno case had begun to cooperate with the government, and that 'it was only a matter of time before Brian and Aitken were implicated.'"

The government's plan to nail Brian and collect his money was taking hold. With incredible audacity, the two agents (Robertson and Bartelucci), at Brian's behest, actually met Robert Kimball — in Nevada State Prison, on February 15 — without the presence or permission of his attorney, Jack Hill. This was a clear violation of his constitutional rights. When Hill found out who these guys were, he was furious. What's more, to gain Brian's confidence, $6 million had already been collected from Tom Sherrett in Portland by the agents, who could have arrested him on the spot except that it would have blown their plan to lure Brian to out of Thailand and apprehend him. Tom Sherrett suspected (correctly) that he had just handed over the money to the government, and decided to immediately flee. After he left, they actually searched his house. Apparently he'd packed out in such a rush that he left a receipt for repair of his motor yacht, the *Lloyd B. Gore*, $277,000 in cash, two pounds of pot, and various sales records. (These receipts and records would be picked up by a sharp-eyed prosecutor in Seattle, Peter Mueller — more of whom in due course).

The Encounter Bay bust

WHEN *Encounter Bay* set its course towards the United States on a summer's day in 1988, the team from Bangkok's Superstar Bar were sailing into a trap. Not only did the group of smugglers include an informant for the DEA, but when the ship neared the west coast of the US, the authorities were waiting.

As the vessel approached land, on June 28, 1988, the US Coast Guard's 378-foot cutter, *Boutwell*, intercepted it. Sam Colflesh, who was piloting, refused to respond to the Coast Guard's radio and public address system orders to stop and prepare to be boarded. At which point, the Coast Guard opened fire. Eventually, after being peppered with .50 caliber machine gun rounds and five-inch cannon fire, the boat was disabled and boarded.

The Coast Guard discovered some 70 tons of high grade marijuana on board, at the time worth an estimated $200 million on the wholesale market and $400 million on the street, according to different media sources. The Coast Guard needed nine large trucks to carry the boat's illegal load away and it took five days to burn it.

The DEA's path to nailing Brian was now clear, once they'd lured him out of Thailand.

All the while, a steady stream of communications was taking place between the agents and the informants. Agent Conklin reported that Brian expected to come to America to spearhead the collection of up to $30 million, with the help of Robertson and Bartelucci. Dennis Cameron, FBI Reno, reported that the DEA "noose was tightening, the warrant was ready and just needed to be signed…once signed that will seal it."

The DEA Plans were in fact two-fold. They knew that Brian was going to Switzerland for medical treatment on his leg. Thereafter, he planned to go on to America, to collect his cash. The plan that Corman proposed to Brian was that he, Corman, would meet him in Toronto, Canada, and that he would arrange a small plane to fly Brian undetected on a short flight across the border into the USA.

Brian departed for Zurich on July 4, 1988. The day before, Robertson and Bartelucci arrived in Zurich to see Brian and discuss his trip to the US. At the same time, though, the DEA "chatter" was all about preparing another option — they were ready to "fire up" a Lear Jet that had been confiscated from the smuggling fraternity in Miami and have it ready to go wherever it was required, just in case Brian hesitated when he got to Zurich. Why? They were suddenly anxious because I had made a lightning trip to Bangkok, just prior to Brian's departure, during which I'd informed him about what Mike Brennan — Tom O'Donnell's former partner — had told me: that Corman was a DEA snitch. This, added to the fact that I'd faxed an *IHT* article to Brian about the DEA's "Operation Pisces" money laundering sting operation — and that Brian had told Corman about both my encounter with Brennan and the article — caused them great concern. They were nervous about Brian having a sudden change of heart and deciding not to go to the States. I believe this is exactly what did happen, and consequently the FBI had Interpol arrest him at his hotel in Zurich.

I had thrown a big spanner in the works of their plan, which I believe had been to arrest Brian after his arrival in the USA, but not until after he had led them to all the millions. I also believe the DEA's and the FBI's daggers were drawn for me in full force from this time onward.

One year later, he was sentenced to 25 years in jail, while the Colflesh twins received sentences of 10 years each. *The New York Times* wrote at the time: "[Brian Daniels] has admitted masterminding some of the biggest marijuana shipments from Southeast Asia to the United States from 1984 to 1988. Among them was the shipment of 72 tons of high-grade Laotian marijuana seized in June 1988 aboard the *Encounter Bay*, an oil-supply vessel, off the Washington coast."

For my part, I had been indicted as a "co-conspirator" in connection to the weed smuggling fraternity, as my name had repeatedly come up in conversations recorded by the snitches. It seemed like only a matter of time before I was truly implicated.

I regretted having stuck my neck out way too far. There was so much activity swirling around me, and I had zero control. I just wanted to wake up and find that this had all been a bad dream, especially for all of my good buddies now behind bars.

The sting at FFS

JUST MONTHS before the siege of the *Encounter Bay*, Jack Corman and the DEA had in fact tried to put the noose around my neck. The date was March 31, 1988 — the last day of business before the long Easter weekend, and prior to the late-night meeting I had with Brennan. It was also a day when — my mind being wholly occupied with other mind-bogglingly serious concerns — a single careless transaction at my office would have a major impact on my life.

I had left for work early in the morning, meaning I missed the telephone call to my home. As I would later read from the tape transcripts, my son Matt picked the phone up at my home in Stanley Village, on the lovely south side of Hong Kong Island. It was the snitch calling.

Matt: *Hello, hello, hello?*
Corman: *Can I speak to Bruce? Is he home?*
Matt: *No, who is calling?*
Corman: *My name is Jack. I am his friend.*
Matt: *You are my daddy's friend?*
Corman: *Yes, is he home?*
Matt: *No…you don't sound like my daddy's friend. You sound like a girl!* (Matt's laughter)
Matt: *No, my daddy went to the office. Good-bye!* (Matt laughs and hangs up.)

Brian had been asking me to please help him to move some money for Corman. One part of me wanted to help Brian as a brother; the other part of me wanted to avoid the whole damn thing because I had a strong negative feeling about Corman. He was one of the few people I'd ever disliked from the moment I set eyes on him.

With these thoughts on my mind, I sensed trouble; I therefore intentionally lingered at the nearby coffee shop so I would arrive at my office late.

It must have been after 11am when I got there. My receptionist, Patty Wong, immediately handed me a bunch of messages. There were more than half a dozen calls from Corman.

I called a meeting of my staff and explained to them that I greatly distrusted Corman. Whatever his request or purpose, we would have to deflect him in such a way that would not make him suspicious.

As I was settling in at my desk, Patty came in and announced that Corman, despite being told I was not in, was now sitting waiting for me in reception. I let him come into my office. He asked me if I'd had any word from Brian to receive, and then transfer back to him, $500,000. I truthfully said I knew nothing about it and was just about to show him the door when fate intervened.

Patty knocked and entered my office. "Bruce, Brian is calling on your direct line and says it is very urgent!"

Shit. Here was Corman, Brian's so-called partner, sitting right in front of me. In another two minutes I would have had him out the door.

Brian asked me to please do him this last favor — to receive the funds from Corman and transfer them to Bangkok via our accustomed same-day underground banking method, all before the five-day weekend.

I was caught between a rock and a hard place, but my gut feeling made me decide against doing what was being asked of me. I decided to call Brian back later and find another way to help him.

Corman left. I had indicated to him I would have to receive the funds before 2pm, which I knew would be next to impossible. Then I immediately instructed my staff, my accountant Y.C., and Patty, that under no circumstances were they to take any money that came from Corman. I told them to tell him it could only be handled by me personally. As for me, I would not be back until 6pm — when it would be too late to do anything.

Turns out I was wrong about them not being able to meet the deadline. Here's how things went down after special Agent Henry Morgan of the DEA in Hong Kong, and Jack Corman, delivered the money to my office at around 2pm.

"At approximately 6:30pm, Corman called Aitken at FFS. The call was recorded. Aitken said that he was expecting to hear from Corman earlier so that in case Aitken couldn't process the money he could give it back. Corman suggested that the problem was with Brian. Aitken said that he was 'not involved' in any way, shape or form. 'This was just dropped on me, it took my accountants a couple of hours to clarify it…I am not in the picture in any way, shape, or form whatsoever, I have no facilities.' Aitken went on to say that through his staff the money got taken care of."

As I was in the process of closing down my business and harbored deep suspicions of Corman, I had decided to have nothing to do with this transaction. Consequently, I had purposely left the office and returned after closing hours. To my horror, however, my accountant — knowing Brian to be my good, long-time friend, being conscientious to provide a good service, and having made similar transfers many times in the past — received Corman's $500,000 cash, and made the transfer to Bangkok.

This single transaction was to later become the sole basis for an indictment against me in Seattle, Washington, one which would eventually pit my wits against a fascistic prosecutor there. In reality, it clearly appears to me that this transaction was a case of government entrapment. The $500,000 was laundered for Brian by the government and came from an account maintained in Hong Kong by the DEA!

The Feds were now in fast-action mode, and most of the action stemmed from the Reagan administration's attempt to end the drug menace by establishing a $200 million Federal narcotics task force. They had the resources to go after non-violent hippie pot smugglers by infiltrating their plans with low-life snitches and fake money launderers.

As mentioned, it was just a month after Jack Corman and the DEA had planted the $500,000 transaction with my office that Mike Brennan warned me Corman was a snitch.

The walls were closing in. Growing suspicions of snitches in our inner circle and the aftershocks of the Reno sting and the siege of *Encounter Bay* were all just too much to bear.

I was sorely in need of a vacation. Everything that was happening and the dangers it imposed on all of us were making me sick. Getting away with Jenny and the boys to Phuket, Thailand, was just what the doctor ordered. My rest, however, would be short lived.

The nightmare saga of 'The United States of America vs. Bruce Aitken' was soon to begin. I just didn't know it yet.

Blow by blow

AS WE have seen, Special Agent Henry Morgan (DEA Hong Kong) and Jack "The Rat" Corman, delivered $500,000 in US currency to the offices of First Financial Services Ltd on March 31, 1988. Here's exactly how the DEA reported their little operation.

"Corman attempted to call Bruce Aitken at the offices of First Financial Services, and at his residence. After several attempts, he contacted Aitken at First Financial at approximately

11:45 AM. Corman told Aitken that he needed to talk to Aitken. Aitken said that he had an appointment for lunch at 12 noon. The above telephone calls were recorded by Corman.

"At approximately noon, Corman met Aitken at the offices of FFS. The conversation was recorded per Operation Pisces standing authorization. He asked Aitken if Brian has explained what he needed from Aitken. Aitken said that he hadn't heard anything. He then started to explain to Aitken about being told by Brian to deliver $500,000 to Aitken. He said that Brian had originally wanted the money to go into an account but he had changed his mind and now urgently needed $500,000 in cash given to Aitken who in turn was to transfer the money to the 'PK 1' account which he presumed was to Vasu Carving in Bangkok. He asked Aitken if he had until 5:00 pm to get the cash to him. Aitken said that 5:00 pm would be much too late.

"Aitken told Corman that 2:00 pm cut-off time was necessary because March 31st would be the last business day until April 5th due to Easter holidays and local holidays. Aitken said a certified check was not feasible because he had closed all his bank accounts.

"Brian then called from Thailand and talked to Aitken… Aitken told him the constraints of the situation and that he would try, but he might not be able to do anything. He then talked to Corman briefly before talking to Aitken again. Aitken hung up the phone a few minutes later. Corman then left the FFS offices at approximately 12:15 PM after telling Aitken that he would bring back as much money as he was able at 2:00 pm.

"At approximately 2:00 pm SA Henry Morgan and SWA went to SECURITY PACIFIC BANK, 6 Des Voeux Road, Central, Hong Kong and met Mr. William Chan, the VP and Manager of the bank. SA Morgan then withdrew $500,000 from account 631-0002798-01 and put the currency in a briefcase. Under the surveillance of Investigative Aide, Teddy So, Corman and SA Morgan then walked to the offices of FFS arriving approximately 2:30 PM.

"Corman and SA Morgan were then told that Aitken had not returned from lunch and that they were very late. Corman and SA Morgan went into Aitken's office and took the $500,000 out of the briefcase and put it on Aitken's desk. After a cursory count by a Chinese male staff, he asked Corman if he would call back in 30 minutes to make sure everything was all right with the money. SA Morgan then asked for a business card. The staff refused to give one out, saying that this transaction was being done through 'Bruce.'"

CHAPTER 22

Trouble in paradise

WE LOVED STAYING at the Kata Thani, a little resort at Kata Beach on Phuket, a part of Thailand known as "James Bond Island" on account of one of the famous movies having been filmed there. It felt like a genuine retreat; but unfortunately there's no outrunning bad news wherever you escape to.

It was 6am on a day in late July and I awoke to a tropical morning breeze softly tossing the palm trees outside our cottage. A shadow from the fading moonlight danced across the ceiling as night turned into day.

It felt so good just to be on a holiday with my family. I had become worried about so many things, and my life had slipped into chaos. Part of my angst stemmed from knowing that, while events were beyond my control, I should have been wise enough to see trouble approaching.

As I practiced tai chi outside to clear my head, I heard the phone ring. It was strange that anyone should call so early, and certainly no-one in Hong Kong knew where we were. I listened to Jenny speaking in her usual friendly voice.

Then she stopped talking.

I waited for her to hang up, and when she opened the door, I could see a look of shock on her face.

"Tim Milner just called. He is on the way over. He said to get today's *Bangkok Post* and read the front-page headline. He wanted you to know that Brian was arrested in Zurich yesterday."

Sweat started to pour down my face; everything about me sank, and a chill ran up my spine. I was intensely sick to my stomach because I knew that life would never be the same. Through my mental fog, I heard Jenny: "Bruce..."

Tim arrived within the hour with a copy of the *Bangkok Post* in hand. My heart sank even further. Brian stood accused of being the kingpin mastermind in a 72-ton shipment of Thai marijuana to Seattle. I remembered the writing I'd seen on the wall the last time I saw Brian — just days before his departure.

"Bruce..." I heard Tim call my name as I finished reading the article in the newspaper. "This is big trouble." Yes, big trouble ahead. No way around it.

I turned to Jenny. "Let's pack up and get back to Hong Kong; we'll deal with whatever happens from there."

I had pretty much wound up First Financial Services and, what's more, I hadn't broken any laws I was aware of in Hong Kong. Therefore, although scared within, I thought I had nothing to worry about. *Right?*

It was early afternoon, as we were getting ready to check out of the Kata Thani, when the phone rang again. This time it was Maria, Jenny's sister in Hong Kong. The Hong Kong police had raided my office and my flat, and had taken all of my records. *All my records? Oh shit!* That meant the records of over 200 FFS clients, all of them under confidentiality agreements.

In a panic to protect my clients, I made a decision: I needed to destroy all the records I kept in storage. I asked Maria to make the necessary phone calls. This decision would later result in serious repercussions.

By the time we had flown from Phuket to Bangkok, we'd decided it would be best for Jenny and the boys to fly back to Hong Kong on their own because I had no idea what was going to happen next. If I returned to Hong Kong, surely I would be arrested. I needed to figure out where I stood.

Alone and adrift

CONSUMED BY a whirlwind of paranoia, I suddenly had another concern — my trusty golf bag. When I imagined it being taken or opened, I felt incredibly sad, and a eulogy flashed through my mind: "Old Faithful, R.I.P." I needed to dispose of it as fast as possible, toss it in a dumpster somewhere as soon as I got back to Hong Kong.

After the family departed, I walked from the international departure terminal to the domestic terminal, took a flight to Songkla in the south of Thailand, and checked into the Florida Hotel. By chance, I befriended a couple of Malaysian fellows who were driving to Penang in neighboring Malaysia the following day. This was a stroke of luck. They invited me to join them, and I quickly figured it would be much easier to cross the border in a private car than on the bus. The night before our planned trip, I assessed my situation.

I had been winding up First Financial for the past year. The "best" accounts I had carried over from Deak were in the export business — the business of exporting Thai weed, that is. My relationships with these exporters had started out innocently enough, and as most of them were naturally friendly people, we got along well — we became friends. I'd also organized my business so no laws were broken — in Hong Kong, at least. Having signed confidentiality agreements with my clients, I felt no compunction to give out any information about them to anyone under any circumstances; not without their specific authorization. I thought I was covered.

But still, I could not sleep soundly. When I woke early the next morning, my first thoughts were of Jenny and the boys — I dared not call home for fear the phone was tapped. At that moment, I felt very lonely, and I wondered if I had made the right decision in not returning to Hong Kong with my family. Foremost in my mind, of course, had been my sons; I could have been arrested at the airport and I did not want them to witness their dad being humiliated in such a way.

At 8am I was already in the hotel coffee shop waiting for the new friends who had given me a ride. I had left them in the bar the night before, as I was in no mood for music or conversation. Reading the newspaper, though unable to focus, I was well into my third cup of coffee when they appeared, slightly hungover but no worse for wear.

Being Muslim, they confided to me, their occasional business trips to Thailand were the only chance they had to have a few beers and let their hair down.

The border checkpoint leaving Thailand and entering Malaysia was only a few kilometers away; but on the way, I perceived my new friends were suddenly concerned about my presence. I sensed they felt there was something strange about my leaving Thailand this way, and I could feel their eyes on me as I handed my passport to the immigration officer. The official took longer than usual to check the computer, then glanced at my picture, stamped my passport and returned it to me.

Driving over the big bridge to Penang, I felt a temporary sense of relief. I soon found myself waving good-bye to my companions at the train station as I boarded the train to Kuala Lumpur. As planned, on arrival I checked into a cheap hotel just before midnight and called a friend's mobile phone that Jenny had arranged to borrow.

To my great relief, she answered the phone. She had arrived home safely with the boys. However, the police had called first thing in the morning and asked both her and Maria to come to the Wan Chai Police Station at 10am. They were asked about my whereabouts, then arrested on suspicion of destroying business records before the statutory time limitation, and had to post bonds of HK$5,000 each.

Jenny said the police seemed like they could hardly be bothered with any of this, except that the request had come from the United States. They made it clear I was the only person they were after.

"Where is your husband and why did he not return to Hong Kong with you?" they had asked. "Did you know that your premises had been searched?"

Jenny said she had no idea about any of it, and that I had continued on a business trip. They said to give them a call when she knew I would be flying back to Hong Kong.

The next day, I took a flight from KL to Kota Kinabalu in Eastern Malaysia, and a few days later took another flight on to Manila, where I had many friends. From the Philippines, I could contact the lawyers involved in the case, men like Robert Kimball's lawyer, Jack Hill. I had to find out what was happening with Brian. And I certainly needed to get some good advice myself.

Due to my total breakdown of any kind of routine, living in small hotels and out of a suitcase, the days in Manila passed slowly. It became difficult to think clearly. I had no appetite. I could not sleep.

After two weeks, Jack Hill said he was in Hong Kong and wanted to see me, along with my newly appointed Hong Kong barrister, Gary Alderdice. They came to see me and both encouraged me to return to Hong Kong as soon as possible. However, I wanted to know more from America first.

The stifling heat in Manila was getting to me. I flew on to Taipei, Taiwan, and checked into a small hotel about one block from the Taipei Hilton, where I had stayed in better times.

By this time, the news had been delivered to me that I had been indicted over the money-laundering fiasco in Reno. A deep depression set in over the following few days as I tried to think. I could stay in Taiwan, of course, out of the reach of America, because the two territories didn't (and still don't) have an extradition treaty. My purpose was not to avoid the problem, but to deal with it from a position of strength.

I felt I had the law on my side, because while the horrendous US indictments charged me with many counts, there was only one — conspiracy to import drugs — on which they could extradite me from Hong Kong, and I was sure they would have to *drop* that charge because there was no case. All the other charges were completely toothless because no such "money-laundering" crimes *existed* in civilized Hong Kong. My conclusion: All I had to do was stay away from America while the case was dealt with in my absence.

Still, anyone who has been indicted knows the feeling of being up against Goliath, and the tremendous weight, which feels like that of the whole world, that suddenly lands on your shoulders. You have to make a choice. You can give up or you can fight like David. I thought of my beautiful family and how blessed I was. I thought of my business. I thought of my stupidity and foolishness. I wondered if I ever would be able to return to the blessed life I had made and had thrown away. Belatedly, very belatedly, I started to pray.

Fuel to the fire

BUT MORE bad news came, and from a very unlikely place.

The last thing I needed was more publicity, or for the ancient Cessna-Milner Affair to be resurrected and regurgitated, but suddenly there it was again, described in excruciatingly minute detail.

The headline on the story published in *The Sydney Morning Herald* on August 29, 1988 hit me like a slap on the face: "Cessna-Milner's Money Mover Raided."

The story read:

"The Hong Kong offices of Bruce Aitken — the American 'mystery-money-mover' in the controversial Cessna-Milner drug affair — have been raided at the request of the US Drug Enforcement Administration (DEA). It is understood that they were part of continuing investigations into one of two major drug syndicates uncovered by the DEA in recent weeks. Although the recent DEA activity is not related directly to the Cessna-Milner case, it might inadvertently prove to be the catalyst for yet another investigation of the nine-year-old affair..."

The paper's extensive report was like a who's who of my personal network. It rehashed and made current lots of information about the past and about my relationships with several account holders at the previously-esteemed FFS.

The report exposed my associations not only with regard to the Cessna-Milner affair but also Howard Marks, Sydney solicitor Morgan Ryan, Tim Milner's kidnapping, and of course Deak & Company — which, readers were reminded, had been identified as a money-laundering organization by the US President's Commission on Organized Crime, in 1984, and was found to have laundered cash for Nugan Hand bank by the the Costigan Royal Commission. Last but not least, it dredged up my brush with the law over the A$60,000 found in my car in 1980.

Messenger boy

IN THE shadows of all this stink lingered one name — Jack Corman.

Corman was the mongrel of a dog who had come to my office on many occasions and tried to entrap me. The first time he came to my office, he was introduced to me by Andy Rogers, an art dealer out of Nepal and Bangkok. Nice work, Andy!

I decided to give ole' Andy a call.

All I said was his name: "Andy." I could immediately hear the surprise in his voice.

"Bruce!" he shouted. "Where are you and how are you? Everyone is concerned about you!"

"Well, Andy (*you arsehole*), you should know why I am calling."

To make a long story short, Andy agreed to fly to Taipei and meet with me to discuss something very important that he could not discuss on the phone — provided I paid his expenses. (Seriously?)

Two nights after the call, I was waiting for him in the lobby of the Taipei Hilton. To make sure he was alone, I stayed at a distance and watched him checking in. Then I startled him by coming up behind him. "Hey you, what is your room number?"

"Bruce," he said, "Shit, you look so thin!"

No kidding? I was down to 140 pounds.

Over the next few hours, Andy would repeatedly express what a great guy Jack Corman was and how he did not know he had been working for the DEA.

So, let me see now just what a great man we were talking about: a cowardly low-life super-snitch who'd set up Brian, my partner Tom, and so many more. Oh yes, Jack was a wonder, all right.

"Get to the point, Andy."

"Well, Jack has a message for you."

The message went something like this:

"*Listen, Bruce, the government knows that you were not a major figure in all of this, and that you had nothing whatsoever to do with drugs. In fact, they are not really very interested in you at all. What they are interested in is your money-laundering expertise, and since you handled so much money that was drug-related, just cooperate and tell them where it all is.*"

Really? All I had to do was give Jack the nod and he would do the rest? In a matter of days, I could return to Hong Kong, meet with the DEA and work out a deal, just like he had, to *roll over on all my friends* and help the DEA set up more stings. Gee, what a deal: roll over on all these good people and then live the rest of my life feeling like a rat!

I laughed out loud.

"Andy, tell Jack, that no-good, low life chicken-shit bastard, to drop dead!"

I could, of course, now clearly hear, taste, see and smell the approaching tsunami.

———— ❧ ————

WHAT TRULY motivated Corman was anyone's guess, but another of his attempts at entrapment illustrates just what a low-life he really was. God knows why, but it seems he just couldn't get enough scalps.

Remember my friend Rakesh Saxena, the Indian financier who single-handedly destroyed the Bangkok Bank of Commerce and caused the collapse of the Asian financial system in 1997?

One Sunday, a couple of years later, Rakesh told me an astonishing story over a couple of drinks.

His wife, Suvanna, had a brother who had become embroiled in some nefarious activities after meeting an American in a bar in Bangkok's red-light district one night.

This American claimed to be very successful in shipping multi-ton loads of high-quality Thai marijuana sticks to the West Coast of America. He and his associates needed an investor for the next load, and asked if Suvanna's brother would be interested. He was.

For an investment of $100,000, he was promised a return of ten times that amount. The meeting to commit to the deal and hand off the money was scheduled for the very next night.

"What's the name of the American?" I asked Rakesh. "I'll check it out for you."

"Great!" he said. "His name is Jack Corman."

"What did you say?! *Jack Corman*? Holy shit, Rakesh! You have to tell your brother-in-law to pull out of the deal immediately! Corman is the number one DEA super-snitch!"

"Oh no!" Rakesh's jaw dropped.

I could not believe Corman was *still* out and about setting traps. That guy really got around! In a state of shock, Rakesh called Suvanna into the room and she immediately called her brother. He did not believe what I told him. "No, impossible!"

He said he had been to the bank earlier that day. He'd completed the withdrawal of his life savings, sold his stocks and converted it all into cash on the black market. The money was now sitting in his briefcase.

Luckily, there was time enough to call the deal off. I returned to Hong Kong and faxed Rakesh a copy of the Florida indictment against Corman that I mentioned earlier and which had by now come into my possession.

When I met Suvanna's brother on a later trip to Bangkok, he thanked me profusely, and even tried to offer me a reward. My reward and his was to keep him from being set up in a sting and spending the next 20 years in prison.

As to how he'd gotten out of the deal, at first he told Corman he was having trouble raising the money. A week passed and Corman followed up again, pressing him insistently. This time Suvanna's brother stated frankly that he had, regrettably, changed his mind. He'd decided he did not want to start in the dope business after all. He did not want the risk of spending his life in jail. It was, altogether, a very narrow escape for him.

CHAPTER 23

The nightmare unfolds

AFTER THE BUST in Reno and the events that followed it, it was apparent to me that I was in a great deal of trouble. Exiled to Taiwan, one thing was clear: I needed a good lawyer. What I really couldn't tell was what exactly in God's name had happened in Reno. I had no idea who had done or said what, or even what passed between Robert Kimball and Ed Seltzer after I had arranged for them to be introduced. I had to assume worst-case scenario in all respects. I felt like the Sword of Damocles was hanging over my head.

I already had Gary Alderdice in my corner, but Kimball's attorney, Jack Hill, now put me in touch with a colleague of his who happened to be in Hong Kong at the time and staying at the Regent Hotel in Kowloon. "Marcus," whose surname I will omit here for reasons that should become clear enough, came from San Francisco and was a very sharp fellow. I took an instant liking to him. Marcus had spunk, and I felt he was a fighter who would clearly make a good defense attorney if I should need one. In early 1988, I needed one.

I placed Marcus on a $50,000 retainer and asked him to monitor the Reno situation and keep me apprised. This he did very well, and as events unfolded he assured me that he had a close, communicative relationship with both the prosecuting US Attorney in the Reno case, and US Attorney Jeff Russell in San Francisco. This gave me quite a bit of comfort.

My occupation had suddenly become self-survival, and it was a full-time job. Not being a believer in keeping lots of paperwork, preferring to do business on a handshake with people who had complete faith in me, and of course my haste to have documents shredded when I heard of Brian's arrest — this all meant my records were pretty basic. I'd made sure all the numbers were correct for audits, but there were sleeping devils in the details, or rather in the lack of details.

First Financial Services Ltd. was now exposed for the whole world to see, and its methods had to be justified under the law. Fortunately, I had done my groundwork in that regard: when I set up the business I had hired a top international law firm in Hong Kong to organize my business so that it could stand up to all legal scrutiny, at least in Hong Kong.

My first task was to detail the whole FFS operation, and to take Marcus through the processes I used for all types of transactions. Glass Radcliffe & Co Ltd, my auditor, needed to prepare all kinds of special opinions and certified copies of everything — client accounts, confirmations, certificates, everything except the rolls of toilet paper.

The list of tasks seemed endless, but the fight was on.

As I had requested in Phuket, Jenny's sister Maria had called our storage company, Crown Pacific, to have all our records from previous years destroyed. Under Hong Kong's companies ordinance, the documents should have been kept longer, and destroying them early turned out to be a big mistake on my part. My motive at the time was simply to protect the confidentiality of my legitimate clientele, just in case the day came when things fell apart. That day was coming at me early.

Fasten your seatbelts

MARCUS SPOKE frankly and did not pull any punches. I liked that in a person, especially a defense lawyer. I recall phoning him one day and discovering he had gone for a walk by the ocean that morning so he could think about how to fight our case. That was very comforting, but the thought of going to trial made me feel quite ill. Criminal indictments do not just go away. They are recurring nightmares.

When he came to see me in Taipei, along with Alderdice, Marcus informed me that we had some major evidentiary problems:

1. The $500,000 transaction that had occurred in my office.
2. The hearsay tapes of conversations in Reno between Harris, Ed Seltzer and the informants.
3. A newspaper article I had read describing the DEA's "Operation Pisces" in Miami, which involved setting people up by providing entrapment money to be laundered. (This was *exactly* what Jack Corman had arranged for Brian, and as soon as I'd read it, I'd faxed it to Brian. He then brought it to the attention of Corman, who immediately brought it to the attention of the Bangkok DEA.)
4. My trip to Bangkok to tell Brian that Corman was a DEA informant.

5. Hearsay from other informants. The list of defendants and others willing to testify against me seemed to grow bigger by the day.
6. Early destruction of the documents in Hong Kong.

I was not feeling well at all. Alone in Taipei, I was unable to sleep and unable to eat. I missed my family, missed my life and felt like a fugitive. I realized it was time to get back to Hong Kong and face the music there. That is exactly what I did.

I returned to Hong Kong on the evening of October 3, 1988 — and was immediately arrested for the offense of "perverting the course of justice" in relation to the destruction of FFS documents. Alderdice met me at the airport and went with me to the offices of the Commercial Crimes Bureau, where I was initially interviewed "off the record" about my alleged offenses against American law. Even off the record, I refused to make any admissions or statements.

The salient feature of this informal interview was that the Hong Kong police passed on an offer, apparently from the DEA, that they were willing to cut me a deal as far as my involvement was concerned. The Hong Kong police could not give any guarantees, but indicated that if I decided to give the DEA my full assistance and act as a State's witness, in return I might not be required to plead to any charges. In addition, there were suggestions of a possible suspended sentence.

Clearly, the US prosecutors seemed intent on making some kind of offer. However, Marcus, who was by now back in San Francisco, told me not to agree to anything until we were able to discuss the matter in person. And although momentarily comforted by a possible way out, I knew there would be no offer I could possibly accept, for one obvious reason: I was not a snitch.

The strength of my legal position was that I could not be tried on 13 of the 14 counts in the Reno indictment because they were non-extraditable. There were *no* such equivalent "money-laundering" laws in beautiful Hong Kong. *This was my ace in the hole.*

Therefore, I simply had to completely avoid the United States until the Reno case of my co-defendants had been tried or otherwise dealt with. After that happened, the first count against me in the drug conspiracy case would automatically fail because it was total bullshit and the prosecutors knew it. The Hong Kong police were well aware of this too — and consequently were treating me with civility.

Marcus wrote to Alderdice:

"*We have received and read the preliminary police reports in this case. It appears our client's alleged role is strictly limited to currency transactions and in no way involved the possession or sale of illicit drugs. Moreover the only direct contact Mr. Aitken had with the DEA was in a currency transaction of a nature which appears to be legal.*

"All other evidence is in the form of hearsay statements of various persons beliefs regarding Mr. Aitken.

"I note that the drug charge (21 USC. 846) in the indictment as concerns Mr. Aitken relates in substantial part to the disposal of monies generated from the sale of marijuana. My assessment is that the government's evidence is quite thin."

I also spoke to Marcus often by phone and the gist of his position (I kept meticulous notes) was that the government's case remained weak. He stressed that any "provisional warrant" was four to five weeks away, after the prosecutors (I preferred to think of them as my "persecutors") made a planned visit to Hong Kong.

Our strategy would be to move for the dismissal of the drug indictment at that stage.

Bottom line, things were well under control and not all bad. Marcus had spoken to the prosecutors, who had agreed not to do anything immediate about the warrant. They wanted to talk to him after they had heard from the Hong Kong police. What's more, with regard to the Hong Kong documents disposal problem there was no evidence, and it was only a technical charge in any case.

I only had one option — unless I wanted to flee to Borneo or somewhere, or become a snitch for the DEA — and that was to fight.

Marcus was also keen to inform me that he was in close touch, almost on a daily basis, with Jeff Russell, the head US Attorney handling my case. Marcus was hoping to gain more time before a warrant was issued, while also making the case that I was not a bail risk.

My daily consciousness was now totally smothered by the nimbus clouds hanging over my head. I knew there was to be an extradition hearing at some point soon, but I was firm in my mind that I would not give any evidence at it. I would simply state: "On the advice of my counsel, I don't wish to say anything at this time; if I am later charged with an offense, I will explain in court."

My instructions from Marcus were exactly as follows: The prosecutor will try to surprise us, so under no circumstances should I agree to be interviewed by anyone. Also, under no circumstances should my wife, Jenny, be interviewed by anyone. Absolutely no exceptions! No provisional warrant had been sent, and none was expected at least for the next 30 days.

In the meantime, we had to wait and see if either Robert or Brian would talk. "Talk about what, Marcus?" I said. "You don't understand. We are all brothers." I was completely at peace.

I had a bit of lucky news, too: Tapes that Jack Corman had clandestinely made in my presence, in Thailand, turned out to be of limited use to the prosecution. At one meeting in Thailand, the recordings were so unintelligible and of such poor quality that the government had simply deemed them worthless.

My position on the tapes was clear: they were *all* worthless. As I told Marcus, they could actually help me because if the government was looking for talk about drugs or money, they wouldn't find it from me.

UNFORTUNATELY, the good news had to swim against a current of more distressing information. According to investigative work being done by a private eye named Jack Palladino, retained by Robert Kimball in support of our cause, I was, in fact, in a perilous position.

Palladino told Alderdice that the count the DEA intended to proceed against me on fell under "Continuing Criminal Enterprise," a law that targets large-scale drug traffickers and is closely related to the RICO (Racketeer Influenced and Corrupt Organization) statutes, whose original intent was to thwart the Mafia.

Sickening news if true. It certainly didn't help that differing indications of the DEA's intentions were now flying around. It made matters confusing and disquieting.

Again on a more positive note, Palladino had interviewed both Harris and Seltzer and had copies of their statements, which he said completely exonerated me. Amongst other things, they explained away why — as revealed in the prosecution's evidence — they had used my name.

Sensing that the prosecution wouldn't file their extradition warrant until some time in 1989, Marcus decided to delay coming to see me in Hong Kong until the new year. We resolved that our primary strategy would be to file a major motion in the court in Reno to block the extradition order — but he said not to get my hopes up. He felt it likely I would indeed be extradited and that I would eventually have to fight my case at a trial. He also recommended that when I got to America I should be co-operative in order to go to trial as soon as possible. His estimation was that I could expect the extradition to take place in around July, and that everything might be finished by about September or October.

Then, to my shock, more unwelcome news. It turned out that the DEA and a team of prosecutors had flown to Hong Kong after the Commercial Crimes Bureau had found a cache of 1986 FFS documents which had not been destroyed. That meant the DEA was now inspecting thousands of pages of my business records.

At one point, I was also contacted again by Andy Rogers, the naive fool who first brought Jack Corman to my office. He had another message for me — from none other than Corman.

"Jack still has an open offer to assist you in some way," Andy told me.

I think Jack must have been feeling the heat because by this point everyone knew he was an informant.

Assist me?

"Yes, thanks for the message, Andy. You can tell him what I said before: drop dead!"

AS INTENDED, Marcus finally arrived with various documents — including records of the informants' degenerate pasts and the three garbled tape transcripts. In the one from when Corman visited my office, I respond clearly to his entrapment attempts: "Sorry, I can't help you in America. Because of reporting requirements, that's one country in which I never touch the money".

Unfortunately, however, my relations with Marcus no longer seemed as watertight as they had been. He said something very forceful to the effect that I had to get my finances together *immediately* to cover his fees. Somewhat taken aback, I said I needed to be brought into the picture first. How could he be talking about higher fees until he could produce some evidence of what had been achieved and where I stood? I wanted to know how he had used my $50,000 retainer money. Clearly, I needed to make an intelligent decision about how much further to take things.

Our understanding regarding fees was that the maximum would be a whopping $300,000 plus expenses for "the whole thing," including our worst-case scenario, a trial. We had put a cap on fees for the sake of my family.

Meanwhile, life had to go on somehow.

The Hong Kong police saw me as I was: a businessman. And I needed to get back to work. Upon Alderdice's request, Inspector Chan — after discussion with Chief Inspector Howard — agreed to return my passport. I could keep it and travel any time by giving them 48 hours' notice.

By this time, I had two months at most until the expected July extradition request. I was very aware of the potential danger. But until extradition, I would keep busy and try to carry on with the business trips I had planned.

Little did I realize what was waiting for me when I made my decision to travel on business to Vietnam in the first week of June.

Guy Coombs, my trusted friend and agent from DHL in Manila, had expressed a desire to visit Saigon with me to look into some business opportunities. The idea was that Tim Milner and I would go there first, and report back to him.

Didn't quite happen that way.

CHAPTER 24

Disaster Strikes

AFTER meeting Guy Coombs in Manila, I arrived in Bangkok late in the evening of June 7, 1989, and cleared customs and immigration uneventfully — oblivious to the fact that the United States of America had just revoked my passport.

The next morning, Tim Milner and I found ourselves caught in the usual Bangkok traffic snarl. I had to go to the Vietnam Embassy to collect my visa for our trip to Saigon but the congestion meant we arrived at the Vietnamese Embassy 15 minutes after it had closed for lunch. We decided to return to the Suri Guest House off Soi 38, where we were staying. It was a beautiful sunny day and I was feeling at peace. In fact, I felt great — considering all the problems hanging over my head.

"Hey, Bruce…!"

"Yo, Tim…what's happening?"

"Something very strange," he said. "The car next to us and the one behind us have US Embassy plates. I haven't seen so many Yanks in one place since the Fourth of July."

We laughed, but suddenly I did not feel so good. But why? I had spoken to Marcus just before I'd left Hong Kong and he'd said there was nothing to worry about. I had notified the Hong Kong authorities of my travel plans, as required.

As we approached the guest house, Tim noticed one of the embassy cars pulling into the parking lot of the Ambassador Hotel, across the street. The other car followed close behind.

Stopping at our accommodation, I went straight to my room, No. 22. In less than a minute, however, the phone rang. It was Sompong, the front desk manager.

"Bruce," he said. "Please come down. There are people here to see you."

Returning downstairs a few minutes later, I saw two Thai Special Branch Police. They approached me.

"Is your name Bruce Aitken? Please come with us."

"What's this all about?"

"You entered Thailand last night on a revoked US passport and you are under arrest."

Surely they were joking.

"You must come with us to see the US Embassy officials. After a talk you will probably be back."

This didn't make much sense — because they asked me to bring all of my belongings.

Tim was in a state of shock. I had entered Thailand the night before without a hitch. Not knowing where I was staying, but *somehow* knowing my plans and itinerary, they had staked out the Vietnam Embassy, waiting until I turned up to collect my visa. How did they even recognize me? I can only assume that Jack Corman was in one of the embassy cars, staying out of sight in typical cowardly form.

I sensed I was in big trouble, and shuddered at the thought that the State Department had canceled my passport. I felt a massive sense of outrage and betrayal: after all, a passport is a very personal thing. And as I was to find out, they had revoked it based on two lies: one, that I was a fugitive, and two, that I was a felon.

In a daze, with desperate thoughts whirling through my mind, I hardly noticed that we had entered a Thai immigration compound, where I was taken into a room to await the American officials. I didn't realize it at the time, but this was the beginning of the most difficult ordeal I would ever face, a nightmare becoming skin-crawling reality.

For the next couple of hours, I was left seated at a desk in a large room. Bantering with the Thai police who brought me drinks and offered me cigarettes, I searched around, in vain, for a way to escape.

Enter the DEA

FINALLY, TWO Americans appeared: Jim Conklin, head of the DEA in Thailand and Mike Seamen, who worked for the DEA in Hong Kong.

Conklin handed me some papers to read and said: "You won't like this very much but you are going to the USA on the first flight tomorrow morning."

Over my protests, Conklin said: "It is people like you who manage money that keep the drug dealers in business. Don't you know that the laws changed in 1986? You should have known!"

They left the room with shrugs indicating I had no rights, and a parting shot:

"Have a nice evening." And with that, the Thai police took me to another office.

I was not allowed to have a Thai lawyer. I was not allowed to make a phone call. And I was not allowed to appeal the decision — an act which would have automatically kept me in Thailand for 60 days.

Eventually, the policeman watching me permitted me to make a local call to an American friend living in Bangkok, Mark Schatten.

I asked him to call Jenny in Hong Kong and let her know what had happened. I was by now experiencing both nausea and some unnamable trauma with regard to what was happening. I just couldn't believe the USA would stoop so low for so little; but my sense of outrage nurtured a seed of resistance and endurance, both of which I would ultimately need to counteract the humiliation I would soon be experiencing.

A policeman escorted me downstairs, past a courtyard filled with women and children playing. My heart sank to the floor. I recalled the vision of my own boys as I'd said good-bye to them the morning before, and remembered my hesitation in leaving my family on that beautiful Hong Kong morning.

I had actually felt like canceling the trip, but instead I'd justified leaving. What was there to worry about? It was just a business trip, and my appointments were already set up. I'd be back in a few days.

Now, as I was being transferred to whatever confinement they had waiting for me, all I could see in my mind's eye was Douglas waving good-bye from the second story window of our home, while Matt ran down the driveway waving until I was out of sight. I'd taken our car from Stanley Village to the Star Ferry, where I'd said goodbye to Jenny, and then jumped in a taxi to the airport. As the cab had pulled away, I'd waved back at my wife and thought how pretty she looked, and how fortunate I was to have such a fine woman. My heart was sad that I had drifted away from her and put her through hell during these last few years. We had just started to heal the wounds I had inflicted.

My thoughts drifted to my flight to Manila, the meetings I'd had there and the late-night, same-day departure to Bangkok, where I'd proceeded to the Suri Guest House, guzzled a beer with the proprietor and was asleep by midnight. I'd had no idea what awaited me the next morning.

Walking across the courtyard, I realized I needed to pee very badly, but decided not to say anything. I was surprised that I was being treated like a criminal: handcuffed, photographed and fingerprinted. My small hand-carry luggage and belongings were taken away, and I was walked into the Immigration Holding Cell.

Bangkok Immigration Detention

THE CELL was something of a microcosm of human survival and suffering under difficult circumstances, and an exercise in human cruelty. I had been naive. It was shocking to
see how the gentle Buddhist Thais treat people who are immigration violators. Shame on
them.

The physical plant consisted of one very large room with a few toilets and two shower
stalls, all to accommodate what I guessed were about 73 hapless souls of various nationali-
ties. I learned that it sometimes housed up to 200 for periods as long as 18 months.

The room had no provision for sleeping. You had to sit on the concrete floor cross-
legged unless you could find a space to stretch out.

It was hot and humid and the ventilation was poor. Everyone had stripped down to
their underwear and rolled their clothes into pillows.

As for food and water, forget it. If you had no money, you were at the mercy of those
who did; they were the acknowledged leaders.

Entering the almost pitch dark room, I surveyed 73 pairs of eyes surveying me back.
A quick tally indicated that most of the population was of Pakistani origin; there were also
a handful of Arabs, two or three Europeans, and a group of Chinese, while the rest were a
mixed bag.

A tall and thin Pakistani, who had a small mattress and a few belongings, immediately
motioned to me to come over and sit next to him, indicating that he was the chief here. He
told me the police had told him to look after me. Not knowing exactly what that meant, I
thanked him and told him straight out that I was capable of looking after myself.

He shrugged and said: "OK, just come over and sign in the book."

As I approached, I saw that he had a large, soiled book, like a telephone book, listing
the names of every suffering soul who had passed through this hell-hole. On page number
108 (an auspicious number in many cultures and traditions — and, incidentally, the exact
number of stitches on a baseball), I added my name to the long list of fellow human suffer-
ers. "Bruce Aitken, Hong Kong, British Crown Colony."

The Pakistani man told me to find a place to sit, and that if I had some baht, I could
buy coffee and cigarettes. With cigarettes, I could also buy tea with a bit of sugar. Looking
around, I squinted in the dim light, and purposely avoided the group in the far corner, an
obvious pocket of homosexuality.

Since I could speak some Mandarin, I gravitated to the sound of Chinese. My new
Chinese friends, economic migrants waiting to be deported, shared their food and encouragement with unreserved generosity.

At 11:30pm, the chief told everyone to stop talking, to only whisper, so we could all sleep. My anger began to swell as I looked around at the group of pitiful, harmless characters I was to sleep with that night.

Did I say sleep?

Short on options

I'D TOLD Conklin before he'd departed our interview that he could go to hell; but if I resisted boarding the plane, I would rot in this room indefinitely, and when I was finally taken to America I would have no chance for bail. I told myself I would eventually be acquitted against these faulty indictments.

It was four o'clock in the morning as I bade everyone farewell and my mind began to focus on the next chapter of this very bad dream. Enter the DEA's Mike Ogilvie, along with Mike Seamens, the Hong Kong agent. The "Two Mikes" would escort me to America.

Ogilvie played the tough guy, refusing me any rights, threatening me with bodily harm, that he'd bind and gag me and do whatever it took to return me to the USA. He wore a brown safari suit, the kind that was in style in the '70s. For his part, Mike Seamens just stood around looking like a cowboy, with his cowboy boots, jeans, and an old shirt with a torn pocket.

Handcuffed and bundled into a car, I watched the sun come up as we drove to Don Muang Airport. It hit me that I was being kidnapped and arrested on foreign soil by fellow Americans.

Having resolved not to resist, I would have no option but to fight the battle in the courts. First, I would have to suffer the humiliation of being transported to America against my will. All I could think about were the boys and Jenny.

Confused, tired and frantic, I wondered if, by taking some action now, I would make things worse or better. I decided to put my faith in God to show me the way to face this dehumanizing battle. I needed to squarely face the United States because there was no way I would ever run away from my problems; and with a family, there was no way I was going to consider looking over my shoulder for the rest of my life. Unbeknown to me at this time, many friends and a Thai lawyer friend were already frantically trying to find me.

After checking through immigration, I waited handcuffed in the departure lounge with my two minders, silently wondering what lay ahead. My children were asleep in their warm beds in Hong Kong. Soon they would be getting ready for school. There were only three weeks of school left and we had been planning a summer of swimming, building models and playing baseball.

Still wearing the clothes I had been arrested in, I remember a very pretty stewardess looking at my face and asking me, as I boarded, whether I was feeling well.

No, I did not feel very well.

The Northwest Orient flight was packed with a group of elderly American tourists, nice white-haired, sweet grannies who reminded me of my mom. They smiled at me until they glanced down at the handcuffs.

The flight landed in Tokyo five hours later. On the way, I was praying for engine trouble, or that the typhoon that was passing by the Philippines would divert the plane to Hong Kong. *There I would be safe.*

In Tokyo, I was escorted by the goons and two Japanese plain-clothed policemen to a waiting room. They offered me an orange juice, and I chatted with them, speaking a few words of Japanese. They politely asked me about Hong Kong and my family.

I sensed that I needed to make some kind of move to find a way out, but if I refused to board the plane, I would definitely be denied bail in America as a flight risk.

When it came time to board the flight to San Francisco, the captain — a tall, handsome Scandinavian-looking fellow — had to take a look at me before I could board. I walked up to him and he gave me a somewhat sympathetic glance and told the goons I could take my seat.

Broken dreams

IN THE days to come, I would remember a dream that had occurred several weeks prior to this disastrous turn of events.

In the dream, I was at Tokyo Airport without a passport, but I did have my permanent Hong Kong ID, and I was boarding a flight to Hong Kong. I don't know why I did not recall that dream when it proved to come true in Tokyo. Was it exhaustion? I can only assume that God did not want me to go in that direction. I would spend a lot of time agonizing over this, and it haunts me still today.

At Tokyo, could I have explained to the captain that I was being kidnapped against my will and did not want to board the flight? I was not technically under arrest, but I had no passport, and I was in transit. Could I have purchased a ticket on my American Express card on Cathay Pacific and returned to Hong Kong?

I remember really wanting to fly home to Hong Kong. Arriving at immigration would have been a bit of a hassle, but in a few hours I could have been walking up the lane to surprise my wife and children.

Afterwards, I agonized over whether I had made a big mistake in not trying, but then I remembered another dream, one in which I was vindicated and was walking away from an American courthouse a free man, armed with a new passport and looking back through an airplane window at the coast of the USA, probably for the last time.

Which dream could be trusted?

In deciding to bite the bullet and return to America, the clincher was probably actually the publicity. All of Hong Kong would have read about my case in the *South China Morning Post*. I would have been ruined, and my children would have suffered as a result. Without a passport, I would not have been able to travel out of Hong Kong, and I would likely have been extradited anyway.

My life was now in the hands of my faith in God.

Had I been wiser, I reflected, I would not have gotten so close to the dealings of some of my friends. All the times I had lived on the edge also flashed before me — all the risks and chances I had taken in Asia. I had been a very lucky man for a very long time. But times had changed and maybe I had not kept up with the changes.

The complexities of my life, my personal faults, being a "dreamer," and being unable to find personal peace of mind — all were factors that had played a part in putting me in that airplane seat headed for America. I had no one to blame but myself.

Yes, if only I had been wiser. If only I could have another chance. Things would surely be different.

Or would they?

CHAPTER 25

Welcome to the USA

AS WE CROSSED the International Date Line, I realized I was going to have to re-live the disastrous day I'd just had all over again: two time zones, two June 9s. The second June 9 would be as horrific as the first, but by then I was numb.

During the long flight from Tokyo, I had occasional conversations with the agents. They pretended to be trustworthy and tried to lure me into talking about my business and contacts. Ogilvie was civil enough, telling me how he had been a New Orleans policeman for over 20 years before joining the DEA. He said he was completely and utterly amazed I had gone to Bangkok.

Ogilvie asked why didn't I renounce my citizenship? Why co-operate? He also tried to advise me that I should separate from the others.

Nice try, guys. It seemed to me I had the best lawyers looking after my interests, both in Hong Kong and the USA. At the Immigration Detention Center, Conklin and Mike Seamens — the "Cowboy" — had both said "bullshit" when I told them that. Conklin told me he had not known I would be traveling to Bangkok, but that he had been notified by the Hong Kong police. When I heard that, *my* response was "bullshit."

On the plane, however, Cowboy seemed to let the cat out the bag when said the prosecutors would probably drop all the charges and indictments against me in return for my co-operation. I said: "That's news to me."

While the agents slept, I slowly opened my briefcase and took out my phone book and various secret papers. Soon my pockets were stuffed full. I went to the toilet, tore all the notes into shreds and flushed them into the antiseptic innards of the plane.

A trial now felt inevitable. The agents told me my attorney Marcus knew the government had a faulty indictment against me. For my part, I couldn't help wondering whether he wanted me to go to trial because it would be in his financial interest.

I recalled Marcus saying: "You are in great trouble and therefore need a first-class law-yer to represent you, to solve your problems — and this requires a first-class fee."

That fee was the $300,000 previously mentioned. The way I saw it, it was food out of the mouths of my family, but I tried to dismiss any thoughts about my attorney's motives by reminding myself how highly I rated him.

UPON ARRIVAL at San Francisco airport, I was met by another group of agents. From here on in, it was all going to get much worse — I was about to enter the American gulag.

As you might imagine, I was really beginning to feel like shit. I had on the same white pull-over cotton shirt with thin blue stripes and the same black pants that I had used as a pillow in the Bangkok immigration jail. After a 17-hour flight, I was at US customs and immigration smelling very foul indeed.

After the other passengers had departed the plane, Cowboy officially arrested me and read me my rights. He also asked me if I wanted to talk to the prosecutors before talking to my defense attorney. If I was willing to co-operate, maybe we could have the whole matter dealt with then and there.

After what they had just put me through, I thought they had a hell of a nerve. And in fact, the torment had strengthened my resolve. I'd already told them I would not testify against anyone, and that contrary to their implied belief, I did not know the whereabouts of any huge sums of money, nor own such sums myself.

I recall Cowboy's words as soon as we cleared US Customs: "For the last time, you can talk to the prosecutor and *maybe* spend the night in a hotel, or you can spend the night in jail. Which will it be?"

My reply was short: "I don't know what the hell you are talking about."

It was a cool morning in San Francisco. Cowboy commented that there was no fairer system of justice in the world than that of the USA. He seemed totally oblivious to the fact that he had just been an accomplice to my kidnapping.

COWBOY and company had a car waiting for me. It was parked somewhere; somehow they forgot where. This in itself was not all that surprising. Meanwhile, I was being paraded around for all to see, like the North Vietnamese used to parade POWs around the streets of Hanoi. Down the escalator, up the escalator. Out the door. Back inside. Up the stairs. Out the front door. Back inside. Down the same stairs, out the other doors. Round and round we went.

After 20 minutes, their legs were beginning to tire; suddenly, they found the car.

They opened the trunk and dropped in my little hand-carry case. This was the exact moment that Cowboy was savoring to compound my misery.

"Oh, by the way," he said casually while all the others laughed. "Did I tell you? I may have forgotten. I have some more good news for you. You just got indicted in Seattle!"

The indictment was a so-called "sealed indictment," which is one that stays non-public until it is "unsealed" by the person being indicted — in this case, me. I remembered that years earlier I had read a book called *Bonfire of the Vanities*, where I'd learned that the ease with which people could be indicted had spawned the saying "A grand jury would indict a ham sandwich."

I said: "Now I know what a ham sandwich feels like." A rogue prosecution, a rogue system of justice, a rogue government. The comment went over their heads.

It was close to noon when we arrived downtown at what I was told was the Federal Building, and I had a sinking feeling as we drove into the underground car park. (My mood contrasted entirely with the agents' by now almost festive spirits: they were so proud of themselves.)

I said to myself: *Don't let the bastards grind you down.*

As we were taking a lift, the door suddenly opened and a lady agent in her mid-30s with blond hair that looked like it hadn't been washed or brushed in weeks, entered. She took a long hard look at me and said: "Got one, huh?" They proceeded to talk about me like I was some object — a piece of dead meat or some dog shit they had stepped in.

Placed into a small cell with only a wooden bench, I waited to be fingerprinted and photographed yet again. As was my right, I asked, and was allowed, to make a call.

A quick calculation through my weariness told me it was about 7am Hong Kong time. It had been more than 48 hours since I was arrested in Bangkok, and I'd had no sleep. But I knew those hours had been even more miserable for Jenny.

When I started to dial the phone, Cowboy told me to be sure to "make the call collect." I told him I knew the government was bankrupt, but I thought they could afford a phone call. I ignored his request. It was so good to hear Jenny's voice. Of course, she asked where I was. I could hear the tiredness in her voice.

"San Francisco, in the Federal Building, awaiting something called an *arraignment*," I said.

My conversation with Jenny was conducted under the stares and bent-over ears of three agents cowering behind me.

I told her I had been indicted in Seattle, too. With a strength found only in my good Chinese wife, she offered me great encouragement and support. I told her not to worry and to look after the boys. That's all that mattered: "Just tell the boys I am away looking after Nana for a few months."

Hanging up the phone, I looked at the listening agents, whose faces had turned dour and mean. By contrast, my own spirit remained unencumbered because I had no fear of their lies and hostility. But I was both exhausted and already contemplating my next trauma, the legal battle ahead.

Who should represent me? Having Marcus on-board had been a good experience for the most part. He had given me confidence that I could weather the storm, but the relationship of trust had changed dramatically. Even with my assets, I'd begun to realize I could not afford him. "Good lawyering is expensive," kept ringing in my ears.

I thought of his second trip to see me in March of 1989, which had accomplished nothing. I had been keen to learn what kind of deal the government might propose and what interest they really had in me, only to be told they were non-committal. But this information contradicted what the agents had been telling me.

At the same time, changing horses mid-stream would be risky — something akin to walking through a mine-field, to mix metaphors.

The arrival of Dan, an associate at Marcus's firm, for my arraignment, gave me a good deal of comfort and confidence. He also informed me his boss would come visit me Saturday morning. It was now Thursday. Since Marcus and I had been drifting apart and unable to agree on fees, I'd really not been expecting anyone.

At the same time, I had suddenly received an urgent message from a good friend who knew of my plight and had made arrangements for a San Diego attorney to represent me. The attorney's name was Michael Pancer.

This was a welcome development. But really I had no idea what to do — except pray. I did: *Dear God, thy will be done — but please take this burden off my shoulders.* I prayed to God as I had many times when I was in trouble in my life; I put my life in His hands.

FOR THE arraignment, the courtroom in the Federal Building was packed. All the DEA agents, plus some other very interested-looking folks with unfamiliar faces, plus the clerk, the prosecutor and the judge — all were evaluating me, and I them.

Nothing much happened. I was asked if I was Bruce Emil Aitken, the indictments were read, and a bail hearing was postponed. Next, I was turned over to the US Marshals office in the same building, but on a different floor.

I had to empty my pockets into a large plastic bag and was allowed to keep nothing except three photos of my children. There was a short list of questions that Cowboy asked the marshal to read off to me. Had I ever been convicted of a crime? No. Was I gay? No. Did I have any contagious diseases? No. The answers were all accepted as No…except one. Was I an escape risk? Cowboy checked Yes! My attorney Dan and I looked on in disbelief. *The bastard.*

Dan asked me: "Why did he do that?" I replied loud and clear: "Because he is an arse-hole."

The old black dude marshal, who was checking me in, then gave me a real evil look and said: "We'll be tough on this one."

I noticed a twinkle in the old dude's eye, though. Finally, after a pause, he turned to me and said the agent wanted to make it damn tough on me by saying I was an escape risk.

"You are from Hong Kong? Well, you don't look Chinese and you don't look like an escape risk to me," he said.

He took my good leather belt as a souvenir and placed it in his drawer. It was theft. I didn't care.

Just like in the movies, I found myself locked in a jail cell waiting for transportation to the Oakland County Jail. But first they put a chain around my waist and threaded it into itself like a needle. Next, handcuffs were placed between my hands and closed around each wrist. And to complete the look "foot cuffs" with a similarly short chain were locked around my ankles.

Cuffed, you cannot move your hands more than six inches in any direction and you have to walk in short steps or else the metal cuts into your ankles. You can't scratch your nose — or anything else. Takes some getting used to.

It was around 5:30pm when I took off in a caged van with three other souls. It was a clear, sunny evening and soon we were smack into rush-hour traffic, heading toward the bridge that connects San Francisco with Oakland. As I peered into the surrounding traffic, I wondered when I would be free, when would I see Hong Kong again. As I watched Americans driving home to their families, I suddenly felt devastated.

OAKLAND COUNTY JAIL was no picnic. After being placed in a cell for two hours, my clothes were taken away and I was issued with prison clothes: blue pants and shirt, socks and rubber sandals.

Then, clutching the photos of my boys, I was escorted into a large dorm with 14 bunk beds and a TV. Fortunately, all the beds were occupied, so several of us were moved to a smaller room with only four beds. This was to be my home for the next five days, while the government decided whether matters were to proceed in Reno or Seattle. (They settled on Reno, where my co-defendants were and where I believe they felt the case against me was stronger. Incidentally, my Reno co-defendants were all anxious that I should be tried separately from them instead of us all being tried together. A lot of potentially damaging evidence against them, with regard to their financial transactions using First Financial Services, could be introduced if we were tried together. I believe this must also have been part of my subconscious reasoning when I'd decided to have those records destroyed.)

I chose the closest lower bunk and introduced myself to the assorted characters before me. I was about to quickly learn how people who have been detained for some time survive having their dignity and humanity slowly stripped away — you make friends without asking too many questions and you learn the routine; and you support and encourage each other not to give up or lose hope against the system. Everyone was suffering silently, but would not give up.

Since I hadn't had a meal that day, I was offered a few crackers and a candy bar, a cigarette. I had no appetite for anything.

Somehow, some time during the night, I fell asleep from sheer exhaustion. It had been three days since I was able to lie down or shower and I didn't care about anything at that moment. Speaking to Dan, I had told him frankly I wanted to fight the case and that my life was in his and Marcus's hands.

The next morning, Friday, was the day before Marcus was scheduled to meet me. It was also the day my other attorney, Michael Pancer, showed up from San Diego. After meeting him, I had 24 hours to make the most important decision of my life.

Michael was someone I liked from the get-go: sharp as a tack and humble in his demeanor. I felt his sincerity. It turned out he could also represent me for less money than Marcus, since there was an indication coming from some of my co-defendants that they would assist with his fees.

On Saturday morning, when Marcus arrived, I was not in a very good mood. I asked him what the hell had happened — he'd told me when we were in Hong Kong that he had a close relationship with the prosecutors and because of that I would be dealt with favorably. What was so favorable that they had canceled my passport so as to have me deported from Thailand?

The meeting quickly came to a head because Marcus became quite angry and surprised when I informed him I was speaking to another attorney. He said something to the effect that I must decide *right now*, and so I did: I chose Michael Pancer. Mightily pissed off,

Marcus left abruptly, huffing and puffing venom while sarcastically wishing me good luck. As I was escorted back to the room, I prayed to God I had made the right choice.

My four temporary soul and cell mates were a real mixed bag. One was in for drug trafficking (smuggling pot), one was a bank robber, one a counterfeiter, and the other a jewel thief. With our different lines of expertise, we could have been a great crew in a Hollywood movie.

The daily routine sucked and so did the food. You had a total of 15 minutes from the time you left the cell to get a tray of food, eat and get back to the cell. I learned to eat quickly.

What left the greatest impression on me, however, was the nature and mentality of the prison staff.

As a general rule, they were all sadists to varying degrees. My feeling is that you have to be a bit weird and unbalanced to gravitate to the prison profession, although I'm aware that a job is a job — and jobs are not easy to find sometimes. For prisoners, the key to some peace of mind is simple: avoid staff in every possible way and they will avoid you; and don't ask for anything because the answer will probably be no. In short, stop existing.

The torture of the Oakland County Jail is that you never see daylight. There are no windows. If you want to know if the sun is out, better watch the weather report on TV.

After a few days, I was becoming disoriented — but I was saved by *tai chi*. I began practicing the Chinese martial art in the small space next to my bunk daily, and it would prove invaluable to my physical and mental health in the days and months to come.

On the sixth day, with ten minutes' notice, at 6am I found myself being whisked off to the caged van again. The driver was a young marshal in his early 20s, assisted by a girl about the same age, who blasted the radio so loud that it would make a dog howl.

The first stop was at a correctional facility near the airport to collect three others, all of us destined for locations unknown. I soon realized why I had been rushed out of Oakland so unceremoniously. To avoid any escapes when transporting prisoners, they kept you in the dark. Something told me this lesson had been learned the hard way.

AN HOUR PASSED as we drove down the highway in the direction of Sacramento. As far as possible, I focused my eyes on the horizon. Soon we approached the entrance to a military installation (I think it was called McClellan Air Force Base) where I observed up-close the coercive power of the US government's correctional machine.

As we weaved our way down immaculate streets, I was reminded of other air force bases I had seen in Vietnam, and of how organized they all were. Stop signs and speed bumps at every intersection. And it occurred to me that America itself was kind of a pseudo-prison.

Everyone had their lives ordered and controlled in various ways by the government (federal, state and local); everyone lived in straitjackets of varying degrees.

The greatest and most valuable freedom in America, I felt, was the freedom to leave and see the rest of the world. I considered myself to be, deep down, a patriot who loved his country the way it was before all this control became baked into the system. At that moment, I would have given anything to have the freedom to go to the airport and board a flight to Hong Kong.

Before I knew it, we had entered the airfield itself and were driving on the tarmac past hangars with fighter jets. I watched several F-16s take off and land. Just then, a car pulled up beside us, and a marshal inside motioned that he and his buddy were the transportation from Reno.

Just as suddenly, a white Boeing 727 landed and taxied right over to us. Simultaneously, several gray Air Force pick-up trucks approached and circled the plane. The occupants of these trucks got out and surrounded the plane, assuming a type of battle stance around the perimeter. Had it been a lot warmer, and had the plane been painted camouflage, I would have thought I was back in Vietnam on Tuy Hoa Air Force Base.

From overhearing the marshals' conversation, I learned that this aircraft had been confiscated by the government from a South American smuggling operation and was now known as "Fed Air," tasked with ferrying federal prisoners around the country like some kind of domestic CIA Air America. Eerie.

Some of the prisoners were taken in the plane, but myself and a couple of others soon found ourselves in the back seat of the marshals' car, bound for Reno.

There wasn't any conversation until halfway through the three-hour trip, which included a stop during which our custodians bought each of us a Coke. These guys were decent and civil, heads above the ones I had met in California. One guy mentioned that he'd almost had the chance to come to Hong Kong to collect me. The other had spent time in the military and had been to Hong Kong several times.

It was good to be out of the Oakland County Jail and I was thankful for small things — like kindness and a Coke.

With some trepidation however, I recalled a weird feeling I'd had two or three years before, when visiting a friend at Lake Tahoe. Driving past a sign that said "Reno," I'd suddenly got a sick feeling in my gut. It had been as though somebody or something — an inner voice, or perhaps my guardian angel — was telling me that I should never, *absolutely never, ever*, go there. If only I had a choice now.

CHAPTER 26

Reno-grad

WE ARRIVED at the Washoe County Detention Center, in the outskirts of Reno, around 1pm. The facility was a brand-new $34 million concrete-and-steel monster with strange small windows and a lot of fencing around it.

They were expecting me. I felt I was considered to be some sort of an alien, a strange creature all the way from the other side of the planet who'd suddenly dropped out of the sky and landed in Reno.

I entered, stepped in front of a camera, and was told to walk to the carpeted side of a large entrance hall. I could use any of the telephones for a collect call, and I could watch TV. Was I hungry? They had water and soft drinks, sandwiches and potato chips.

The place was high-tech, which unsettled me. It felt like a space-age, computerized people processor. But it was very clean, and the people were civil enough. I could not help but wonder what lay ahead for me in the labyrinth that extended behind all the automatic glass and steel doors I could see.

I wondered: should I consider myself lucky to be entering this wonderful place, on which society had obviously lavished a fortune to look after its growing number of misfits? I was soon to learn that good luck had nothing to do with it, however. Here, all you had to do was jaywalk and you could find yourself a guest of the State for a few days.

Jaywalking? Hilarious. I roared inside with laughter, envisioning the whole population of Hong Kong being stuffed into paddy wagons for jaywalking. (Pedestrians in Hong Kong are quite notorious for criss-crossing the city's streets with no mind for traffic lights.) I shared the joke, but no one laughed.

Another way to land here was to be caught in public with an open can of beer in your hand. God forbid!

No doubt about it, America had become a hypocritical police state, with common sense nowhere to be seen. I was beginning to feel a knot in my stomach. *What kind of justice could I receive in such a place?* Just a few miles down the road, in California, possession of a joint would earn you a fine at the time; here, it was a felony. I felt nauseous. Claustrophobia was setting in and my breathing quickened.

Entertainment in the waiting area, as in the rest of the place, consisted solely of TV, the mind-numbing electronic teat, which in itself made you feel ill. It seemed to be non-stop police-state garbage (violence, crime, police interventions, followed by more violence, more crime, more police interventions). *Miami Vice* is child's play compared to watching real-life roadblocks waiting for drunk drivers, or real-life drug busts on *America's Most Wanted* and *The Reporters*.

In Reno in 1989, you could smoke cigarettes anywhere you liked, gamble your money away and fornicate until your testicles fell off (prostitution remains legal there to this day). But just don't walk across the street with a Goddamn open can of beer! Have some decency and use your common sense: put it in a paper bag or else you'll ruin our children!

WHEN MY name was finally called after about two hours, I was asked a few questions and fingerprinted yet again. Down the corridor, I turned into a small lobby with a row of plastic seats against the wall, across from a supply room with a wall-to-wall shelf counter, and a row of shower stalls. I was asked my size, handed clothes, told to take a shower and place the clothes I had on into a plastic bag.

The clothes on my back were in fact the same unwashed clothes that I had been wearing when I was arrested in Bangkok — I'd had to put them back on when I left Oakland. That would explain why everyone was staring at me when I came in.

My first real shower in two weeks felt so good — that was until suddenly the marshal barked: "Grab your family jewels and cough!" Since he could not see into my cubicle, I decided to cough only. *Screw you!*

After passing through more doors and checkpoints, I arrived at Housing Unit #2. My first impression was that this place was not very crowded.

The unit was a large, diamond-shaped room with a 20-foot-high ceiling. Around the perimeter were two floors of cells, with metal stairways on both sides. In all, there were 56 rooms, each identified in large orange numerals.

The central area was occupied by an elevated platform divided in half; each side had plastic chairs and tables, and one color TV.

Before entering and being assigned to Cell #23, I was directed to a small conference room to view a ten-minute video describing life at the facility, and given an *Inmate Information Handbook*. Looking again at my new attire, I started to dislike the color orange.

Having some space and privacy was a bit of a respite. The last time I'd lived alone and spent time with myself was in Vietnam many years before. What would I learn about myself? What would I dislike? This was a chance to do some soul-searching that would test my mettle, but the truth was I did not know if I could handle it.

I felt enormous pressure; the fabric of my mind and philosophy of life should have been well-developed by now, giving me an anchor of sanity. But peace of mind was something I had not had since the previous September, when I'd phoned Jenny from Manila and learned of the Reno indictment. I knew it was all bullshit, but how do you get out of this kind of bullshit? The government does not play with a full deck and the odds are stacked against you. A grand jury really *can* indict a ham sandwich.

Many thoughts were to cross my mind in the privacy of my cell's square footage. If I had been wiser I would not have gotten into this mess in the first place. I was not guilty in my own opinion, yet I now *felt* so very guilty. I did not have Jenny to rely on. I did not have my sons' companionship. Over the weeks that would pass, the times I felt the most overwhelming grief were the times I thought of my children. Of course, they needed their dad. But oh, how much more I needed them: the closeness, the physical contact, tickling each other, watching them sleep.

Our family had made some wonderful summer plans. And although we were not an especially religious family, I had just gotten into reading a beautiful children's Bible to the boys at night before they slept. We had planned to swim, cycle, and hike. Just the week before I went to Thailand, I had purchased two nice folding tents, good enough for us to camp in the country park. We had models to build. Oh, my boys — my love and my life!

I resolved that whatever happened I would not let the bastards grind me down. I thought to myself: *I am going to kick their ass in court. This experience will not destroy me.*

Even though I had not been able to walk away from the money-smuggling business as I had planned, I was determined not to let this ruin me. Even though I had been a fool, I had to believe in myself. I believed it was not too late.

Bail

THE FOREMOST objectives in my mind were bail and getting out of jail. It was now June 1989. Since my return from Taipei to Hong Kong to face the indictment, every step I had taken on the advice of my lawyers in the US and Hong Kong had been calculated to create a favorable situation for bail. I never anticipated I would spend a single day in prison. I thought I'd done everything properly.

I had been charged in the Reno indictment with only one count that was extraditable. Having been basically kidnapped and returned to American soil, however, I was now facing all 14 counts, plus the newly unsealed indictment in Seattle. The nightmare I'd dreaded had become a reality. *Lord, this time you've given me a mountain to climb.* What the government had done to me was outrageous — but clearly they thought it would force me into some kind of co-operation.

The first order of business ahead of the hearing was to prepare for an interview with a person who would check on my background and make a recommendation about bail. Her name was Mary Callahan and she had a reputation for extreme bias in favor of the government. Her report was crucial.

Somehow, I sensed that the tide was very much against me. I was not the first person the USA had kidnapped — and I had learned that no one previously kidnapped in similar fashion had been granted bail, as all were considered flight risks, a danger to society, or both. The purpose of going before the magistrate was to request that my bail hearing be delayed until my Hong Kong barrister, Gary Alderdice — whose familiarity with my case I valued immensely — was able to fly from Hong Kong and appear on my behalf. It was important to show that I was aware of the indictment, was taking legal advice in strict accordance with the letter of the law, that I was not a flight risk, and that all along I had been waiting for the extradition notice to come to America and face the charges.

I slept badly the night before speaking to Mary Callahan, and as I sat down with her, my voice was raspy. In 15 minutes, we covered my whole life, and I discovered that my intuition had correctly told me the obvious: that Callahan had already formed a prejudicial and biased opinion about me before we even met.

The day of the hearing came and the magistrate, a lady named Atkins, listened to both the prosecutor (who read the charges) and my attorney, Michael Pancer. I agreed to a delay and to being incarcerated for another two weeks to allow time for Alderdice to arrive. I also needed the time to prepare myself. What if bail was denied? Reno was beginning to feel like a pit of quicksand.

Prison rules

BEING CONFINED in a maximum security prison entails not only restrictions to one's physical movement but a new social environment too. Verbal communication among the incarcerated is a given, but there are a few important rules to follow. Survival can depend on understanding them.

The most important of all these rules, and you can forget the rest, is never, absolutely never, under any circumstances, discuss your case with other inmates. For that matter, don't discuss it with the marshals either.

The reason for total secrecy is that prisons are awash with informants. Yes, snitches are lurking everywhere. These are desperate people who will lie and swear under oath to anything if it helps them get closer to their day of freedom. Apparently, the prosecutors and judges just love to set such scum free.

In jail, snitches are usually pretty easy to tell because they will be given better facilities and treatment than the general population, but they get no respect. Once they're known to be snitches, whenever they transfer to other prisons or end up returning to prison, they are marked just like cattle are branded.

Going green

AFTER FIVE days in Housing Unit #2, I was suddenly transferred to Housing Unit #3. Thankfully, this required my clothes to be changed from orange to British racing green, which is so much easier on the eyes. Most of the folks in my new quarters had either been found "guilty as charged" or were awaiting sentencing (or, like me, bail.)

I was one of about a dozen Federal prisoners being housed in this State facility. Since the Federal government pays the State something like $77 a day for Federal prisoner maintenance, the State does not like to let us go. Yes, the profit motive is alive and well in the correctional system.

I was still wearing bright orange when they took me to HU#3, however, so I had to stand there looking like a luminous traffic cone in a field of green grass. As I stood at the entrance surveying the crowd, I saw about 75 tough-looking characters sizing me up. I couldn't wait to get into my green suit and blend in with the crowd.

The place was full, so I was told I had to share Cell #9. I made my way there and the door buzzed open with the loud, sickening sound only a prison door can emit. I heard a murmur of voices coming from the direction of the TV in the common area and I could feel the inmates watching me. I thought: *Oh shit! They must be putting me in a room with either a maniac or a raging faggot.* I put my mattress and the few personal belongings I had on the floor.

It turned out the inmate there was another Federal prisoner who had been in and out of court for over a year. He was also meticulously clean, and I soon saw the humor. I was sharing a room with a *real* "Mr. Clean" — the cell was so spotless I didn't even want to pee in the toilet for fear of messing the place up.

My roommate for the night (the very next day someone transferred out of the unit and I was moved to Cell #39) offered to share his food and his books, and turned out to be a very decent fellow, uttering no complaints that someone was sleeping on the floor and taking up 90 percent of the cell's remaining space.

A few days later, another prisoner arrived who turned out to be a co-defendant in my case, a colleague of Robert Kimball's and in fact a friend: Tommy Tuttle. Meeting him in these circumstances brought on a heavy flashback. One night in Toronto, while Tuttle and I were having dinner, I believe around '85 or '86, I'd had a weird premonition that one day we would be seeing each other in a prison somewhere. It was around the same time as my Reno premonition while holidaying at Lake Tahoe. Again, I wished I'd heeded what these portents were telling me.

Strangely enough, quite a few of the inmates were familiar with our case. I was told to forget about getting bail from Magistrate Atkins, and that my barrister might as well stay in Hong Kong. I was also told to go through the motions and set up a good case to get bail on appeal from a real judge in the 3rd District Court of Appeals in San Francisco — just spend a few more weeks in jail and then get bail. Atkins was a prosecutor's mouthpiece through and through.

I was also told that she bolted for her chambers for a shot of Johnny Walker Black every time there was a recess. That would explain her bulbous red nose.

CHAPTER 27

The battle for bail

THE DAY finally arrived for my bail hearing, and I entered the courtroom with a heavy heart. I studied Magistrate Madame Atkins' face intently. Her black judge's robes contrasted with the gray bouffant hair that surrounded her round face and pale skin that had never seen sunshine. She had that red-faced, alcoholic look.

While I had suspected the next four hours would be an exercise in futility, I was shocked at how biased and unfair she actually was. She was absolutely a prosecution mouthpiece and *only* a prosecution mouthpiece; an anathema to the system of justice that America stood for — or the one I remembered, anyway.

Gary Alderdice had flown in from Hong Kong and met with Michael Pancer and me the night before the hearing. We had become good friends over the nine-month ordeal and it was great to see him. A New Zealander, Gary was familiar with the evidence in the pre-trial discovery and knew that I was no criminal. He flew all the way to Reno for a modest fee and returned to Hong Kong immediately after the hearing.

Gary also brought me two letters from Jenny that I had to speed-read, and some beautiful color drawings from my sons. This greatly raised my spirits and I wanted to retreat into the privacy of my cell to read them over and over. The top of the drawing read: "To my beloved Dada." I needed to cry. However, the marshal took the drawings and letters away, and I was never to see them again. The pervert wanted to apply more pressure on me, but in fact the opposite happened — it made me stronger. (*Truth be told, it really, really, really pissed me off.*)

Besides the presence of Alderdice and Pancer, my dear friends Mickey and Chato Howard, from San Diego, had braved all to come as character witnesses and even to offer their home as surety. Surely no better friends existed on the planet. Against the advice of his lawyer, Mickey had also come to visit me the week before.

The government had two prosecutors, Jeff Russell and Brian Sullivan, supported by an assortment of spooks in the gallery, and the tomato-faced Atkins.

When the prosecutor from San Francisco, Russell, had the floor, I tried to catch his eye to see what kind of person he was; but he totally avoided looking at me. He was like a dangerous robot. The Reno prosecutor, Sullivan, at least exchanged a nod with me. A human. I felt no animosity; they were doing their jobs.

I quickly realized, however, that I was in a war and the courtroom was the battlefield. Russell took the offensive — and was *extremely* offensive. He proceeded to vomit out an arsenal of lies and deceit, portraying me as a monster, a danger to the community and a flight risk, someone for whom a life sentence in prison would be warranted. He was an artist with a poison brush. I find it amazing that in a courtroom they don't make the prosecutors take oaths in front of everyone.

Indictments had been returned against me by two grand juries, he roared, as if this in itself had some magical credibility to it. I had that "ham sandwich" feeling, again.

Russell "pre-offered" most of their discovery and I felt the hearing dramatically shift gears from being a bail hearing to a trial.

My sins as outlined by Russell were as follows:

1. I was a "foreigner," having left the United States over 20 years before and lived in Hong Kong for the last 16. (Oh, no!)

2. I was a person who traveled a lot. Here, he showed a copy of my passport, with its multiple additional pages, recording my travels since 1985. Just *look* at all the stamps, over 34 countries! (I ask you: Since when was "traveling a lot" a crime?)

3. Informants said that I had identified them as being informants to one of my co-defendants.

4. An informant had executed a financial transaction in Hong Kong at my office in the amount of $500,000. This, Russell said, was money-laundering. "In fact," you are looking at the Meyer Lansky of money-laundering," he declared, referring to the legendary organized crime figure, known as the "Mob's Accountant," who — along with his associate Charles "Lucky" Luciano — was instrumental in the development of the National Crime Syndicate in the United States. All attending the court gasped out loud, and with what seemed like malice aforethought, stared at me as if I had just landed from outer space.

5. When I became aware of the indictments, I did not rush back to the USA to face them immediately.

On and on he went, presenting a bent and twisted version of the truth and facts. What a pervert!

Next, Alderdice took the stand. He certainly was an excellent witness on my behalf. He had been a prosecutor in Hong Kong for 14 years and knew what he was talking about, having just handled two US extradition cases.

He went on to explain how he and I had met in Manila; how I had first called him *from* Manila; how he did not know me before that date. He said that on learning of the indictment, I had acted immediately to obtain legal advice.

When we met in Manila, he added, we discussed my options and I was well aware that I could have chosen to stay in countries that had no extradition with the USA. I could have stayed in the Philippines; I could have stayed in Taiwan, a country that has no extradition with anyone; I could even have gone off to live in Vietnam.

Instead, I returned to Hong Kong, to my home and to my family. To do so was to knowingly face the extradition process. I had complied to the letter of the law with the Extradition Act and, what's more, I had always co-operated with the Hong Kong police. He reiterated the fact that they had returned my passport to me so I could travel on business at any time.

Additionally, Alderdice's testimony mentioned that I had not been charged with "perverting the course of justice" in Hong Kong, although the police wanted me to plead guilty to "not maintaining proper records."

When the prosecutor took his turn again, he stressed that my records had been destroyed, contradicting an earlier statement that he had in fact been able to examine records of mine for1986 and 1987 in May in Hong Kong and deemed them to be intact.

I was the last person to be called to the stand, and by that time I was not feeling at all well. I was very emotional and told Michael Pancer that I did not think I would be able to control myself. He said I would be a good witness for myself and we proceeded.

Michael began by asking me some questions about my background, my family, where I grew up — and my life suddenly began opening up before me. With every eye in the packed court-room staring at me, *suddenly I could not speak*. I had to turn away from the court because I almost choked on my emotions. My body had simply had enough… the lies, the humiliation, and the anger. I felt like I was about to experience convulsions. A five-minute recess was called so I could drink a glass of water and regain my composure.

NEXT, THE prosecutor asked me questions under cross-examination. When it got to First Financial Services, he asked if I had taken deposits of cash — and a fog seemed to descend.

My mind went totally blank, and I couldn't understand the ramifications of the question. My attorney instructed me not to answer. This was entirely beyond the scope of the bail hearing.

Prior to this, there had been another heated exchange regarding who had told me about my indictment. My attorney objected, saying even he did not know the answer to that question — and again that the matter should be saved for trial. The objection was *overruled,* and I had to answer. I couldn't think! I answered that my wife had called me in Manila and told me, and the questions stopped there, because anything relating to who told her would have been hearsay. *God must have put the right words in my mouth.*

Soon, four hours had passed and it was 6pm. The prosecutor reiterated that I was a flight risk and a danger to society. My attorney reviewed our efforts to address the problems legally and pointed to the fact that I was a decent person.

Magistrate Atkins obviously needed time to write an opinion and consider the evidence. I also sensed she was in dire straits for another stiff drink.

The following day, after being chained and shackled and put through another humiliating check-out, I was thrown in the prison van and taken back to the courthouse holding cell — which was of the kind with bars that you see in old western movies.

Pancer had already gone back to San Diego and sent an assistant, and the prosecutor did not bother to attend. I was inwardly pleased that my attorney had chosen not to be present. It showed that we knew what to expect from a kangaroo court.

At the same time as we drove up to the courthouse, Atkins pulled into the building's parking lot. She could not look me in the eye as I shuffled along in shackles. In fact, I could sense she felt extremely uncomfortable; maybe she had a conscience after all. She bristled when the marshal's car radio suddenly came to life, crackling loudly, asking where the hell we were.

One said: "I don't think he will be released today." The one in the car replied: "Well if he is, I'll only have to re-arrest him and send him to Seattle!" Laughter!

In the cells, I was greeted by a tall black marshal who asked: "Is this guy coming from the laundry?"

Somewhat bewildered, the other marshal replied: "No, from court."

"No, I mean, can this guy take care of the laundry, as in 'money?'"

Really funny.

———— ❦ ————

SOMETHING sinister was unfolding, no doubt about it. Clearly, the government wanted something, but whatever it was, I could not accommodate them. Although they knew I had absolutely nothing to do with drugs, they falsely assumed I could lead them to tons and tons of cash belonging to my clients.

The drug counts in the indictment were 100 percent faulty. Moreover — and not to belabor the point — it seemed to us that the remaining money laundering counts would surely have to be dropped without any equivalent counts in Hong Kong, because otherwise they were non-extraditable. (That they had gone to the trouble of canceling my passport and kidnapping me on such flimsy counts nevertheless meant I was now fighting for my life.)

How had they managed to kidnap me? It was accomplished with a phony letter from the US Consulate in Bangkok to the general in charge of Thai Immigration requesting that I be deported, based on two lies — first, that I was a fugitive and second, that I was a felon. The idea that I was any kind of danger to society seemed preposterous.

A political issue

ON THIS point, we reached out to an expert witness named Leon Richardson, a friend and prominent Hong Kong businessman who, better than anyone, could explain how Deak & Company handled cash in Hong Kong.

He replied in a letter: "Mr Alderdice, I realize the severe problem Bruce Aitken is facing in the US." And he emphasized: "At this time, money laundering is an exceedingly HIGH POLITICAL ISSUE in the US… the administration is doing everything possible to go after others such as what they are trying to pin [on] Bruce Aitken.

"I think they would not listen to any facts even if you or I told them that what Bruce Aitken did in Hong Kong was not illegal and was not money laundering, due to the fact that Bruce is a US citizen."

Leon really put my nightmare in perspective.

The courtroom, as we awaited the bail decision, was crowded and hot, and the room smelled of stale air and government injustice. My breathing quickened, and although I already knew the forgone conclusion, I steeled myself.

After a reading of the facts, Magistrate Atkins stated: "I have considered the cases and exhibits provided by both sides and feel that I have no other choice but to detain you, Mr. Aitken, where there is a presumption to believe the person has committed the crime where the maximum term of imprisonment of ten years or more is prescribed…"

And for good measure, she added: "Even assuming that the Government had 'kid-napped' defendant Aitken in Bangkok, Thailand, and brought him before this court, such action would not justify the dismissal of the Indictment against him. Under the Ker-Frisbie Doctrine, the personal presence of the defendant before the Court gives the Court complete jurisdiction over him even though the defendant may have been abducted, illegally arrested or improperly extradited."

She continued: "There were a number of contacts over the next weeks and months between the government and attorneys for Mr. Aitken in an effort to have him return voluntarily to stand charges, but this was to no avail.

"In about March 1989, [Marcus] traveled to Hong Kong to meet with defendant Aitken and after his return to the United States he advised the government that his client was not interested in working anything out."

"Contrary to present counsel's contention, there was absolutely no agreement of any kind between the government and defendant's former counsel [Marcus]."

Being denied bail, a basic right of a citizen of the United States of America as guaranteed under the Constitution, was a humiliating, degrading and depressing development that deserves analysis.

It had a devastating effect on my respect for the US justice system and revealed how its henchmen operated. But the truth remained that the two indictments against me were faulty — and they knew it.

CHAPTER 28

Prison Notes

AH, PRISON. It is an experience that most sensible people fear and dread, and with some justification given the worst-case scenarios that are portrayed in the press and in Hollywood movies.

At the same time, along with the loss of freedom and the fear of violence, few environments, as I have stated, present such an opportunity for you to test your personal mettle. On the list of "life experiences," at least I can scratch this one off.

I soon learned that most of the people in prisons stand in stark contrast to the stereotypes portrayed in movies and other media. Most inmates I met were non-violent, ordinary people who had done a lot of different things in their lives. It just happened that these things included committing crimes and being unlucky enough to get caught.

RETURNING ME to my cell after the failed bail hearing, a fat Italian marshal named Lou said to me: "Why don't you just tell them about your friends and where all their goddamn dope money is, and then you can go home to your children?"

I remember telling him that I was innocent and would fight to the end, and that I would never let the bastards grind me down. We discussed Vietnam and for some reason he got very angry. He was under the impression that I had been working with the enemy in *North Vietnam*. He was a vet who had been wounded, and had been rewarded with a Purple Heart for a scratch on his forearm. I have no idea where he got that story about me but it goes to show that lies spread quickly in prison.

ALL PEOPLE in prison are under great pressure. Some cope well. Others suffer a lot; you observe and pity them, but you have your own suffering to bear. You turn to your faith. If you have not developed faith in God before you arrive, then chances are you are in big trouble. It is really the only thing that will save you, your spirit, your humanity, your sanity. In my case, I should have been much better prepared.

A lot of my woes had to do with being surrounded by so many stressed-out men all day, men with serious problems who were under immense pressure. Rainy days made everything worse. I felt like I needed a miracle.

On the face of things, the charges against me spelled doom. What's more, my loved ones were on the other side of the planet. Loneliness had really set in.

Against all that, my karma was good and many people were rooting for me. I knew I needed to pray for my tormentors, for those who were persecuting me. I had to force my mind to think pleasant thoughts, think about things that were true, noble, right, pure, lovely, and honorable. I knew it was the only way I could find peace.

EVERY MORNING, a little bird came to visit me, perching on my small, barred, slanted "window." I had the habit of giving my eyes a rest from the constant interior glare by gazing out into the distance, where I could see a highway and cars going to and fro on it. This little bird, tiny and free, seemed to take pity on me in my human cage, and it brought back one of the most pleasant memories I had.

Some years earlier, when I'd gone to Chiang Mai in Northern Thailand with my son, Matt, we visited a Buddhist temple, at the base of which was a very large bird cage filled with several dozen songbirds. Their lovely little chirping sounds were irresistible. For a donation of a few baht the door of the cage was opened and all the birds were allowed to fly away, leaving you with a feeling of goodness in your heart. It really didn't matter that the birds would fly back to the cage in time for their next meal and to wait for the next kind-hearted person to again set them free.

I wished the same thing could happen for everyone in the prison.

ONE OF THE marshals, "J.D.," was actually a good-hearted person, and would often ask after my family. He said he knew it was tough. The government had endless resources at its disposal and was hard to beat. He gave me some sound advice, though. He said that although the jail was not bugged, if anyone were to ask what we talked about together, the answer should be "Hong Kong and tai chi." He told me he had heard about my case and that the government was clutching at straws. If I was innocent, great; and if I wasn't, don't tell anybody.

One day I was called down to collect a big box of evidence from the prosecutors. There was a message to call Michael Pancer immediately. He said he would come to see me in the next few days, and that he had reviewed everything. He sounded very confident and upbeat.

In the meantime, I needed to sit tight and try not to watch the endless violence on television. No matter what I did, my mind raced, and I sometimes felt I was close to the edge. I was 44 years old, facing 20-plus years in prison. *Could this be possible?* In Reno, I reflected, yes it could be.

OF COURSE, I was also terrified of having a bad influence on my sons. I spoke to Matt and Doug one day. "Mommy is coming to America to see you," Doug said. "Can Matt and me come too?"

He asked if I was staying at the same hotel as Mommy. I badly needed to get bail.

Jenny came from Hong Kong on two occasions. What a woman. What a wife. She looked great, but I was not allowed to give her a hug.

I had been busy reading through three big boxes of the "discovery": evidence connected to the cases in Reno and Seattle, all bullshit about me and my fellow defendants. I didn't feel sorry for myself, but I did feel sick. It was so obvious they were trying to apply maximum pressure to break me. Thank Heaven for Jenny. She kept me thinking positive.

As she left for Hong Kong, of course there were tears. And when she was gone, the blues hit me hard — but all I ever had to do was think of her and I would bounce back. Jenny's words gave me strength and restored my faith: *"We are proud of you."* Every time I read Jenny's cards and letters, I had to steel myself:

"On days when you are low, just try to think of the fun things and good times you will be sharing with Matt & Doug. These two wonderful and precious boys are the source of your joy and happiness. You must fight to the end! Don't for a moment give up hope. Remember you are now at the bottom. You have no choice but to go up. Yes, it will be very painful to fight against a mountain of fabricated lies, alone, without the family around. We are not physically with you but you are always on our minds and in our hearts. Be strong, keep your chin up, let your spirit flow free and you will win. Try meditation and to relax and be calm; take it easy, Bruce…we all love you. Love, Jenny"

A positive lesson in all of this misery was about perseverance — to wait without giving in to feelings of impotence or anger, to wait with a sense of purpose. To do this, I had to practice correct thinking, but I really had to *work* at it to overcome the things that were trying to drag me down. I discovered that my free spirit was not built for being in prison for very long, and despite my efforts, I began to feel more and more like a caged animal.

CHAPTER 29

Help, I need somebody!

ONE THING WAS becoming clear to me: if I didn't win this case, I was a dead man, and that's all there was to it.

My horror at the thought of not seeing my children grow up sparked me into action. I knew I needed to get reference letters for the next bail hearing, but I didn't feel I could ask Jenny to help because she was under enough pressure already. With a feeling of desperation, I decided I would have to reach out to my friends in America and elsewhere, tell them of my predicament, and ask for their help.

With the assistance of Mike Pancer and my mom, I contacted several of my old friends and associates — everyone from my old colleague Ron Langa in Orlando to Father José in Japan. (My list also included friends I'd got to know in Guam — Mickey Howard, Steve Deutsch, Chuck Nordquist and Roger Slater — as well as some other old Florida buddies, namely John Schofield, Jim Wooten and Norm Wolfinger, who was by now a prosecutor himself.)

The response was overwhelming. Letters and faxes started flooding in, all framing me in a positive light. Ron Langa said he almost fell off his chair with concern at my predicament — and immediately faxed his recommendation. What affected me profoundly was his willingness to do even more than I had humbly asked him. I told him I already appreciated his letter very much.

"I know that," he said. "But what more can I do?"

He said he would pray for me. I could not have asked for more at that moment.

When my mom called Norm Wolfinger, he immediately wrote me a wonderful recommendation. Others on my list even pledged to attend my hearing.

With the help of my Florida friends, who were horrified when they saw the indictments, we also got in touch with former Senator Lou Frey. He raised my case with contacts of his in Washington, DC, and held a meeting with the local FBI and DEA, whom he knew well. John Schofield, also well-connected among Washington's power elites, was told I had been offered the witness protection program — which came as news to me. John said what they wanted was my cooperation. Since it was not forthcoming, they were trying to make me sweat. Lou Frey confirmed that the Government's tactic was to keep me in prison until I broke down.

I was sweating, that's for sure. But the outpouring of support I got at this time from friends and colleagues meant the world to me — and it strengthened my resolve not to give in.

LIFE IN prison didn't get any easier, though, and one night in particular I really hit what felt like the bottom of the barrel.

I was having a terrible time with myself and could not seem to shake the doldrums. I tried walking outside in the cage, but I couldn't stand it for long. I'd walk for maybe ten minutes, then go inside and drink more coffee. I felt the walls closing in on me. Around and around I went in my head until I thought it would explode, along with my heart, which felt like it would burst with frustration. I was terribly lonely.

In a state of despair, I placed a collect call to my mom, although it was almost midnight in Orlando. At age 86, Mom was a fighter and firmly believed in her son. In fact, she had been praying for hours that I would call because she had some news to tell me and she was very excited. John Schofield and Senator Lou Frey had told her they'd been able to pull some strings on my behalf in Washington.

Unfortunately, this turned out to be a case of one step forward, two steps back. Shortly after, John received a call from an "Agent Coombs," working for either the DEA or FBI, telling him to back off because Bruce Aitken had been photographed on board the *Encounter Bay*, the smuggling ship that had been seized in the DEA's sting in the summer of 1988. He told Frey that since I was not co-operating they were going to throw me in prison until I broke down.

Lies, lies and more damn government lies! God damn it! What was I to do? Their game got dirtier by the day.

In the face of such mendacity, I needed to get a hold of myself and keep a clear head. I could show no weakness. I had by this time made it a daily habit to write home. I would write two letters — first, one about my frustrations and how miserable I was feeling. I would then tear that letter up and write another one that was positive in every way — no use putting Jenny under more pressure. Yes, I was going through a personal hell, but I had to fight the matter at hand, and make the right moves.

One day, my legal mail included a very interesting letter addressed to the Government about having the Seattle indictment dropped. Michael Pancer correctly pointed out to the Justice Department that the two cases against me were, in essence, based on the same set of facts, and therefore, one should be dismissed.

The letter gave me real hope for a breakthrough.

Another development around this time seemed more likely to complicate matters. To my surprise, it transpired that Crown Pacific, the storage company which had been tasked with destroying FFS' records from 1987, had managed to overlook ten boxes. It seemed to me that having this evidence back in play could either make things much worse — or much better.

Either way, I felt sure there was some *karma* at work.

Flight risk?

SOMETIMES something happens that's unconnected to whatever has been consuming your entire focus but which turns out to change your whole outlook around. That's what I experienced when I started talking to a fellow inmate, Mike.

When Mike first appeared at the table where I sat for breakfast, it took us some time to break the ice: he was a naturally quiet and reserved kind of guy. When we did, however, I got to know a lot about him and his amazing background. Turns out all I had to do was introduce the topic of Vietnam and we were soon good friends.

Mike was an amazing person and an experienced pilot. While flying a Falcon Executive jet from Canada, he had suddenly been ordered to land at Reno airport — where he found himself detained and the plane impounded. I can't remember him telling me why (maybe there was some kind of alien aboard the aircraft); but, anyway, instead of phoning a lawyer, he opted instead to use his one call to contact his partner in Los Angeles. This partner promptly flew to Reno with a spare set of keys, and while the paperwork was still being done, filed a new flight plan and took off with the evidence — the Falcon jet. Amazing. I loved this!

Mike also told me about his experiences in Vietnam, where he'd been a Phantom jet pilot in the US Navy, flying off aircraft carriers in the Gulf of Tonkin and on missions over North and South Vietnam. He had been shot down — not once, but twice.

I told him about my interest in flying. I had been working on my private pilot license in Australia before a certain A\$60,000 legal problem in the country had discouraged me from returning there. He told me he and his business partner could use a good pilot to fly a chartered Falcon out of Singapore, and encouraged me to re-apply myself. At first, it sounded like a fantasy.

What happened from that point on was truly a work of inspiration, as I placed myself in the hands of "Roger That" Mike. From scratch, and using all the paper and cardboard we could scrounge up, he created an entire pilot's course for me, including lessons on aeronautical engineering, flight instruments and navigational equipment, and a pilot's test.

Mike was a great teacher. He would give me various assignments, then we would sit down at night and I would "fly." The deputies in the prison were so impressed with this activity that they gave us the use of the lawyers' conference room — a glass room next to their station which they could see into. When it was time to wrap things up for the night, they would come round and say: "Time to land the plane."

I believe this diversion was a gift given by God to help me through those difficult days when it felt to me like time had stopped and my suffering threatened to become unbearable.

In a couple of months, I completed Mike's course. I took his test — and passed with flying colors. Afterwards, we talked about me undergoing flight training on the outside and going to work for Mike and his partner. Sadly, for reasons we'll come to, that plan never materialized.

----- ❦ -----

FROM MY diary: "I am writing tonight because we are in *lockdown*; after dinner a spoon was missing and 'life' will not return to normal until it is found…"

Fortunately, I had had some fantastic conversations with Jenny and the boys earlier that day to sustain me. And the letter I had received from Jenny also reassured me: "I'm sure that *something* will be happening soon." She emphasized the need for strength, courage and persistence, and to look for the light at the end of the tunnel. She only asked that I not give up hope.

"Every time you are down, you must get up and start all over again. It is tedious but in the end you will reach your goal and be vindicated. The boys, you and I have a strong bond and it will pull us through.. Call whenever you need to talk to us, write also.

Love, Jenny

"PS: Bruce, I know that lately you have been feeling low and depressed, which is natural. But I want you to shape up, for our future with the boys. You have your whole life and your future at stake. You simply can't give up. If you do, I will not forgive you. Please get out of any depression you may be getting into. Take things one day at a time, do it for the boys. We love you!"

I composed my own poem: *"For God has sent me a trauma of a grave and heartless kind, to test my strength of being and the fabric of my mind. I search my soul to find the answer, how I will survive. It's my faith and love of family — that's my goal to stay alive."*

THE MONTHS passed, with my hopes being raised and dashed. Late fall of 1989 arrived — and along with it a great impatience. My final appeal for bail was due to be heard in the 9th Circuit Court. (To spare you the suspense, it would be another unsuccessful bid. In all, I was denied bail three times, but based on what? I was deemed to be both a flight risk because I "traveled a lot" and a danger to society because I had access to other people's money, essentially.)

Michael Pancer told me not to get my expectations up, and they were certainly lowered when I discovered that the Reno prosecutor, Brian Sullivan, had another desperate move up his sleeve: he had found a new snitch. Sullivan told the judge that this new witness, named "Bender," had delivered money to my office in Hong Kong with Tom Sherrett on one occasion and was prepared to testify against me. All of this completely out of the blue.

This panic move by Sullivan might have been connected to the fact that Robert Kimball had just won his case, partly thanks to an embarrassing blunder. It turned out that (as alluded to in chapter 21) government agents had visited him while he was incarcerated in Nevada State Prison, in 1988, without the permission or presence of his attorney. This was a clear violation of constitutional rights: schoolchildren could have figured that one out.

The next curve-ball came mid-November when, one day, I got a call at noon informing me to be in court at 12:30pm. There was no advance explanation given as to why, but it transpired there was a motion to transfer my case to Seattle.

After the court hearing, I was brought back to detention by Lou, the fat Italian marshal I mentioned in the last chapter. He asked why I was in court again, to which I sarcastically replied: "For the monthly airing of the innocent."

He said if I were innocent, all would be okay, and if I weren't, then the time I had already spent inside would count against my sentence. He asked my opinion of the prosecutors. I told him they had a sleazy job but that they were doing it quite well.

Back at the jailhouse, just before dinner, it happened again. For the second time in one day, a fork had gone missing and we were back in lockdown. All I could think was, *I have to get out of this place!*

When I later spoke to Michael, he said again not to get my hopes up for the 9th Circuit Court because there was little chance of winning on appeal and he didn't want me to get disappointed yet again. (For the record, I was not getting my hopes up — by this point I'd learnt there wasn't such a thing as justice any longer in the United States. What's more, I had seen first hand how utterly and morally corrupt our system and government had become.)

———————◦❦◦———————

AS I WAS facing this ordeal, in my prison reading I had the chance to consider the words of Louis Brandeis, US Supreme Court Justice (1856-1941):

"If the government becomes a lawbreaker, it breeds contempt for the law; it invites every man to be a law unto himself. It invites anarchy. To declare that in the administration of the criminal law, the end justifies the means — to declare that the Government may commit crimes in order to secure the conviction of a private criminal — would bring terrible retribution."

I also found useful the words of Congresswoman Edith Green from Oregon:

"The misconception behind the existence of the CIA is a simple one, as I see it. The misconception is that it is possible and proper to turn over to a group of men the kind of authority and power the U.S. Constitution was specifically designed to prevent. In fact, the very existence of the CIA is a monument to the failure of recent and present generations of foreign policy makers in government to take the basic philosophy of the nation seriously.

The main work or principle that emerged from the work of the Philadelphia Constitutional Convention was that the biggest danger to human freedom was represented not just by bad men at the heads of bad governments but by good men who were put in positions where they were able to operate outside the law.

"The founding Fathers didn't have to be told that extraordinary situations would arise in which extraordinary authority might be required. What concerned them, however, was that the existence of such situations might stampede and mislead men into creating a mechanism that in itself would be subversive of Constitutional government."

How right they both were, and still are. (Does the more recent "Patriot Act" ring any bells?)

———————— ❖❖ ————————

SOON, there was more talk of a deal being offered if I pleaded guilty to some technicality.

"Depends on what the technicality is," I told Michael.

Seems I could save a bunch of money from going to a costly trial, and return to my family with just some damage to my reputation, if I only gave the pit-bulls a few crumbs to satisfy their blood-lust.

Michael came to see me as my co-defendants — Ed Seltzer, William Harris, Robert Kimball, Tommy Tuttle, Brian Daniels and David Bose — were tabling their offers before Sullivan. We spent an hour and a half going over everything, and for once I was able to stay upbeat. Michael and the lawyer representing my co-defendants, Ed Chesnoff, were to meet with Sullivan later that day and we agreed I would call Michael back at home in San Diego at around 8pm in the evening.

The hours after our meeting were spent in a mood of high anxiety as I waited for 8pm to roll around. I held my breath as I dialed Michael's residence. He initially said that things had not gone as well as planned, but that there were some positive points.

In essence, the government was reasonably satisfied with the proposed financial settlement with my co-defendants. They would collect a sizable sum of between $10-30 million, in addition to the $7.6 million they already had from the Reno sting.

The sticking point was the time in custody. Because of the drug charges, my co-defendants were looking at a mountain of time between them.

From me, they were asking for less but still too much: eight years. They said they wanted me to serve some years to learn my lesson. I knew that if I succumbed I would almost certainly lose focus and at some point "auger in," to use the polite term for crashing a plane into the ground.

Eight years, eight years… the number struck me in the gut. In eight years it would be 1997; Hong Kong would have reverted back to China and I would still be in prison! I was feeling mightily pissed off and my temperature rose vertically.

The positive news was that the Seattle prosecutor, Mark Bartlett, did not want me to transfer there, and he agreed to go along with whatever was decided in Reno with regard to a settlement.

I was crestfallen, but in a moment I told myself: *the real war has begun.* Michael indicated to me that their offer had been made tongue-in-cheek, and said he wished I had been there. It was like they had just gone through the motions so their superiors would be satisfied.

Next time, we would get closer to reality. Steve Swanson, a former DEA agent whom Pancer had hired as an investigator, had some insight and came to discuss matters in depth. He suggested we make a counter-offer: I would accept 18 months, of which I would have to do 12, less what I had already done; and after a period of bail, I should be allowed to do the remainder on a farm.

I told them that I would not make such an offer because the government were hypocrites and I wanted to fight. *Let's go to trial and defeat them!*

Finally, Michael cleverly said he would write to them and tell them I wanted bail before I would consider any type of settlement.

"Okay, let's go to trial!" he added. "Good man."

Michael knew I was standing up for principles, and he confirmed that he thought the case was a winner. There was no deal to negotiate. For me to have pleaded guilty at that point would have justified all the unjust actions of the government. No, thank you.

I prayed: *God please give me courage and see me through this most difficult time in my life.*

To fight, I desperately needed a carrot to dangle before the government, however, and Steve came up with an approach that made sense to all of us. This concerned the many clandestine payments which I not only knew about but had made, *for and on behalf of the US government*, while working for Deak & Company in Asia.

I gave Steve the particulars about payments to John Clutter of Lockheed, CIA involvement in the whole affair, and the commissions paid to Japanese generals — all of it clearly sanctioned by the US government.

At the same time, the following letter was tabled from Ed Chesnoff, to Sullivan, on November 30, 1989:

"As to Mr. Aitken, his attorney could only recommend a plea bargain that allows for his release from custody. He may have served the equivalent of an eighteen month sentence depending on credits for time served. Mr. Aitken has not agreed to any deal at this time, but his counsel would recommend a plea bargain in which Mr. Aitken was released from custody pursuant to a no contest plea to a currency violation. (Mr. Aitken has indicated to counsel that it is his firm belief that all the charges against him should be dismissed.) Mr. Aitken is the only defendant that has not had his motions heard. If he prevails as to the motion to prohibit

admission of co-conspirator hearsay pursuant to the Silverman decision [see Silverman vs. United States, 1961], *there would be no trial evidence left from which he could be prosecuted."*

Then, in December, Michael told me some very good news about the so-called informant "Bender" in San Diego.

He had spoken to Bender's attorney and discovered that Bender had never made the statements Sullivan was claiming — statements to the effect that I had said I would hold the money Bender and Sherrett brought to my office in 1986 until the "mother ship" was loaded. These accusations had, at least in part, been the basis for denying me bail, and it turns out Bender wasn't even making them — perhaps because they had no basis in truth whatsoever. He did maintain that he brought funds to my office. However, this was far less damaging testimony.

The unraveling of the Bender information was a huge moment.

Status anxiety

NOT LONG thereafter, something called a "status conference" was held. I was brought to court, along with my co-defendants, to listen to the attorneys and prosecutors thrash matters out.

As a result of the conference, the government's offer to me was suddenly boiled down: If I pleaded guilty to one felony count — a currency violation — I would serve five years, with four and a half of those suspended, and pay a fine of $250,000.

Bullshit — the whole system of fraud and greed on which US justice is clearly built — was prevailing. It was clear to me that the government and prosecutors had never actually wanted to go to trial. Back in prison that night, however, I had a visit from Dwayne, Steve Swanson's partner, who said the offer was actually very good and that I should not be too concerned as there would be help coming with regards to my fine from the other defendants.

"Focus on the fact that the deal will get you released immediately," I remember him stressing. "Get out, go home and never come back; it's a great deal!"

I spoke to Jenny about it. Like me, she was not happy. It was giving the government several more pounds of flesh than I could bear. I had dreamed of being home for Christmas, but would instead be happy to bide my time and treasure the Christmas drawings I received from Matt and Doug.

That same day, a new deputy locked us in our cells for 24 hours. He was a real sadist.

I refused to eat. Mentally, things were going badly.

CHRISTMAS PASSED and New Year passed before Steve came to visit me again on January 3. We went over some accounts and had a very frank talk. Then I spoke to Michael, who said things were happening fast. He must have ruffled some feathers, because all the defendant attorneys were now in Reno talking to Sullivan. Michael and Chesnoff came to the jailhouse the following day.

Steve, after pleading with me no end to accept the offer, laid out the stark reality. "Look," he said. "They just can't drop it, not after they have made you serve almost ten months and practically destroyed you!"

I looked him squarely in the eye for a full minute before I replied. My mind was racing.

"OK, OK, I will consider it," I said, as the possibility of going home took shape in mind as more than just a fantasy.

The main point was that all my co-defendants and the government had now agreed terms — and their deals would fall apart if I did not also agree. This was something like government blackmail. It was all or nothing. Again, that's how the system is rigged.

"Bruce," he said, "Frankly, you may not think so, but the biggest danger you face is going to trial."

A trial would be dangerous for two important reasons, as he saw it.

First, sentencing guidelines. If I were found guilty under new government guidelines, there would be little flexibility and I could very well be sentenced to 20 years.

Second, facing a jury of "peers" from Reno would be to my great disadvantage, given the amounts of money involved and the nature of the drug charges. I would not stand a chance against all those cowboys trying to understand what I was doing in Hong Kong. They would tend to side with the government. To go to trial in Reno would be an absolute and total disaster.

By now, Steve was almost screaming at me: "Look man, I am from Reno. There is no way in hell you are going to win here. There is no fucking way in hell. Do you *get* it? There is absolutely no question in my mind that the jury here will not hesitate to find you guilty. The judge will have no choice. You'll be doing 10-20 years for sure. *Wake up!*"

The marshall on duty tapped on the glass of the Attorney conference room indicating to Steve that the whole floor could hear him shouting. In a softer voice, he continued: "If you accept this deal, although it is not perfect and you feel humiliated, you can get out of jail next week. If you miss this chance, with no bail, you'll rot in here for most of the next year, even before you get to a trial! Accept, and others will help pay the fine."

We also contemplated all the possible people who potentially would turn against me. These included my former friend and client Brian Merrill (who had been indicted because of the *Encounter Bay* bust, and who could testify that I knew about the shipment and tie it to the $500,000 dropped on my office), as well as Howard Marks' partner, Philip Sparrow-hawk (who had been arrested alongside Marks in Vancouver in 1987 in a marijuana bust). And who else? Who else? Who else?

Again, Steve pleaded with me: "Man, please don't blow it. Trust me! This is your one and only 'get-out-of-jail' opportunity!"

ON TOP of everything else in the government's plea bargain, there was also a diabolical and confidential caveat that had been thrown on the table in the negotiations between my attorney and the prosecutors: I was to be debriefed about my knowledge of money-laundering methods.

Via my lawyer, I swore that, *as far as I directly knew*, none of my clients — the names of whom the government had obtained from my files, via the Hong Kong police — were involved in the drug business; none, absolutely none. I would, therefore, not be telling them about anyone, nor would I testify against anyone. I would not, even though several of my clients had decided to sing like birds against me. So what was the big problem?

As I weighed my options, something in my consciousness kept screaming "Beware!" But Steve's words kept ringing in my ears, too. The thought of not seeing my sons grow up always sent a tremendous shiver down my spine, and when I came to my senses, it was a no-brainer. They were right. I should take the get-out-of-jail card.

I also considered the advice from Gary Alderdice in Hong Kong, who thought Michael had performed a miracle to create this chance for me to extract myself from the jaws of the monster. In time, I would come to realize that he was absolutely right. In a letter about my case addressed to Jenny, he wrote: "I am not trying to influence Bruce who maintains his innocence to plead guilty to something he strongly asserts that he has not done. I am trying to point out the factual realities of the situation. I believe Michael Pancer has achieved all he can in negotiating this proposal and I can see no reason why Bruce should not accept it."

All in a trance

I DID not sleep well on the night of January 12, 1990, as court proceedings were to begin at 11am on January 13.

The US Marshals who drove me to court applied the usual customary harassment.

"Hey, Aitken, how do you like it here in Reno? How's the family doing in…where is it? Hong Kong? How come you don't live here in America? You got no patriotism, man?

Man, why don't you just tell the prosecutor where all the Goddamn money is and you can go home?!"

Once at the courthouse, I tried to focus on what was being said but it felt almost like I was in some kind of trance. Before I knew it, it was 5pm, and the judge was accepting the Plea Agreements.

I was sentenced to time served and the fine, most of which would be paid by my co-defendants. In effect, everyone got their deal.

In a statement on my case, it was recorded: "Through a plea agreement, the government has offered Mr. Aitken the opportunity to be placed on probation after a term of incarceration. This short term of incarceration has already been satisfied by the approximately two hundred and fifty days of custody Mr. Aitken served in Reno, Nevada. Mr. Aitken anticipates returning to his family in Hong Kong. Mr. Aitken is considered to be one of the less culpable individuals in this money laundering case and that participation reflects his favorable deal with the government."

Later, on January 16, 1990, my Hong Kong barrister, Gary Alderdice, informed Chief Inspector Howard of the Hong Kong police that all indictments in the US had been dealt with by way of the prosecution accepting a plea of guilty for aiding and abetting others in the laundering of money. "His sentence was imposed to enable him to be released immediately from custody. He has been in custody and his entire personal and business life has been completely disrupted as a result. I would hope that having regard for all the circumstances of the case, the Commercial Crimes Bureau can safely and correctly take a decision to his benefit, in other words, that the Hong Kong 'holding charge' should not proceed."

On reflection, had I not traveled to Vietnam in June 1989, I believe I could have avoided the whole nightmare. By the same token, had I not taken Steve's advice and instead used my stubborn fighting-Irish nature to fight the case, and had I ignored Michael's frank appraisal that the government saw me as a major launderer of narcotic funds, I may well have spent 20 years in prison. But in both instances I had made the choices I had made and this is where I had finally ended up, a battered but a free man. A born optimist, I hoped that somehow some good might come of the trauma I had experienced.

CHAPTER 30

A taste of freedom

STRANGE TO RELATE that as I listened to Judge Harold McKibben accepting my plea, and those of my co-defendants, I remember feeling that I just wanted to be out of the glare of the situation — and alone in my cell. Truth be told, I had already become somewhat institutionalized.

Nine months had passed, but in reality it had seemed much longer because of the prison environment — something akin to being in a psycho ward. I always suspected they put something in the food to make your mind dull. But you had to eat.

The hearing had taken six hours. Then, suddenly, I was back in the marshals' van being taken back to jail for the last time. The marshals were speechless.

I had not yet been checked out, so to all intents I was still in custody, shuffling along in leg irons and handcuffs.

During the 30-minute drive back to the detention center, we ran into heavy traffic. I sat in silence, experiencing a totally surreal sensation of relief, mixed with unbelief, something like detached awe. Feeling as if a weight had been lifted off of me, I no longer had any animosity towards anyone.

Was I guilty?

Technically, perhaps, of many things. However, my conscience was clear. I looked out of the van window at the freezing tarmac and smiled at the marshals.

As I was processed in and buzzed back into the "comfort" of Housing Unit #3 Main Wing, dinner was just winding up. As I entered, escorted by one of the marshals with my release papers in his hand, the buzzer rang loudly.

There was a moment of utter silence as I faced the other 90 good souls living in that unit. I paused for what seemed to be a moment frozen in time, and gave them the thumbs up. Pandemonium broke out in the form of a massive roar! The duty marshal announced loudly that everybody better shut the hell up or they would be locked down for 24 hours.

I was not given a chance to say good-bye to anyone. Instead, I was told to hurry.

"Get your personal belongings from your cell and get back here in five minutes, and don't talk to anyone!"

My cell door buzzed open. In ten minutes, I had all my belongings: a box of legal pads, two books, my notes, and photos of Jenny and the boys. That was about all.

The reinforced windows in the jail's cell doors were placed at such an angle — no doubt engineered that way by some sadistic moron architect — that you practically had to place your face against the glass and squeeze your eyeball sideways in order to see anything on the other side. As I walked down the metal stairs, I felt many a squeezed eyeball wishing me well. I turned to each cell that I passed by and again gave everyone the thumbs up. The roar continued until I cleared the unit.

That good-bye was an exhilarating experience. It was a magical sound that I shall never, ever forget.

I HAD not seen my personal belongings in 250 days. Upon checking out at about 8pm, I was handed plastic bags containing my wristwatch, roughly $2,500 in cash, and some Thai baht left over from when I was arrested in Bangkok.

There was my favorite blue polo shirt, rolled up and wrinkled. I recalled that I had worn it for about five sweaty days in a row, including on my flights from Asia. It had never been washed. I stared at it for a moment and chose to put it on. I'll leave just as I arrived, I decided.

It was cold outside, but I did not give a damn! They offered to let me wait in the lobby entrance until my lawyer picked me up, but I preferred to wait outside, alone in the snow. It was about 20 degrees Fahrenheit (minus six degrees Celsius). Although I was shivering like hell, I was at peace.

So many thoughts flooded my brain. I could not wait to call my mom in Florida, to call Jenny, to soak in a hot bathtub and have a good meal and an ice-cold beer. I would soon be booking a flight to San Francisco to arrange for a new passport and take the first available flight to Hong Kong.

MY FEELINGS of euphoria soon mingled with new anxieties, however — because I knew surviving probation for the next four and half years would be like navigating through minefields. The Seattle prosecutor, Peter Mueller, a man I privately thought of as "the Nazi," was a particular worry. The prosecution had heaps of evidence and documents about what I *supposedly* did and what I *supposedly* knew, and it was obvious that he was absolutely furious I was getting out of jail.

At the same time, mysterious "others" had been arrested and were ready to testify against me at the drop of a hat to earn less prison time. Only people like my Reno co-defendants had the guts and integrity to remain silent, and for that, some were now paying the price of being incarcerated for many years.

Accepting the plea had been the most difficult decision of my life, but I was certainly aware of my good fortune in the fact that a plea had been offered at all. Mueller had been away from Seattle (an absolutely amazing stroke of good fortune, fate and karma for me, as I was to learn about later) when everything was being decided, and it was all signed off in his absence by US Attorney Mike Bartlett, forever bless his soul.

Ultimately, the government knew it would be difficult for me to go against my friends and force them into deals that might be worse. Per the Plea Agreement: "If any defendant chooses to withdraw his individual plea of guilty, as set forth, the entire plea agreement as to each and every other defendant who is a party to the Joint Plea Memorandum shall be null and void, at the discretion of the US attorney."

The others had all negotiated and agreed their own pleas, and I knew that for some of them that involved forfeiting additional funds for time off. William Harris, aka "Sir William," had broken like a twig early on and had paid a lot of money.

The tipping point to my decision to take the plea had been the fact that if I did not, *nobody* had a deal. I could have no idea what further dramas might lie in wait on the other side of the hill.

———————— ⬦⬦ ————————

AS I CHECKED in at the crowded lobby of the Reno Hilton, trying to look as inconspicuous as I could while wearing a smelly, wrinkled short-sleeve polo shirt in the dead of winter, I must have been a wretched sight. To my surprise, the counter staff gave away no sign of noticing, handed me my key and told me to have a nice evening.

I immediately called my mom. Through the entire ordeal, I had been worried about her more than anyone. Her son in prison? If anything had happened to her, I am sure I would have never been able to recover.

My room in the Reno Hilton overlooked a busy street strewn with glittering lights. I sat on the edge of the bed and dialed. She picked up on the fourth ring.

"Hello, Mom."

"Oh," with a sad voice. "Hello, Brucie." (I would always be her little boy.)

"Mom, are you okay?"

"Oh…"

"Cheer up, Mom! I'm out! I'm calling you from the Hilton Hotel in Reno."

Silence. My mom started sobbing uncontrollably, and it was at least ten minutes before she could even speak. I was crying, too. She was just unbelievably happy and relieved.

"I'll be going to San Francisco, Mom, to get a new passport, then going home to Hong Kong. Then I'm coming back to see *you*!"

Next, I called Jenny.

Jenny answered the phone on the first ring. She was so surprised, but pleased it had happened so unexpectedly.

"I'll get to Hong Kong as soon as possible."

Next came a long-awaited soak in a hot bath tub. The feeling was surreal: I was suddenly able to do what I wanted — which at that moment was *nothing*. But, of course, my mind wandered over various facts and scenarios, including that some of my friends had gotten sentences of 20 years. I reflected on how the system *tries* to break people and I kept thinking about all of the inmates back in the detention center, both the ones who dreamt of their coming freedom, and those who had already come to terms with being sentenced to decades, or for the rest of their lives.

As I dried myself, I snapped back to reality. I had to focus on myself, and the meeting I was required to attend the next morning at the Federal Building. Hello probation.

I DID NOT sleep well, and again my first thought of the morning was for my friends still in prison. I went for a jog through a small park, where I was startled to come upon a couple of empty beer cans on the path right next to a big pool of blood. *Shit!* What the hell could have happened here last night? I really needed to get the hell out of Reno!

Not knowing what to expect, I arrived at the office of the head parole officer, Wayne Momerack, before my scheduled 9am meeting. If I had been a minute late, I figured they would send out the marshals.

Mr. Momerack was expecting me.

"How long have you been in Washoe County jail?"

"Since I arrived on June 15, 1989."

"What! Since the day you arrived!?"

"Yes, sir."

He seemed surprised and sympathetic to my having had to spend my entire stay in Reno doing "hard time" in Washoe.

Because I would be living in Hong Kong, my probation would be "unsupervised," meaning I would have to complete a monthly form advising Mr. Momerack of what I was doing and listing my income. That was it. Should any inquiries come up regarding my probation, he would be the person who would communicate with me. To my recollection, we shook hands and he said good-bye and good luck.

We did not meet again, although at times I was concerned that it would be reported to the court that I was not sending back the monthly income report in timely fashion or not declaring sufficient income. To my mind, Wayne Momerack was a very decent fellow doing a tough job well. I liked him.

That evening I also had the pleasure of having dinner with J.D. Wallace. J.D. was the marshal that I had come to know, trust and respect, whose kind words of support — *"Hang in there, man!"* — when I was at rock-bottom always gave me the strength to snap out of it.

That first day, I spent a lot of time feeling like I was disembodied, living in a dreamlike world. Just 24 hours earlier I could not so much as have my own spoon, and yet, there I was now with J.D., sharing a happy, peaceful evening. I even had a dinner knife! It was getting late when J.D. and I heartily shook hands and wished each other well. I had found a real friend, a kindred spirit. I knew God had sent him to help me — God bless you, J.D.

TWO DAYS later, I went straight to the passport office. Based on the documents I was given by the government on leaving jail, obtaining a new passport should have been routine. But what can I say? When dealing with the government, nothing is quite routine.

The first task was for them to enter my name in their computer. Well, as soon as that happened, it was like I had triggered a state of emergency. I thought I was about to be re-arrested. "We have to check this out! Wait right here and do not leave," they said.

"No sweat," I said. I didn't intend to leave without my new passport.

Calls were made to the prosecutor in Reno and to the State Department in Washington. I sat silently, saying to myself: "Go ahead; knock yourselves out!" After about an hour, they had done just that — knocked themselves out. Then, finally, in a calm and friendly manner, they presented me with a brand-new US passport.

With the new document in my possession, I bade the passport officials a quick farewell and took a taxi straight to San Francisco Airport. It was now almost noon. I had made a reservation on the direct non-stop Cathay Pacific flight to Hong Kong, departing at 6.15pm, and I planned to be early.

The feeling was absolutely surreal as I checked in, made my way to Customs and Immigration, and found the departure gate. I took a seat until the other passengers arrived and it was time to board.

As I waited, my emotions fluctuated wildly. I had strong flashbacks to June 9 the year before, the day I had arrived from Bangkok in handcuffs and was unceremoniously paraded around the same airport like a piece of meat. The feeling of overwhelming joy that I would be seeing my family at Kai Tak Airport in Hong Kong was coupled with disbelief. Finally, aboard the plane and strapped into my seat, I heard the roar of the engines and felt the force as the 747 accelerated to rotation speed and lift-off. I was going home.

Sayonara America

TAKING THE deal and getting out of jail, in spite of whatever battles lay ahead, did turn out to be the right decision. With some half a dozen "friends" waiting in the wings to testify against me, it would have been almost impossible for me to have survived a trial in Reno.

Agreeing to accept the felony conviction and fine was a lot more than the government deserved, but I knew they lamented letting me off easy, and would likely try every way they could to get me back in jail. However, I would soon be back in Hong Kong and had every intention of spending as little time as possible in America for many years to come. If I was served a subpoena, I would rather just *disappear* — and it seemed to me Vietnam was as good a place as any to fade into. In time, everything would pass away.

I admit I did not anticipate the insane tenacity to come from the Seattle prosecutor, Mueller. I was a money launderer, so what? Were my clients involved in smuggling drugs? He said so, but technically his guess was as good as mine. I never saw any drugs. I only saw cash. Talk of drugs was non-existent. (Of course, in reality, I knew otherwise. I was not a fool.)

I could tell my version of this truth, but I believed without a shadow of a doubt that the government was not at all interested in hearing the truth from "the Meyer Lansky of money laundering."

CHAPTER 31

Out of the frying pan

WITH ACCUSTOMED Cathay Pacific punctuality, my flight touched down in Hong Kong on time. It was 8:15pm on Tuesday, January 17, 1990.

I have almost no recollection of immigration or waiting for my luggage except for walking quickly out the sliding exit door, turning left, as I had probably done hundreds of times before, and looking up at the crowd awaiting arrivals at the bottom of the long ramp.

My eyes instantly found both of my sons — Matt, age 10, and Doug, 8. They flashed me huge smiles, ducking under the divider and running full speed up the ramp into my awaiting arms. With tears of joy, just like I had imagined it, we broke into fits of laughter, as Jenny watched us in delight. She looked both radiant and worried at the same time, knowing that the future ahead would be wrought with uncertainty.

For the moment, though, we could all enjoy a quiet celebration. The worst was in fact over — and I had come home to the family.

⬧⟨3✦E⟩⬧

BEING released from the prison gulag should have been the happiest day of my life but in reality it didn't mean I was free.

For one thing, I would have to return to court for formal "sentencing" in a few months' time; more than that, though, my situation dictated that a new and stressful chapter lay ahead. For the next four and a half years, I was under probation and would have to fight tooth and nail on a daily basis to escape being thrown back in the hole.

It quickly turned out that the devil was in the details of the plea agreement, details I was not initially made aware of. On the day of my release — January 13 — I took heed for the first time of the *exact wording* in the plea.

As far as the charges against me went, I had nothing to hide. I was about to find out, however, that the government now expected me to tell them all about everything I had done for my clients.

Before sentencing, I'd had to agree to face a debriefing in Reno prior to my departure from the US — and another, if required, in Seattle. The government wanted me to throw them a crumb, but this crumb-throwing went against all my principles. The idea made me feel sick.

Ironically, in prison I'd had peace of mind simply from not feeling compelled to communicate with the government and from refusing to participate in its witch-hunt. But even after I'd been released from jail, there were still people champing at the bit to testify against me, and I could see that I now faced one battle after another.

When I voiced my concerns, Michael Pancer again stressed that the deal we had taken was the best he could have possibly negotiated. He assured me we would get through both meetings with the prosecutors, and that I could then put this experience behind me forever. It would be a piece of cake — all I had to do was tell the truth. Of course, in theory, he was absolutely right and I respected that. But still, I knew I would have to use every bit of strength and wit to survive the years ahead without falling foul of any government traps.

FIRST STOP had been Reno, right after being released and visiting my parole officer, and I got through that meeting with ease, offering and saying nothing. Maybe it was all just a face-saving exercise, like my legal team had said.

I was asked stuff like whether I had plans to go to Vietnam — and was told to keep the government informed of anything worth reporting back. *Don't hold your breath.*

The Reno prosecutor, Brian Sullivan, was civil. I smiled when his wife suddenly appeared at his office, stopping by to see what I looked like, I guessed. I must have been the number-one dinner table topic in the Sullivan household for quite some time.

During our meeting, Sullivan played a tape that Corman and Christensen had made while meeting with Brian and me in the coffee shop at the Hyatt in Cha Am, Thailand, in 1988. Not one word was mentioned about drugs or money laundering. The tape completely exonerated me.

To everyone's credit, the meeting felt more like a formality than an interrogation. It was even somewhat cordial.

One strange thing sticks in my memory, however. As we talked, my mind drifted back to an occasion when Brian and I were in Thailand and had gone to visit a temple, where we each — separately — had asked a Thai monk about what lay in our futures. When we later compared notes, our faces turned ashen: the monk had told each of us we would go to prison.

The Seattle pissing contest

FOLLOWING my return to Hong Kong, in late February I flew back to America to see my mom — and made a point of facing the Seattle prosecutor, Peter Mueller. Let's get it over with, I thought to myself.

Michael Pancer made the arrangements, and — to ease the tension — took me to a Seattle Supersonics basketball game the night before. It was a great gesture, but I couldn't concentrate much on the game.

On meeting with Mueller, my first impressions were that his office was cluttered with files, and his pale face etched in a way that suggested a dour, driven personality. With his whining voice and dour demeanor, he reminded me of Jack Corman, another squeaking balloon that made your skin crawl.

I also felt his tenacity and zeal to do his job. No mistake, Seattle was the complete opposite of Reno, and it did not take long before the kitchen got hot. The challenges facing me with regard to the content of the plea agreement were becoming perfectly clear.

I immediately realized that I had to find a way to dance around Mueller, and engage him in a pissing contest. My best efforts to do so made him mighty angry and he was soon spewing venom. There was no meeting of minds; we were worlds apart — as far apart as night and day.

Before our interview, or perhaps I should say my interrogation, Michael Pancer had forcefully commented that any violation on my part would not be determined by Mueller (God forbid) but by the judge in Reno. Mueller reluctantly conceded the point. However, as matters proceeded, he repeatedly accused me of holding back information, and I realized he was determined to revoke my deal. I knew he wanted so badly to incarcerate me and even to charge me with additional offenses. *This was war.*

I really had not anticipated the guy's insane persistence. For the last two decades I had lived in Hong Kong and abided by Hong Kong's laws. Were my clients involved in smuggling drugs? He had no more proof than I did of this. I never saw any drugs. I only saw cash, and talk of drugs was non-existent. (Of course, as mentioned previously, I knew implicitly what was really going on.) I could tell my version of this truth, but it was patently obvious that the government had made up its mind that I was beyond contempt and wouldn't listen to anything I said. Mueller's methodology was to go over all the client records I had at First

Financial, one by one. But he was wasting his time. From the beginning, I had consciously blocked out any trace or memory of anything that could incriminate anyone. I had always been determined that absolutely no one would suffer because of my explanation of First Financial's accounts. I kept my answers short and refused to confess any knowledge. This was difficult for Mueller to swallow, and he became more furious by the moment.

"Sorry, Mr. Mueller," I would say. "Truthfully, I have no idea about the business of this person and I certainly do not have any idea of the whereabouts of his money."

I was beginning to sound like a broken record — because I was deliberately speaking like one. I could not wait to get out of there and return to Hong Kong.

When I did return to Hong Kong, after two weeks in the US, Mueller kept up his dialogue with Michael Pancer. The communications relayed to me from Michael usually began with the words, "Bruce, Peter Mueller says the government has information that you knew about [so and so]. Blah blah blah…."

I had to say the same thing over and over, restating my intentions, which I crystallized in a letter to Michael Pancer and Gary Alderdice in April:

"I want to mention that in spite of all the difficulties I was facing in prison, I would never have entertained any agreement if I thought my statements could hurt anyone, especially since the questionable people I know have already been dealt with. So far, this has been the case. I will never testify against anyone!"

Knife in the back

WEEKS and months passed, and Mueller continued to bombard me, via Michael, with questions about each account. I confirmed they were all clean as a whistle and not tainted with drug money that I had any direct knowledge of.

As I have stated, I was never so rude as to ask my clients personal questions about the source of their funds. Deak & Company had taught me well: never listen to hearsay. I was not paid to be a policeman. I was operating out of Hong Kong, following Hong Kong laws.

Dancing with Mueller was not easy, though. At one point, he asked me about my client and friend Brian Merrill — who had been indicted in Seattle because of the *Encounter Bay* bust — and his connection to the drug business. I gave him my canned reply that Merrill was a "really fine fellow, excellent sailor and yachtsman and not drug-related that I have explicit personal knowledge of." Merrill had only had a small account with FFS.

Soon after, Michael Pancer called and told me that Mueller was on the warpath because I had "lied" about Merrill. In an apparent effort to save himself in Seattle, Merrill had informed Mueller he was prepared to testify against me. Merrill claimed I knew he was involved in smuggling drugs, and that the money in his account with First Financial Services was *all* from the sale of drugs.

Sad — all I felt was sad. This was totally out of character for Merrill. I could only assume he had been put under unbearable pressure.

Mueller immediately accused me of violating the plea agreement. And to make matters worse, it came to me that another defendant and client had supposedly expressed his willingness to roll over on me. Now I was in very big trouble, facing a nightmare potentially as big as the one I had experienced the previous year.

Michael told me he had talked with Brian Sullivan in Reno and learned that Mueller now had very grave misgivings about the workability of the plea agreement — namely around "Aitken's violations."

Mueller told Michael that he had been flimflammed in that I did not cooperate with the government. To quote: "The problem is that there is no guarantee that Aitken is potentially subject to any meaningful penalty for the violations."

It was really touch and go. Michael was very concerned and thought the situation had suddenly turned from bad to perilous. He said he hoped we could get back on track and keep me out of jail.

To top it all off, Mueller also had questions concerning Howard Marks. He emphasized that Marks had just been handed a 25-year sentence and was likely to be debriefed. Michael informed me that Howard's brother-in-law, Patrick Alexander — the guy who had introduced me to Howard — was also now in jail and may also be debriefed.

"In other words, we don't want another Merrill situation!" Michael said with great concern.

I assured him not to worry about Howard Marks, a brother of the highest ethics and integrity.

Michael deadpanned: "These are not all of the government's many areas of concern, but they are the main ones."

I thought to myself: *This is unbelievable! How did this happen?* Suddenly, I was finding myself besieged by a pile of dog shit from Mueller and Sullivan.

With more and more people coming out of the woodwork to potentially rat on me, Michael was wisely looking for a chance to go back and correct any "mistakes" and save me.

One option now proposed by him was for me to admit that I had not disclosed all the relevant facts concerning Merrill, that there had been "a breach of the agreement by Bruce Aitken," and to pledge that I would be fully co-operative and truthful in the future. This would open me up to the agreement being changed to my disadvantage, however. Various eventualities spelt out to me by Michael involved me serving the full five years in custody — and possibly more.

I suddenly felt like I was walking on paper-thin ice. But while I sincerely appreciated Michael's efforts to fight the ton of incriminating garbage Mueller had puked up, I knew I could never bring myself to say I had lied, or sign any stipulation to this effect. Such an action would always be alien to my chemistry.

What to do, then?

I called on every fiber of my being and decided I would, once more, fight the bastards. I pointed out that all of Mueller's questions about what I knew about Merrill related to ancient history.

I told Michael: "I will never stipulate that I did not disclose all relevant facts about Merrill and will not agree to a full five years in custody. I will never agree to let Mueller unilaterally decide and take this matter out of the hands of the judge. I do not agree to the changes in the plea agreement about testifying against individuals in Seattle and Reno. I will not sign any such statement agreeing to the changes."

In closing, I added: "I hope you will fully support me in this big fight because I think it has only begun!"

When Michael responded that he had no problem proceeding, I was relieved. "I am happy to fight for you," he said. A real trooper.

In his meeting with Mueller, Michael was shown enough of Merrill's transcript to convince him that we would have big problems prevailing at a hearing concerning whether or not we'd complied with the plea bargain. In addition, he was absolutely convinced there were many other Merrill situations just waiting to happen. Mueller wrote to Michael: "The government considers that Mr. Aitken, pertaining to his denial of any involvement by Merrill in the illegal drug business, has breached his plea agreement. I told you the Government has no interest in his 'cooperation' if it is not given wholeheartedly without reservation. We have spent enough time cross-examining and fencing with this individual, while he endeavors to tell us only those things he thought we could otherwise prove and held back the information he believed we didn't have, or couldn't get otherwise."

What I did not tell Michael, or anyone for that matter, was that I'd sworn to myself that — if it became necessary — I would do a runner; I would go to Vietnam and stay there indefinitely. That would mean they would have to kidnap me again, and I felt sure they would find it very difficult this time. Why? Because I would have no problem getting a visa to live in Vietnam while working to develop international sporting events, as was my plan.

More importantly, America and Vietnam had no official diplomatic relationship or mutual consular representation. America couldn't touch me there.

⋅⟨⟩⋅

WE RECEIVED yet another sour letter from Mueller. He said he had requested that a date be set for a hearing on revocation of my probation. However, he also dangled an unexpected offer:

"It occurred to me that provided he is truthful and cooperative in the future, there might be one circumstance in which the government could agree in advance *not to seek imposition of a prison sentence on account of Mr. Aitken's plea violations relating to his knowledge of matters concerning Merrill. That circumstance would be if he can now proffer and provide current useful information of major importance to law enforcement, such as information leading to the apprehension of a major fugitive like Thomas Sherrett or the Shaffer brothers, or significant information relating to the current operation of an important drug smuggling enterprise."*

In short, they wanted me to turn super-snitch.

Michael broke down my alternatives:

1. You can admit to the court that you held back information about Merrill and hence have violated the plea agreement. The government will tell the judge that they are going to give you an opportunity to continue to cooperate; but they can, if they wish, ask the judge to revoke your probation. The government would agree, however, not to pursue the charges in Reno or Seattle unless you again violate the conditions of the plea agreement.

2. Your other alternative is to not admit that you held back information about Merrill. In that event, the government would set a hearing date at which they would try to convince the judge that you did hold back information. If they were successful at the hearing, they would then institute the charges in Reno and Seattle; and in addition, they would try to prevent you from withdrawing your plea. They would also ask the court to sentence you under the plea agreement to the full five years in custody. This will then be followed by prosecution in both Reno and Seattle.

"It is my recommendation that you choose the first alternative," he said. "I know these are not ideal alternatives, but they are our only choices."

I reflected, again, that the problem went back to the wording of the original plea agreement — which I had only had a few minutes to consider before accepting. There was no meeting of minds in the agreement, and I don't believe I would ever have considered it had it not been a make-or-break deal covering all of the co-defendants… or, come to think of it, if I had ever been granted my constitutional right to bail. The government's use of coercion as a policy is shameful.

Telephone conversations between myself and Michael Pancer reflected my disgust at the debacle. I knew Michael was right, but I couldn't accept what he proposed. What the hell to do?! Mueller told Michael the government had at least nine or ten additional major problems with my statements, because everything I'd said was "no."

My real dilemma had to do with my upbringing in our neighborhood in New Jersey, when it was still the good 'ol USA. Ingrained into every sinew of my being was the fact that you never, absolutely never, snitched on anyone. I kept thinking: How had we become a nation of snitches? Screw the prosecutors!

There was more, of course, that I did not tell them, but this was largely circumstantial: thankfully they did not ask the right questions; and truthfully, I did not remember a lot of what they were hoping to hear.

I was in a war of wills and wits and did not know where to turn for relief. It was a depressing time. Luckily help would come from an unlikely source, delivered, I believe, by an act of God.

CHAPTER 32

Time to disappear

THE ENDLESS HARASSMENTS of the Seattle prosecutor made it increasingly hard for me to lead a normal life. I would wake up in the middle of the night, in a cold sweat, at the thought of going to trial and the high stakes gamble I was caught up in. Should the jury foreman, at the critical moment the judge asked for a verdict, utter the word "guilty," I would be inside for the next ten years at a minimum. Shaking myself back to reality in bed, I would pinch myself. "I'm out. And I'll do whatever it takes to stay out!"

To distract myself from this stressful situation and to embrace one of my main passions — outside of money laundering — Tim Milner and I had found a reason to make several return trips to Ho Chi Minh City (as Saigon had been renamed after the war). We were working on a wild idea that we had presented to the Saigon Sports Department: an international marathon. I had always enjoyed long-distance running, and this project offered the perfect escape and respite from the incessant whining and threats of the tenacious Mueller. I started flying to Saigon regularly to work on organizing the marathon.

One morning, the phone rang at around 7am. I picked it up and immediately recognized the voice on the other end. The news that I was back in town had reached the ears of my good old friend Tom Sherrett — who was by this stage a fugitive on the run from the US agencies. He was calling from the hotel lobby.

Tom had in fact found me by checking the names of passengers arriving in town on Vietnam Airlines. Few Americans were visiting Vietnam at the time.

Over coffee and breakfast, we shared our respective predicaments. Even though it was not a happy time, I was happy to see him. Tom was tired, but that wasn't surprising: being a fugitive takes its toll. He was looking for solutions but knew that back in the US he faced a nightmare indictment and a very long prison term. He knew that the government had interviewed me — and that the government could not be trusted.

289

I assured Tom truthfully that, no, I knew nothing and had said nothing about his Vietnamese lady-friend and her brother being involved in his business or in carrying money to Hong Kong. At the same time, I felt nervous knowing that I was in an extremely sensitive position should it ever become known that I had met Tom while on probation.

The meeting would turn out to be something of a blessing, however: a carrot I could dangle in front of the prosecutors. A CIA agent I had previously met in Hong Kong had asked me to keep in touch should I ever come across any information about American fugitives or MIAs in Vietnam. I knew that Tom was a major fugitive of interest to the American agencies — and as mentioned in the last chapter, Mueller had offered to let me off the hook if I could provide "information leading to the apprehension of a major fugitive like Thomas Sherrett…"

Later that year, almost ten months after my breakfast with Tom in Saigon and with Mueller still snarling away like a dog at a bone, I suddenly realized that informing the government of the meeting was the only carrot I could offer them in order to buy time. I also knew this would do no damage to Tom, as I was sure that he would be long gone from Vietnam. He is a good friend and would understand.

When the moment came, I spoke to Michael, told him I had information, and asked him to pass the message on. He did.

The effect was electric. Mueller came back almost immediately, saying that his office was "very interested in apprehending the fugitive in question" and would like to receive the information from me as soon as possible.

There was a catch, though. Mueller said he would agree to final dismissal of all the Seattle and Reno charges, but only if the information I provided resulted in the fugitive's apprehension. If I provided relevant information and assistance that did not lead to an apprehension, the charges would remain. In short, he wanted my proactive assistance — and results, not just information.

After all we had been through, Mueller still didn't get it. I was mightily pissed off at him and had had enough of his vindictive bullshit over nothing material. I was beginning to hope that he would have a stroke. But I kept my guard up. As in a boxing match, I had to win the fight one round at a time. The skills I had learned in tai chi kept coming to my rescue: let your opponent expend his energy, and give him little or nothing in return.

More twists and turns

THE DAY arrived, some time in July 1991, when I had to fly back to the US for formal sentencing in Reno. I did not relish the thought of going back there.

The court hearing is etched in my memory. Present were Judge Harold McKibben, Michael, the prosecutor Sullivan, and a menagerie of assorted government types.

I listened intently as Judge McKibben read and accepted the plea agreement and sentence. I replied that I consented to both, and at the conclusion he asked me if I had any statement to make.

This was it — my chance to make a statement; you could have heard a pin drop.

"No, Your Honor; I have nothing to say."

Just as had happened when I'd appeared in court before, my mind had gone blank. I really could not think of anything to say.

After the hearing, Mueller tried to order me to meet with DEA Agent Conklin, Corman's handler in Bangkok. I refused. He really just could not get it through his thick skull that I would not lift a little finger to help him. Back in rabid dog mode, he later expressed his feelings to Michael: "I am quite unhappy with Mr. Aitken's evident uncooperative attitude and am nearing the end of my patience in dealing with him!"

I flew back to Hong Kong while we awaited the judge's final sentencing. By now, I was seriously considering taking my family and moving to Saigon on a permanent basis.

The month was August. The Seattle prosecutor's office sent two photographs of Tom Sherrett and simply asked that I show them around Saigon. I showed them to Tim Milner.

"Tim, have you seen this fellow in town recently?"

Tim dutifully replied: "No, not me; never saw the guy before."

I reported back: "No developments."

The passing of time was my best weapon, and I knew something would eventually have to turn in my favor.

It did. Out of the blue, and after weeks of silence, Michael sent me a fax. The words were like printed gold.

"Our war of attrition seems to be turning somewhat in our favor. The government did not wish to keep our trial indefinitely on calendar in Seattle. Hence, they are willing to dismiss the case...

He went on: *"[Once] it is dismissed, it is my understanding that they would have to reindict the case to prosecute you and that would be an impediment to their ever going forward with the case. Hence, please sign the enclosed waiver as it is greatly to our advantage to do so."*

I couldn't believe it. It seemed to me the government must have finally realized just how weak the Seattle indictment actually was, even with Merrill's testimony against me. They'd renditioned me all the way from Thailand, but now they had run out of road. I signed that beautiful document as fast as I could, and for the first time since I was released from prison I felt at peace. I was in heaven. It was a miracle.

The decision read:

DISMISSAL OF INDICTMENT
United States District Court Western District of Seattle, USA, Plaintiff v Bruce Aitken, Defendant

Pursuant to Rule 48(a) of the Federal Rules of Criminal Procedure and by leave of court endorsed hereon the United States Attorney for the Western District of Washington hereby dismisses the:

SUPERCEDING INDICTMENT
Against: **Bruce E. Aitken,** Defendant
Dated this 9th day of September 1991
Mark Bartlett

I was suddenly looking forward to the New Year: 1992. Jenny and I spent New Year's Eve having a quiet dinner at home. Our sons were doing well in school; but we were living on savings, and the cash was getting lower all the time.

My life had changed dramatically over the last couple of years, and so had my financial situation. There aren't too many job openings in the classified ads for former money launderers, especially ones who have a felony conviction, and I felt a slight sense of panic at the thought of being broke and unemployed at the same time.

I would also have the specter of probation hanging over my life until 1996, along with worries about prosecutors continuing to hound me.

Another 'Merrill'

BACK IN Saigon, in early January, I was enjoying a beer at the roof-top bar at the Hueng Sen Hotel when Jenny called. Her voice was full of concern. She had received an urgent fax from Michael. The sickening knot returned to my stomach.

To no-one's surprise, Peter Mueller had not forgotten about me. He had told Michael that the information we'd supplied to him about Tom Sherrett had proven to be totally worthless, and now he was apparently preparing to take some further action in my case.

Mueller made it known that a man named Philip Sparrowhawk had been singing about me. This Sparrowhawk claimed he had given money to me on numerous occasions on behalf of Howard Marks and Robert Kimball, as well other persons associated with another unnamed "individual" about whom I had seemingly given false information.

Sparrowhawk's statement from the Metropolitan Correctional Center in Miami read: "I have known Bruce Aitken since approximately 1984. I was sent to his office by Kimball to deliver $75,000 cash, which represented the purchase price of the 3.5 ton shipment of cannabis going to Australia. I have visited (with cash) Aitken's office at 1415 Connaught Centre, 1 Connaught Place, Central, Hong Kong on approximately 10 occasions, and have also met Aitken in Bangkok and Toronto. Aitken told me that he was an American citizen who operated several financial and investment businesses in Hong Kong, including First Financial Services. Aitken is known to have the nickname 'Brubaker' from Kimball."

Sparrowhawk had a memory like an elephant. I imagined Mueller must be salivating over all the information spewing out against me. To quote Michael: "Mr. Mueller said it would be the government's intention to use this deposition at a hearing in Reno to revoke your probation and at a trial in Seattle where you will be prosecuted for giving false statements to government agents."

I was, of course, worried about Mueller's intentions. Just when I had begun to see light at the end of the tunnel regarding my future prospects, suddenly "another Merrill," only far worse, appeared out of the woodwork. Just when I thought Mueller was down for the count, up he jumped right at the count of ten. I was secretly beginning to have a hidden respect for his sheer resilience. When we met in person, he seemed not a bad sort, just unhappy and dour with some kind of massive chip on his shoulder. I even felt a bit of pity for him.

At first, I couldn't for the life of me remember anyone named Sparrowhawk — but then I realized I knew him well under his alias "Brian Meehan." I always thought he was a nice guy, soft-spoken and likable. Even if he'd snitched on me, I would never snitch on him, I told Michael.

Again, I imagined how pressured and desperate Sparrowhawk must have been to have given them anything on me. I could forgive this transgression, but the violations enumerated in the Sparrowhawk deposition were totally overwhelming — and they frightened me.

I needed a miracle — again. *Surely God was tired of me asking!* And indeed before anything of the sort could land on my lap, a five-hour deposition of Sparrowhawk led to the possibility of new charges against me. Michael wrote to me outlining several points of concern:

- *Repeated statements by you that you terminated FFS in 1986.*
- *Statements* [from others] *indicating that the closing of accounts were not accurate.*

- *Statements concerning associates of Kimball and Howard Marks that did not mention Sparrowhawk or a guy who came to visit with funds for Richard Kimball.*
- *Statement that you did not know who delivered the false passport of Kimball.* [This referred to a passport which Kimball kept, under the name "Robert Bland," in my safe.]
- *Failure to disclose knowledge of facts relevant to the Vancouver case* (the sting in which Kimball, Sparrowhawk, Howard Marks and others were all busted for trafficking marijuana, in September 1987.)
- *Failure to reveal Wylie as false identification of Kimball.* ("Wylie" was the name on another fake passport used by Kimball.)
- *Denial of facts or knowledge of Denbigh's and Marks' involvement in drugs.* (John Denbigh was another associate of Marks who was caught up in the Vancouver case.)
- *Failure to disclose a $1,000,000 cash transaction with Sparrowhawk in Canada.*
- *Failure to disclose knowledge of the Sparrowhawk bank account.*

Think! I told myself. *How the hell am I going to get out of this one?* I kept a suitcase packed so I could make a quick exit.

Months passed, and I heard nothing back from the prosecutors. In fact, I spent almost that entire time hunkered down in deep prayer. I could hardly believe the silence from Peter Mueller.

Eventually, Michael received a call from Assistant Attorney Mark Bartlett informing us that the delay was because of an act of God, a blessing and a miracle for me — that intervention of good fortune, fate and karma I mentioned earlier: "Peter Mueller was involved in a very serious automobile accident two months ago." He had been out of the office for that period of time.

I felt no personal joy in hearing this news. But still, Mueller had told Bartlett he intended to prosecute me for false statements when he returned — unless I provided information of some importance to the government. Even injured, Mueller kept coming after me.

Several more anxiety-filled months passed, slowly destroying my brain cells. Michael wrote: "I have not heard anything recently but it is hard for me to believe that Peter Mueller will let you slide."

So ended 1992, a year in which success could only be positively measured by several miracles that had allowed me to stay out of the United States and out of jail.

Then one day, in April 1993, I had an unexpected break. Michael received a letter from Bartlett.

It read: "I wanted to write you a brief note concerning your favorite client and my favorite 'cooperating' witness, Bruce Aitken. Although Mr. Aitken has consistently withheld substantial amounts of valuable information from the government in violation of his Plea agreement, he is like 'a cat with nine lives' that always gets one more chance."

Bartlett went on to explain that an assistant US attorney named Charles Stuckey would be traveling to Southeast Asia as part of an investigation into "the Sherrett conspiracy," referring to my friend Tom. They wanted to meet with me during their visit.

He continued: "I view this as Bruce's last chance, a chance that in all honesty, he does not deserve. If Bruce, however, undergoes a change of heart and provides truthful, honest and complete assistance, our District will forgive his past sins."

Michael responded that he honestly thought there were no conditions that would prevent Mueller from going after me. He'd put quite a lot of work into building his false statements case and Michael didn't think he would abandon it. "But apparently there is a good chance we can put the whole matter behind us. It is quite possible that your 'truthful, honest, and complete assistance' will be easy to give, hurt no one and as a result, as Mark Bartlett says, 'our District will forgive his past sins.'"

The individuals being indicted with Tom Sherrett were his friend, Vo Minh, and her brother Vo Qui, and I immediately felt relieved and happy because I could finally tell the truth — which was that, contrary to what Stuckey and Mueller wanted to hear, they had not brought money to my office from Sherrett. Doing so also gave me the chance to pay Tom back for the way I'd used my knowledge of his presence in Vietnam to stall Mueller's pursuit of me a couple of years earlier.

I had been asked about Vo Minh and Vo Qui before by Mueller — in Seattle, in 1991 — and stated clearly and truthfully that I only ever saw them in Hong Kong on two or three occasions socially when they were there with Sherrett. I was not aware of any business they did, and I had no business relationship with them.

In that light, any comments from me then or now would surely only help them in their defense. I promised Michael I would put my best foot forward and tell Stuckey what I knew.

That the government was willing to forgive my past sins in return for this statement was another timely, desperately needed miracle; I thanked the Lord — and the prosecutor, too.

In late September an investigator named Al Santos visited me in Hong Kong. He was not like Mueller; he was decent. I told him straight up and politely that I had no knowledge of Tom Sherrett's Vietnamese friends other than having met them briefly, and only socially. As I have said, I was delighted to be actually telling the truth.

To say I was glad to see the back of 1993 would be a great understatement. It had been yet another year living with Mueller's sword hanging over my head.

I felt I was aging rapidly.

CHAPTER 33

Hallelujah!

I SPENT 1994 and 1995 quietly scratching out a living and filing the monthly probation report stating my income — which, by the way, was steadily on the decline. The months passed uneventfully until the day I had been waiting for finally arrived.

United States District Court
District of Nevada, Probation Office
JANUARY 30, 1996

Re: TERMINATION OF PROBATION

Dear Mr. Aitken:

Thank you for your monthly supervision report for December, 1995. We would like to confirm that your expiration date from supervision was December 6, 1995. You have completed the supervision term as ordered by the court and we would like to express our congratulations. Best wishes in all future endeavors.
Sincerely
(s)
WAYNE L. MOMERAK
Senior US Probation Officer

I was *THRILLED*.
There were several steps the government could have taken to prevent my termination, but — hallelujah! — they had chosen to take none of them.

I was free, finally. Michael said that the prosecutors in Seattle were still threatening us with a "false statements" case, but given the passage of time he believed the case was pretty much dead. There also remained a chance I would be subpoenaed to testify in one or other of a number of pending cases against individuals who might offer to testify against me

"When all of the prosecutions in Seattle are over, I believe I could then tell you that the matter is totally behind you," Michael said.

It's about the money, stupid

AS I THOUGHT back on the years of being chased by prosecutors and by America's alphabet agencies, one thing stood clear. I'd learned that crime does not pay — *not if you get caught.*

The smugglers of weed and of art, and the people who laundered the proceeds, were generally just in for the money. We were decent, non-violent folks for the most part, and loyal to our friends. The karma, I felt, was harmless.

The government, for its part, created the criminality and the parallel cottage industries that fed off it: the judicial system, a booming business in prison construction, and the complex of agencies and agents. All were motivated by the same thing we were: *money.*

Some of my friends did time, others lost their lives; life kept rolling on. And with the passage of time and some reflection, I can honestly say I feel no bitterness towards anyone involved. My family suffered enormously, of course, and that hurt. However, only one person bore the responsibility for that state of affairs and that person was me. I had spent my life blatantly violating currency regulations.

I resolved I would try to make it up to the people I loved in the future.

Reflection and revelation

AFTER MY probation ended, I seemed to drift like a ship without a rudder. Nothing seemed to matter. I felt utterly lost. My positive outlook was evaporating, along with my savings.

What skills did I have? What talents did I possess? I took inventory and found myself sorely lacking. A mild panic set in and I turned to my last resort to show me the way: my faith. My spirit was hungry, and the material world was slowly ebbing from my consciousness.

In searching for answers, I realized I could offer my services as a consultant of sorts, so I tried to put together some deals on a fee basis; but they were few and far between. I yearned for the good old days. In laundering money, I had stumbled — *or was it fate?* — on one of the best professions in the world. Now it was impossible for me to continue in that vocation.

What do you do after you've lived like that?

Picking up the pieces, I felt there were also lessons to be learned about the realities of human life, human nature and survival. I had lived my life believing I could control my destiny, but I'd come to develop serious doubts about that.

As I attempted to work out a new plan for my life, I took stock of myself with a palpable and terrifying sense of foreboding. Beads of sweat formed on my forehead at the thought. I desperately needed to secure my family's future.

It was now 1997. The years I had spent on probation had been totally consumed by one battle after another to avoid incarceration, shattering any real hope for a new direction in my life.

"Mike," my pilot friend and instructor in prison, had made me a fascinating proposal once I'd gained my freedom. Corporate aviation was expanding fast in Asia and he said his company would be expanding. After a few years' training, I could be based out of Singapore, flying a Falcon 500. I would have to begin training immediately in Aspen, Colorado, however, and the one place I wanted to stay away from as much as possible was the United States. Instead of spending my probation years learning to fly and accumulating hours, I had to stay off the radar, in Hong Kong and Vietnam. Therefore, this option never materialized.

The 'Vietnam Follies' as Tim and I affectionately came to refer to our sports promotion business, had also run its course for me personally. It was quite the adventure, lasting from 1990-1996. We organized some amazing events, including International Marathons in Saigon and Hanoi in alternate years, as well as a world-class Surfing Championship at China Beach, Da Nang, a Bryan Adams Concert, a Hong Kong to Nha Trang Yacht Race, and more. In fact, the biannual Hong Kong-Vietnam Yacht Race has become the stellar race in all of Asia.

Tim and I could laugh at some unique memories, such as bumping into United States Army General Norman Schwarzkopf and the legendary American journalist Dan Rather in Saigon on the Rex Hotel roof garden. We were there to announce our groundbreaking Saigon '92 Marathon. They both freaked out. The US embargo of Vietnam was still in operation. What were we thinking? Two former convicts, too!

We'll always cherish the sight of over one million spectators lining the streets for those marathons. And I will forever remember a poignant meeting at the VN Ministry of

Veterans Affairs, when one American and one former Viet Cong wheelchair athlete discovered they had both been injured on the same day in the same battle. They embraced. Not a dry eye to be seen. War, what is it good for? *Absolutely nothing!*

I had been spending more and more time in Vietnam, away from my family, however. There were no international schools there for the boys, so I decided to look for work in Hong Kong, while at the same time searching my soul for some meaning and purpose.

Returning to Hong Kong, I mysteriously and inexplicably found myself drawn to church, my last resort. I had heard it said that to serve the Lord is the highest calling and in my search for peace and happiness, I began to attend Sunday Mass. Suddenly I was giving praise to God — and making new connections. Through a friend I met at St. Joseph's Church, I secured a much-needed employment opportunity, consulting for a Russian-based company that made chips for watches and calculators. Prayers answered.

This job kept me busy for several years. I'd travel to Moscow and Minsk, in Belarus, for friendly business negotiations, all followed by a lavish party at the company *dacha* outside Minsk. I surreptitiously learned that by taking the overnight train, I could make several trips back and forth between Minsk and Moscow on a single-entry Russian visa. It seemed the train ride, but not the airplane flight, was considered domestic, with no customs or immigration. In a way, I was back hustling.

Despite this employment and my ongoing interests in Vietnam, I couldn't shake the feeling that my life was going nowhere. I had totally lost interest in work — or in anything else, for that matter. The world had changed dramatically for me — and I just felt *off* all the time.

I needed something to anchor me and give me hope for the future.

Turning point

FINALLY, the Lord called on me to serve. After my baptism on December 15, 2000, I attended a rally in a packed Hong Kong Stadium. It was hosted by El Shaddai Prayer Partners, with the charismatic founder Brother Mike Velarde in attendance. That lit a spark in my spirit.

Teaming up with two long-time friends — Kamran Hashmi, a Muslim turned Baptist pastor, and Jacqueline Chan, the Chinese wife of our mutual friend, Illyas Butt, peace be upon him — we decided to open a kiosk in the open-air space next to the Macao Ferry Terminal in central Hong Kong. And so, "Happy's Kitchen," cleverly named by my son Matt and a little "Chinglish"-sounding in a way that struck a chord with local sensibilities, was born.

Illyas and I had been great friends ever since the first day we met, around 1975, when he came to Deak & Company to change some money. I always enjoyed visiting him when he was at his home in Lahore, Pakistan, and in fact he was my initial introduction to the bank BCCI, both in Karachi and in Hong Kong.

With a stage right in front of the kiosk, on weekends we invited choirs and bands to perform praise and worship music, drawing huge crowds. Simple Pakistani and Filipino food was served. Our policy: help yourself, no price; just leave what you want in the big glass jar. Beggars joined flocks of domestic helpers, all served by volunteer waiters who were in some instances their weekday employers.

All was well until the SARS epidemic hit in 2003. The fearful Hong Kong public, all wearing face masks, evaporated into the night, taking Happy's Kitchen along with it. What to do? We prayed.

The idea came to me to play our beloved "praise" music on the radio instead. On Palm Sunday, April 6, 2004, the *Hour of Love* radio program was born. It has been my vocation until the present day.

CHAPTER 34

Epilogue

AMERICA CHANGED SO gradually it felt like no one noticed or cared. But I cared.

It seemed to me that I had grown up in America's golden age. I was eight years old when the Korean War ended in 1953. In school, we pledged allegiance to the American flag, said the Lord's Prayer and read verses from the Bible. God had not yet been cast out of the schools and people's lives. Life was lovely. We were poor, but so what? There was baseball, and there were cats and dogs on the streets of Hasbrouck Heights, New Jersey. If we could recite a Bible verse, we could swim on hot summer days in our neighbor Mrs. Earl's pool, one of the big rubber ones. But no verse, no swim! Those were the rules.

It was a life of honesty and integrity, ethics and justice. America was the greatest country in the world. I believed it wholeheartedly because it was true. There was absolutely no doubt in my mind that America would go to the rescue of anyone in need and suffering injustice. With particular gusto, America would first and foremost always be the champion of the underdog. Always!

Things were about to change, though. Remember Vietnam and the peace rallies? "Make love, not war." Well, the pot-smoking hippies were right about that, but they lost America's internal war to the nerds in the government.

My life as a professional launderer of money gave me many wonderful experiences. I traveled the world over, logging more air miles than many professional pilots. I was blessed to meet lots of amazing people — most of them good people. Money was made and money was lost. It was the main commodity in my professional life, and one that was oftentimes very heavy to carry around.

Other people's money, given to me on a handshake, accentuated a feeling of personal satisfaction because of the high degree of mutual trust involved. My own money was, therefore, hard-earned. The lessons I learned at Deak & Company served me well. As far as I was concerned, at bottom there was no evil in cleaning money, and cleaning it was technically a "tort" rather than a crime.

Other people's ethical objections to cleaning money never haunted me because I felt I was doing it for the right reasons — to support my family and to help others in need.

Unfortunately, however, it was often my fate to take the road of risk instead of the road of wisdom. That, in turn, put individuals around me in danger. Greed, pride and reckless-ness around risk caused actions to be taken that did more harm than good. In the circles in which I moved, principles were forsaken for the sake of money — and some even discarded their honor, inflicting pain and suffering on others.

My epiphany, a baptism of desire to cast off these difficult memories, changed every-thing.

I grieved for my past mistakes, and I felt the wretchedness in my soul. I extended an in-visible spiritual hand through the cosmos and touched those I'd hurt along the road of life — and I asked for forgiveness. A new peace was born in my heart. Suffering and failure had happened for reasons that would turn out to be valuable for the development of my soul.

Prison showed me where justice was lacking in our world. The helpless feeling of loneliness that encompassed me made me feel as if my luck had run out. That experience weighed all the more heavily on me because of the suffering I knew others were experienc-ing as a result of my decisions. The effect on my wife and children, my co-defendants and my best friends, made me realize that I had lost my innocence. Those tough times showed me I'd lost the confident swagger that had always seemingly put me in the right place at the right time. They also taught me important lessons about survival, and to be brave. They reminded me that I was a fighter.

The horror I felt while I was on the run in Taipei gave me a sense of solitude, but it also filled me with all-consuming thoughts of my family and an unquenchable longing to see and touch them. The loss of my freedom and the feeling of shame that gripped me caused me to panic at the thought of never seeing them again. My brief "fugitive life" was not romantic. It was unbearably lonely. I learned that suffering is the way we test, realize and value our love.

I also learned the value of real friends and how rare they are, those individuals who would put themselves out on a limb for you. And I learned some things in prison, too, about human relationships. In prison, you cannot hide, and you must be tough. Friends are there if you look out for them. It is not hell.

Another lesson I had reluctantly learned was to forgive and not to hate those who hurt you. Snitches are abominable, but they are the minority and they will always have to live with themselves, hostage to their own fates. As I have said a thousand times, where I came from you did not, under any circumstances, inform on anyone. My real friends shared this bond and a history of loyalty and integrity that can only be understood by survivors of our experience.

My spell on earth so far had been shaped to a large extent by events, some of which had been within my control, some not. I had lived an exciting life. The black market held an irresistible glamor and once I entered that world, people were drawn into my orbit like a magnet, and I theirs. I think it was my destiny to be in it. I had lived to tell the tale and got out, but because I'd had that life nothing would ever be the same again.

My dreams now became bigger: I knew I wanted to change the world in some way. Everything up to that point had just been a prelude and preparation to make a positive impact before my days ran out.

What I have discovered is that when all is said and done, all you need is love.

———— ·❦·❦· ————

HOW TO change the world?

Now is the time for the silent majority in the whole world to peacefully rise and use the powers of the spirit. In our clarion call to action, let us examine ourselves until we find the Holy Grail in our lives — our true power and charisma and collective destiny. We must relearn the spiritual language that has been forgotten, each person in conversation with God.

When we are true, God responds to our desires and eliminates our fears; as we come to understand our lives in the Spirit, we are changed into forces of goodness and caring and forgiving, an open river of flowing grace. Such grace cannot be measured in a material sense, because happiness, joy, goodness, trust, and truth cannot be measured — but they can become our life experience. We can make it hard, but it's easy: focus on love and forgiveness.

We have the power to make the world a better place if we surrender to the simple life, dedicating ourselves to our families and to society. These endeavors open endless possibilities and can create a positive collective fate for humanity, changing the world by each and every kind thought, each and every act of love, reaching out towards the universal good.

I had gone through a lot to learn these powerful lessons. Arm in arm with fate, the events of my life unveiled to me that to serve the Lord is the highest calling; that the best thing in life is to get high — not on drugs, but on love.

"If all the religious traditions worked together to combat the brokenness in our world, there would be a tremendous outpouring of goodness and love, of compassion and mercy, of forgiveness and reconciliation, and of justice, respect and dignity for all. The result would be universal peace." — Scarboro Missioner Raymond O'Toole (1938-2019).

Final Thanks and Thoughts

THANK YOU for reading my very personal tale.

I hope you have gained some insight into my life and times, and the problems faced by people who have had the unfortunate luck to be thrown into the court systems — people who are up against the government.

I broke the law, made a bunch of money, lived a lifestyle very few ever get to experience, and, like Icarus, flew too close to the flame and came spiraling down to earth.

Luckily, it worked out for me in the end. I am free. I have my life, my lovely family and my friends. It could have worked out very differently.

My life as a successful money launderer taught me many lessons, the most important one of which is to value the spiritual over the material; people over things.

For that, I am eternally grateful.

I've spoken much about my faith, and it was partly responsible for the decision to write this book.

The other impetus was more circumstantial than spiritual. Some years ago, I remember sitting one day in an office I shared with a friend. I had my head in my hands and was wishing I had some money to launder, when the phone rang. It was the United States Consulate in Hong Kong. I could not believe my ears.

"Yes, Mr. Aitken, that's correct. We have received 17 boxes of documents from the United States addressed to you." Seventeen? That is too many. "Where do you want them delivered?"

The boxes arrived, and what a treasure trove it was. Not only were all my documents there, but the clerk who packed the shipment had been kind enough to include all the associated FBI reports, DEA reports, DEA handwritten notes, CIA reports, "snitch" handwritten notes, and more.

That's when it really occurred to me: Some day, God willing, I must try to write a book!

Baseball at Florida Southern 1967

Bruce at grand opening of American Express office in Chu Lai, Vietnam, circa 1971

Bruce in Dirk Brink's office, circa 1977

Tony Pong, Bruce and Nicholas Deak in Hong Kong, 1976

Bruce in Moscow, Russia, 1970s

Bruce in Sydney after a pick-up, 1980

Bag full of cash

The Sydney Morning Herald

BEYOND THE CESSNA-MILNER AFFAIR

How the deals were done

The sixth man, mystery money-mover

Former police chief Wood likely to face at least one charge

Mr Wood ... further police inquiry material under review.

'$50,000 paid' in Cessna Milner case

EXCLUSIVE
By ANDREW KEENAN

Timothy Milner ... arrested after drug importation.

Newspaper cuttings from the Sydney Morning Herald

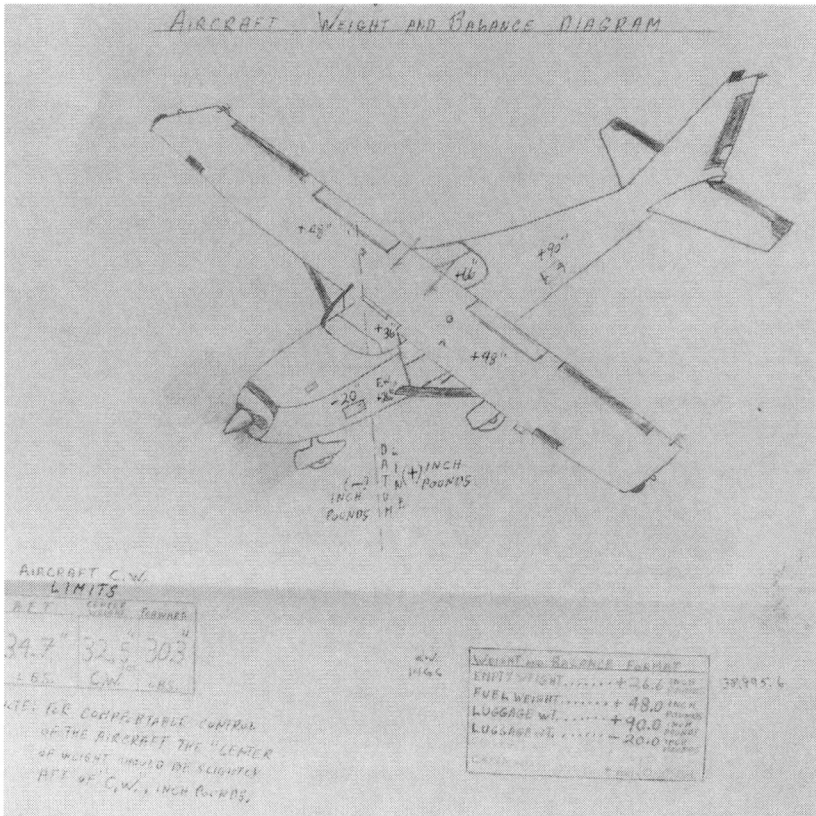

Learning to fly in prison

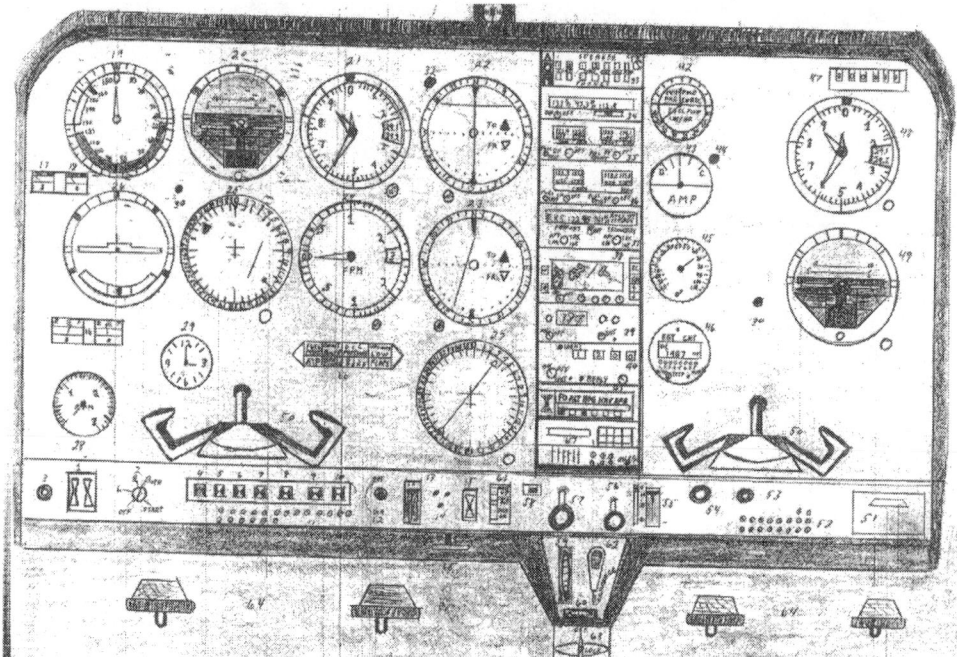

5 June 1967

Mr. Bruce E. Aitken
Box 101
Florida State College
Lakeland, Florida

Dear Mr. Aitken:

I have learned with pleasure of your decision to accept a professional position with the National Security Agency.

In extending my congratulations on this occasion, I also wish to express my appreciation for your patient cooperation during the sometimes tedious procedures which necessarily preceded the establishment of our common interest.

Between now and the time you begin your association with NSA, our National Cryptologic School will work closely with the management officials in the office to which you will be assigned in order to provide for your professional development, both to your satisfaction and to the benefit of the Agency.

During your first week at NSA, we in the Office of Personnel will conduct a series of orientation programs which should answer many of the questions that may have come to mind since your visit to the Agency. However, if you feel a more urgent requirement for additional information, please advise Mr. Russell K. Kimbro of the Employment Division.

I wish you a safe and pleasant journey to NSA, and I look forward to seeing you upon your arrival.

Sincerely,

WILLIAM M. HOLLERAN
Director of Civilian Personnel

NSA letter

Bangkok, Thailand
June 8, 1989

Police Major General Kriengkrai Karnasutta
Commander, Immigration Division
Royal Thai Police
Soi Suan Plu
Bangkok 10120

Dear General Kriengkrai:

I am writing to inform you that the U.S. passport number
Z4979990 and any other U.S. passports in the possession of
Bruce Emil Aitken, an American citizen, who was born on
February 7, 1945, in New Jersey, U.S.A., has been revoked by
the Department of State. This action is based on the fact that
Mr. Aitken is the subject of a United States Federal arrest
warrant, issued on September 13, 1988, by the U.S. District
Court for the District of Nevada, charging him with conspiracy
to distribute marijuana, in violation of 21 United States Code
846. He is also charged with conspiracy to defraud the U.S.
government and to launder money, as well as interstate travel
in aid of racketeering.

Mr. Aitken is a fugitive felon who has entered Thailand
without a valid travel document on June 7, 1989. Accordingly,
the Embassy would appreciate your assistance in returning Mr.
Aitken to the United States. If you consider Mr. Aitken
deportable as an undesirable illegal alien, the United States
Government will pay the costs of his transportation and provide
agents to escort him to the U.S. It would be greatly
appreciated if Mr. Aitken could be held in custody until such
arrangements are finalized.

The Government of the United States would welcome the
deportation of Mr. Aitken. However, because of the limitations
imposed by U.S. law, we would not be able to guarantee
reciprocity if the situation were reversed.

Mr. Aitken is described as a white male, 173 centimeters
tall, weighing between 75 and 80 kilos, with brown hair, hazel
eyes, and possibly wearing a beard or moustache.

I wish to express my deep appreciation for your assistance
in this matter. You are most welcome to contact me or Consul
Carmen Martinez if you require additional information on this
case.

Sincerely,

Wesley H. Parsons
Wesley H. Parsons
Deputy Consul General

Revocation of passport

Made in the USA
Columbia, SC
02 June 2022

61235691R00198